The Roots of Revolt

A conceptually rich, historically informed, and interdisciplinary study of the contentious politics emerging out of decades of authoritarian neoliberal economic reform, *The Roots of Revolt* examines the contested political economy of Egypt from Nasser to Mubarak, just prior to the Arab Uprisings of 2010-11. Based on extensive fieldwork conducted across rural and urban Egypt, Angela Joya employs an 'on the ground' approach to critical political economy that challenges the interpretations of Egyptian politics put forward by scholars of both democratization and authoritarianism. By critically reassessing the relationship between democracy and capitalist development, Joya demonstrates how renewed authoritarian politics were required to institutionalize neoliberal reforms demanded by the International Monetary Fund, presenting the real world impact of economic policy on the lives of ordinary Egyptians before the Arab Uprisings.

ANGELA JOYA is Assistant Professor of International Studies at the University of Oregon. Her research focuses on the impact of neoliberal globalization on the lives of workers and peasants. She is currently researching grassroots responses and alternative models of development among the anti-extractivist movements in North Africa. She is the author of numerous articles in journals such as *British Journal of Middle East Studies, Journal of South Asian and Middle Eastern Studies, Mediterranean Politics, International Journal of Middle East Studies* and *Review of African Political Economy* and has conducted fieldwork in Egypt, Tunisia, Palestine, Jordan and Turkey, Greece and France.

The Roots of Revolt

A Political Economy of Egypt from
Nasser to Mubarak

ANGELA JOYA
University of Oregon

CAMBRIDGE
UNIVERSITY PRESS

CAMBRIDGE
UNIVERSITY PRESS

University Printing House, Cambridge CB2 8BS, United Kingdom

One Liberty Plaza, 20th Floor, New York, NY 10006, USA

477 Williamstown Road, Port Melbourne, VIC 3207, Australia

314–321, 3rd Floor, Plot 3, Splendor Forum, Jasola District Centre,
New Delhi – 110025, India

79 Anson Road, #06–04/06, Singapore 079906

Cambridge University Press is part of the University of Cambridge.

It furthers the University's mission by disseminating knowledge in the pursuit of
education, learning, and research at the highest international levels of excellence.

www.cambridge.org
Information on this title: www.cambridge.org/9781108478366
DOI: 10.1017/9781108777537

© Angela Joya 2020

First published 2020

Printed in the United Kingdom by TJ International Ltd, Padstow Cornwall

A catalogue record for this publication is available from the British Library.

Library of Congress Cataloging-in-Publication Data
Names: Joya, Angela, 1980- author. | Cambridge University Press.
Title: The roots of revolt : a political economy of Egypt from Nasser to Mubarak /
    Angela Joya.
Other titles: Political economy of Egypt from Nasser to Mubarak
Description: First Edition. | New York : Cambridge University Press, 2020. |
    Includes bibliographical references and index.
Identifiers: LCCN 2019038886 (print) | LCCN 2019038887 (ebook) |
    ISBN 9781108478366 (Hardback) | ISBN 9781108745758 (Paperback) |
    ISBN 9781108777537 (ePUB)
Subjects: LCSH: Protest movements–Egypt–History–21st century. |
    Self-immolation–Political aspects–Egypt. | Egypt–History–Protests, 2011–2013. |
    Egypt–Social conditions–21st century. | Egypt–Politics and government–21st century. |
    Arab Spring, 2010-
Classification: LCC DT107.87 J69 2020 (print) | LCC DT107.87 (ebook) |
    DDC 962.05/5–dc23
LC record available at https://lccn.loc.gov/2019038886
LC ebook record available at https://lccn.loc.gov/2019038887

ISBN 978-1-108-47836-6 Hardback

Contents

Figures and Tables

Figures

Tables

Acknowledgements

I am grateful to many organizations and individuals for their support over the many years that it has taken to research and write this book. When I first began researching the topic of social conflict and social change in Egypt in 2005 as part of my doctoral thesis, I was supported by generous grants from the International Development Research Center (IDRC) as well as the Social Sciences and Humanities Research Council of Canada (SSHRC). After arriving at the University of Oregon in 2014 as an assistant professor in the department of International Studies, I began work on this book. I am grateful to the Department of International Studies and my colleagues at the University of Oregon for their support over the years. I am also grateful to the University of Oregon's *Underrepresented Minority Recruitment Program* major grant, which allowed me to take time off teaching and carry out further research and fieldwork in Egypt in 2014 and after.

The research and writing of this book spanned many years. While at York University, I learned the foundations of critical political economy, state theory and theories of social change from Leo Panitch, Greg Albo, David McNally and George Comninel. In the field of Middle East political economy, I have benefited immensely from the research and support of Ray Bush, Raymond Hinnebusch and Adam Hanieh as colleagues whose works have been insightful as I worked through my own arguments in this book.

Over the years, other colleagues in Middle East Studies and critical international political economy have provided moral support and encouragement and have either read or listened to aspects of the arguments developed in this book: Adam Hanieh, Jillian Schwedler, Mark LeVine, Sune Haugbolle, Laryssa Chomiak, Koen Bogaert, Sami Zemni, Habib Ayeb, Ted Swedenberg, Hendrik Kraetzschmar, Paola Rivetti, Lucia Sorbera, Estella Carpi, Gennario Gervasio, Ashraf El

Sherif, Brecht de Smet, Sabine Dreher, Hannes Lacher, Sam Knafo, Julian Saurin and Ingar Solty.

At the University of Oregon, Michelle McKinley, the director of the Center for the Study of Women in Society, has shown unwavering support for my research, by discussing it and publicizing it.

I owe a big thank you to the staff at Cambridge University Press and especially my editor Maria Marsh who received the manuscript with great enthusiasm and sent it out for review. I am grateful to the anonymous reviewers for their constructive feedback, which helped sharpen particular aspects of the book.

Over the course of my fieldwork in Egypt, which began in 2005, I was welcomed by friends, colleagues and ordinary Egyptians. In Cairo, I met Soad Hamed, who not only introduced me to colloquial Egyptian Arabic, but also took a leap of faith and decided to accompany me on my first major fieldwork journey across various governorates in Egypt. Her generosity, kindness and support over the course of this first leg of fieldwork enabled me to feel comfortable knocking on doors in villages and small towns across Egypt and interviewing ordinary Egyptians. I would also like to acknowledge the support of Dr. Emad El-Din Aysha, a dear friend over many years as I kept returning to Egypt. Dr. Emad's network of friends and colleagues at Al Gumhuriyya and at the American University in Cairo (AUC) helped me navigate my way in securing important documents and accessing officials relevant for my research. The staff at the AUC's Social Research Center allowed me to borrow their documents and resources. I would also like to thank Pr. Tewfik Aclimandos for the fruitful conversations in Cairo and for introducing me to relevant policy makers.

I feel a sincere gratitude towards all the ordinary Egyptian men and women across the country, in villages and in the big cities that were always willing to speak with me and share their life experiences and their struggles. It is their stories that breathed life into theories of political economy and social change that constitutes the core of this book.

Finally, my family has provided emotional support over the course of this research. I could not have completed this book or the research for it without the support and love of Geoff, my husband who has never tired of patiently listening to me and asking me questions, which ultimately helped me in developing and polishing the arguments in the book. During my absences over the years, Geoff has been there for our girls, Sophia and Mischka, keeping them happy, caring for them and ensuring that I do not feel guilty while being away from them.

I dedicate the book to the ordinary Egyptians in rural and urban Egypt whose struggles against injustice and inequality inspire me. Their resilience in the face of numerous challenges provides hope for a better world.

1 | *Neoliberal Authoritarianism in Contemporary Egypt*

The Purpose and Scope of the Study

Over the span of two weeks in mid-January 2011, reports of numerous self-immolations were surfacing in Cairo. On January 17, Abdou Abdel Monaam, a small restaurateur, set himself on fire in protest against a law preventing restaurant owners from buying subsidized bread, forcing him to buy bread at five times the subsidized price. On the same day, Mohamed Farouk Hassan, a lawyer, railed against rising prices before setting himself on fire. These immolations, clearly in emulation of the events that sparked the uprisings in Tunisia, sought to ignite the fires of popular protest against the Mubarak regime in Egypt.

On January 25, 2011, on a day intended to commemorate Egypt's police forces, tens of thousands of Cairenes flocked to Tahrir square in a self-declared "day of rage." The popular call of "*ash-shab yurid isqaat an-nizam,*" meaning, "the people demand the overthrow of the regime," kept getting louder as the protest picked up momentum over the course of the day. A rare event in the Arab world, the escalating protests shook the foundations of the Mubarak regime, which had ruled for more than three decades. Those on the streets represented people from all walks of life: doctors, pharmacists, teachers, tax collectors, factory workers, tech-savvy youth, women and the unemployed. The outpouring of public anger that filled squares in the main urban centres was broadcast around the world by Al Jazeera. At least two sets of demands captured the media's attention: civil and political rights, and an end to police brutality. What the media did not sufficiently cover were the demands for "bread, freedom and social justice."

The Egyptian uprising fell closely on the heels of similar events in Tunisia, leading scholars and media commentators to try to identify the causes that could explain both cases. Ragui Assaad (2011) argued that Egypt was unable to turn its youth bulge into an opportunity owing to its inability to implement economic policies that would transform the youth bulge into human capital. Adeel Malik (2011) echoed this analysis and blamed the persistence of "a development model based on a leviathan state and greased by oil and aid windfalls." Ali Kadri blamed the uprisings on increasing unemployment, under-employment and inequality, resulting from failed economic policies, broken political institutions and a corrupt elite (Partridge, 2011).

While these analyses shed light on the conditions that afflicted the Middle East and North Africa region (MENA), we learn little as to how these conditions came to be, why they intensified over the past three decades and the relationship between market liberalization and worsening socioeconomic conditions and intensifying social conflicts. Focusing entirely on "Middle Eastern" factors disconnected from global developments ignores the fact that, soon after Egyptians occupied Tahrir Square demanding "bread, freedom and social justice" and an end to Mubarak's authoritarian regime, the Occupy Wall Street movement would occupy Zuccotti Park to protest increasing inequality and call for an end to corporate rule in the United States. In Athens and Madrid, the *Aganaktisménoi* (the Indignant Citizens Movement) and the 15-M movements were protesting the imposition of austerity in the wake of the global financial crisis. Far from being limited to Egypt or Tunisia, popular uprisings against what critics refer to as *neoliberalism* – and the dominant economic forces that imposed and benefitted from neoliberalism – really did seem to be "kicking off everywhere" in 2011 (Mason, 2012).

There is a need, therefore, to situate the region within the developments underway in the broader global economy. Doing so enables us to better understand the relationship between domestic processes of socioeconomic change and political conflict, and changes in global institutional structures and processes of capital accumulation. Ignoring the effects of neoliberalism on the region determines how we understand the prehistory of the Arab uprisings. Focusing solely on internal factors for the uprisings marginalizes the role of international actors – particularly the International Monetary Fund (IMF) – in the reshaping of the socioeconomic relations of Egypt. This book tells the story of the dramatic social transformation that took place in Egypt in the context of the development of new strategies of capital accumulation occurring under the rule of Hosni Mubarak. While not an analysis of the Egyptian uprising per se, the book focuses on the dispossession and the dislocations resulting from the neoliberal policies implemented at the behest of the IMF, the World Bank, and a rising class fraction of neoliberal oriented capitalists within Mubarak's ruling National Democratic Party (NDP) from the 1990s onward. While the Egyptian chapter of the Arab uprisings played out with its own national characteristics, it was very much a part of larger processes of change and contestation in response to decades of neoliberal globalization.

Capitalism and Democracy in Mubarak's Egypt

Under Mubarak, Egypt has undergone a dramatic process of economic liberalization in response to the economic crisis experienced by most states in the MENA region during the mid-1980s. During this period, most countries in the MENA were burdened with staggering levels of external debt resulting not only from trade deficits incurred through import substitution industrialization, but also from the aggressive monetary policies pursued by the US Federal Reserve – the so-called Volcker Shock of 1979–1981.[1] The second oil shock of 1979 aggravated this dramatic increase in debt, ensuring that it would escalate into a full-blown debt crisis. As a result, inflation, unemployment and poverty ensued. By 1986, Egypt's unemployment rate stood at 14.7 percent, its trade deficit stood at $1.3 billion and inflation reached 23.8 percent (Ikram, 2006, p. 211).[2] As a result, many commentators believed that the statist model of economic development put in place in many MENA countries after the attainment of independence was no longer able to deliver the goods to its citizens and became delegitimized in the eyes of reformers and citizens alike.

By the late 1980s, a new elite consensus – the *Washington Consensus*[3] emerged as the basis of the new development project of the international financial institutions. The Washington Consensus identified the postcolonial developmental state and its interventionist policies (extensive state

---

[1] The Volcker shock refers to US Federal Reserve Chair Paul Volcker's decision to dramatically increase interest rates, beginning in 1979. This was done in response to the decreasing value of the dollar over the course of the 1970s.

[2] During the same year, unemployment in Tunisia stood at 16.1 per cent, Morocco at 16.3 per cent and Algeria at 16.9 per cent (World Bank, 2018t). Growth averaged 6.5 per cent throughout the 1990s (World Bank, 2018f).

[3] The Washington Consensus was formulated by John Williamson in 1989–90 as a background paper at a conference at the Institute of International Economics with the main goal of assessing the relevance of development economics as it had been practiced in Latin America.

ownership, public subsidization of basic goods, wealth redistribution schemes, etc.) as the reason for the crises afflicting the Global South. To resolve these crises, policy-makers proposed numerous structural adjustment policies. First, dramatic reductions in public expenditure through a general tightening of fiscal discipline would eliminate deficits and lower outstanding public debt. Second, the privatization of state-owned enterprises and the elimination of public subsidies would create new markets in the private sector. Third, the deregulation of economic activity would increase business competitiveness. Fourth, the liberalization of interest rates would facilitate the growth of financial services in the private sector. Fifth, the reform of the tax system would reduce the economic costs of doing business. Sixth, trade liberalization would enhance comparative advantage, and decrease the costs of imports and outstanding trade deficits. Seventh, the liberalization of foreign direct investment would stimulate growth by opening the economy to foreign investors. Eighth, public funding for infrastructure, education and healthcare would increase economic returns and enhance income distribution. Ninth, a competitive exchange rate would stimulate export growth, helping to reduce the trade deficit. Finally, the concerted protection of property rights would send positive signals to foreign investors and stimulate growth.

Table 1 *The Washington Consensus*

Policy	Intended Outcome
Fiscal discipline	Eliminate deficits and reduce public debt
Privatization	Attain fiscal discipline and create markets
Deregulation	Increase business competitiveness
Interest rate liberalization	Stimulate the growth of finance capital
Tax reform	Reduce the costs of doing business
Trade liberalization	Enhance comparative advantage and reduce trade deficits
Liberalization of foreign direct investment	Stimulate growth through foreign investment
Fund infrastructure, education and healthcare	Improve income distribution
Protection and enforcement of property rights	Provide security for capital
Competitive exchange rate	Stimulate the growth of exports

This so-called consensus effectively rationalized policies that had already been imposed on countries in Latin America, starting with Chile after the coup that established the Pinochet dictatorship. Williamson effectively provided a coherent policy framework for the neoliberal model of development that would be imposed on the rest of the Global South over the course of the 1990s.

In response to this debt crisis, Egypt, as well as other MENA states like Tunisia and Morocco, implemented numerous structural adjustment programs (SAPs) intended to liberalize the economy. These SAPs were promoted by the international financial institutions that were instrumental in consolidating the Washington Consensus and bore a striking resemblance to the liberal reforms being pursued in other parts of the Global South, such as Mexico, Argentina and Chile from the early 1980s.

Many scholars of the Middle East viewed the neoliberal reforms of the period in a positive light, believing that they would resolve the economic problems of the region and promote democratization. There are two important elements to this literature. The economic argument rests on an assumption that markets are more efficient than the state in the allocation of capital, resources and labour. Against the statism of the postcolonial period, market-based development will result in higher levels of growth and job creation. The political argument rests on the assumption that promoting economic liberalization restrains state power – and the authoritarian tendencies of the Egyptian state in particular – and empowers civil society, which then becomes the agent of democratization.

The economic argument in favour of economic liberalization rested on the general belief that eliminating the constraints on capital – through both deregulation and privatization – would enable firms and entrepreneurs to respond to price signals, rather than political objectives, and increase the efficiency of their economic activity. This increased efficiency would lead to increased productivity, which would stimulate domestic and foreign investment. This increased investment would result in general economic expansion – both in the sense of growing existing businesses and creating new ones – and generate job growth, which would drive down Egypt's high unemployment rate and increase rates of participation in the labour market.

During the 1990s, the proponents of economic liberalization were numerous. Following in the footsteps of Francis Fukuyama's (1993) pronouncement that the collapse of Soviet communism was akin to the "end of history," numerous liberal economists celebrated the triumph of capitalism. The World Bank's resident economist in Egypt, Marcelo Giugale (1993) argued that structural reforms – entailing the removal of subsidies for consumer goods, privatization of public corporations and liberalization of trade and finance – were unavoidable if Egypt wanted to return to economic growth. Jeffrey Sachs, the architect of "shock therapy" in the former Soviet Union, promoted substantive privatization of Egypt's state-owned enterprises, arguing that such radical liberalization was Egypt's "only real choice" to grow its way out of an economic crisis that was the result of its post-colonial statist growth model. Once reformed, Sachs argued, Egypt "could well become one of the fastest growing countries in the next decade" (1996, p. 30). Waterbury and Richards (1996) lauded the prospect of economic liberalization in the Arab World and supported the Washington Consensus, believing that it would correct the failures of the growing trade deficit sustained by foreign borrowing that ultimately drove up inflation.[4] El-Erian and Sheybani (1997) argued that investment would be stimulated by reforms that increased the ability of firms to generate capital, access foreign exchange and repatriate profits. High levels of taxation, strict labour laws and other "rigidities" would discourage investment and undermine the prospects for growth. Alonso-Gamo, Fedelino and Horvitz (1997, p. 29) argued that "most of the empirical work performed so far has shown a positive impact of openness on growth." Excessive government intervention and price distortions from subsidies discourage trade and investment, and therefore growth and employment. More specifically, large public sector deficits "tend to slow down growth, by reducing available credit to the private sector and crowding out private investment" (Alonso-Gamo et al., 1997, p. 29). As such, they conclude that "the progressive liberalization process underway in the region could play a crucial role in raising the growth potential of Arab countries" (Alonso-Gamo et al., 1997, p. 27). Finally, Maskus and Konan (1997, p. 275) argued that "Egypt's greatest potential gains come from removing its administrative trade barriers while adopting globally free trade." All were in agreement that the general

---

[4] However, in the 2008 edition of their book, they confessed to uncritically supporting economic liberalization.

liberalization of the Egyptian economy was the only way to resolve the country's economic problems.

Other scholars viewed economic liberalization as a necessary and sufficient condition for the expansion of freedom and the curtailing of authoritarian state power. Insofar as economic liberalization imposes constraints on the state and empowers the forces of civil society, it was argued, market-led reforms weaken authoritarianism and strengthen democracy. In this sense, the proponents of liberalization in the MENA region resemble the proponents of democratization in other parts of the Global South that proliferated in the 1990s as part of Huntington's so-called *third wave* of democratization. For Harik (1992) and Luciani (1994), economic liberalization will undermine the rentier character of many Middle Eastern states, particularly those dependent on oil rents that support the repressive nature of these states. Henry and Springborg (2001, pp. 6–8) linked the lack of development in the region to the prevalence of bloated state sectors, dependence on oil rents, the power of authoritarian elites and the general weakness of civil society. Economic liberalization, they argued, would undermine the economic basis of patronage and clientelism that supports authoritarianism by eroding the regime's monopoly over resources and assets. Liberalization would, therefore, strengthen civil society and chip away at the crony capitalism rampant in the Egyptian economy. As the state recedes, a middle class grows in its place, which has an interest in further democratization. Insofar as capitalist forms of private property are at the root of liberalization, private property and privatization facilitate democratization. Beach and O'Driscoll (2003, pp. 27–28) viewed economic liberalization in Hayekian terms, arguing that it would bring "democratic capitalism to the Arab world" because the "system of private property is the most important guarantee of freedom, not only for those who own property, but scarcely less for those who do not." According to them, the wide dispersion of economic ownership (allegedly) constitutive of capitalism precludes the ability of any individual – or institution – attaining enough power to control the lives of others. In this way, capitalism is necessarily democratic.

However, the 1990s was a difficult decade for the MENA region and Egypt in particular. On average, growth rates were lower than they were in the 1980s, official unemployment remained high (8 percent in 1999) and income inequality remained higher at the end of the decade than it did at the beginning.[5] Indeed, after initially supporting the Washington Consensus, Richards and Waterbury (2008, p. 261) later argued that there was no "strong evidence that countries that embraced much of the Washington Consensus performed markedly better than those who eschewed many of the recommended changes." Politically, Egypt was not faring much better. The emergency laws that Mubarak implemented after the assassination of Sadat in 1981 were still in effect, the main political opposition – the Muslim Brotherhood – was still formally banned, hindering the competitiveness of parliamentary elections, and executive power remained unelected and unaccountable. On top of this, political tensions increased with the Luxor massacre in 1997.

During this time, some critical scholars pointed out that economic liberalization in the MENA region was neither reducing unemployment, poverty and income inequality, nor was it facilitating democratization. As early as 1995, Farsoun and Zacharia warned that increasing social polarization resulting from "increased inequalities among the social classes" will "undermine the social basis of democracy in the Arab world" (1995, p. 275). What is being established in the Middle East, they argue, is a process of "[e]conomic and political liberalization ... imposed by ruling elites from above while the repressive state agencies that existed heretofore remain intact in the new electoral regimes that are used to suppress (and in some cases, as in Jordan and Morocco, co-opt) all opposition" (Farsoun and Zacharia, 1995, p. 277). In the case of Egypt, Mitchell (2002, p. 282) argued that liberalization "did not remove the state from the market or eliminate profligate public subsidies." Rather, "subsidized funds were channeled into the hands of a relatively small number of ever powerful and prosperous financiers and entrepreneurs." In the case of Tunisia, King (2003, pp. 3–4) argues that "economic liberalization ... coincided with coalition politics that changed a populist authoritarian regime to one ... designed to bolster large landowners and the urban bourgeoisie." As a result, "accelerated marketization in Tunisia has been associated with the hardening of authoritarianism" (King, 2003, p. 5). These critiques, however, were marginalized during the market-based euphoria of the 1990s.

---

[5] In 1990, the Gini coefficient was at 0.32 while in 1998 it had increased to 0.328, after a decrease in the middle of the decade.

Resilient Authoritarianism and Networks of Privilege

As the time lag between economic liberalization and democratization in Egypt grew, and as the continuity of neoliberalism in the context of the post-revolutionary military rule of General Si-Si became increasingly clear (Joya, 2017), studies of "resilient authoritarianism" have become more prominent. Demmelhuber (2011, p. 146) argues that during the 1990s the Egyptian elite "recognised the desirability of reforms, but were concerned that these reforms might ultimately undermine their power, their privileges and their political logic of authoritarianism." In a similar vein, Wurzel (2009, pp. 98–99) argues that structural reforms have been "designed and implemented in order to stabilize the authoritarian regime in the face of increasing economic and political problems." In other words, political considerations took precedence over the proper implementation of the structural economic reforms needed to "lay the foundations necessary to make the national economy more competitive on the international scene" (Wurzel, 2009, p. 99).

In an earlier study, Albrecht and Schlumberger (2004) argued that the democratization literature is rooted in teleological assumptions of political development. Rather than asking why democracy has failed to take root in the Middle East, scholars should turn their focus to the persistence of authoritarian political systems. This process in turn requires shifting focus from searching for "changes in regime *type*" to "changes at the subsystemic level," that is, "changes *within* a regime" (Albrecht and Schlumberger, 2004, p. 385). Albrecht and Schlumberger identify five core strategies employed by authoritarian regimes to implement "change for stability" at the subsystemic level to "*foreclose the emergence of autonomous social forces*" (2004, p. 386 emphasis in the original).[6] This focus on subsystemic changes has given rise to the use of network analysis to demonstrate the ways in which

---

[6] The first is the establishment of structures of legitimacy and strategies of legitimation, which include the incorporation of a democratic discourse in daily political life. Second, the circulation of elites within the political system to ensure the existence of an adaptable ruling elite. Third, the creation of Western-style institutions – electoral laws, constitutional reforms, political decentralization and so on. Fourth, co-optation of potential social threats to the stability of the political order, such as trade unions, social movements and other interest groups and civil associations (including business associations). And finally, the use of external influences to transform constraints into opportunities.

the Mubarak regime controlled in reform process by co-opting the Egyptian business elite.

A network refers to a "regular set of contacts of similar social connections among individuals or groups" (cited in Wurzel, 2004, p. 102). Network analysts substitute "interaction" for individual action, owing to the extent to which individuals are "embedded" within their networks. This is meant to introduce an element of "sociality" that is said to be absent in traditional economic approaches to class. For Heydemann (2004), the networks of importance here are "networks of privilege." As the term suggests, networks are more fluid than relations of class, given the extent to which the latter are defined in relationship to property. In one of the more insightful network analyses of Egypt's reform process, Sfakianakis (2004, p. 78) argues that liberalization "provided space for new networks to emerge in an institutional and social environment that had long sustained privileged ties between business and state." The reform process, however, "did not operate as a zero–sum game pitting one set of business actors against others, based on their fixed positions within the Egyptian political economy" (Sfakianakis, 2004, p. 93).

The networks associated with Egypt's liberalization process are, therefore, highly fluid to the point where network analysis threatens to become a descriptive narrative of the rise of new elites within the various networks of privilege in Egyptian society, rather than an explanation. For example, Sfakianakis (2004) argues that once the "whales of the Nile" had used their access to the regime to benefit from liberalization, they then became opponents of further liberalizing reform. The members of this new network, argues Sfakianakis, sought to "delay economic liberalization but also to prevent competition outside their ranks from prospective domestic competitors" (2004, p. 93).

Yet this overstates the extent to which Egyptian business elites sought to stall further reform and obscures how the business opportunities pursued by these elites related to a broader regime of capital accumulation. What is absent from network analysis is an understanding of how these business networks are situated within the changing strategies of capital accumulation characteristic of Egypt's relationship to the global economy during the so-called globalization decade. As will be shown in Chapter 3, the liberalization process gave birth to a fraction of Egyptian capital that coalesced around the construction, tourism and real estate sectors. While network analysis sees this either as a relatively contingent outcome of the competition between networks of businessmen, or as a result of cronyism and authoritarian politics, it can be better understood as an emerging strategy of capital accumulation linked to various transnational interests that are dependent upon processes of what Harvey (2003) calls accumulation by dispossession, to be discussed in the section on "Accumulation by Dispossession."

There is, however, another sense in which the network analysis used in the authoritarian resilience literature fails to decisively break from the assumptions underpinning the earlier liberalization and democratization literature. Like the democratization literature, there is an implicit assumption that economic liberalization is supposed to empower the growth of an independent, democratically oriented business class. The fact that capitalist development has occurred under the auspices of the authoritarian regime of the NDP contradicts the fundamental contours of what Wood (1991, pp. 2–8) calls the "bourgeois paradigm" of capitalist development. For example, El Tarouty's (2016, p. 56) study of businessmen, clientelism and authoritarianism in Egypt is intended to show how "different types of co-option of parliamentary businessmen prevented them from playing a democratizing role, and thus helped renew Mubarak's authoritarianism." In this way, the resilient authoritarianism thesis seems to be the opposite side of the same coin as the liberalization/democratization literature of the 1990s.

Capitalism against Democracy

The problem with these responses, however, is that they fail to address the assumptions at the heart of their interpretations of liberalization and democratization. The literature on economic liberalization assumes that the neoliberal growth model is sustainable in the sense that it results in "inclusive growth." Rooted in supply-side economics, it presumes that granting capital greater mobility, access to resources and discretion over their workforce will result in a growth of investment that creates jobs and benefits workers, thereby decreasing unemployment and inequality. However, as some critical minded liberal scholars pointed out at the time, the 1990s was a period of dramatically rising inequality and discontent in the context of modest increases in growth across the globe – *despite* the dramatic increases in productivity (Rodrik, 1997; Stiglitz, 2002). This being the case, it stands to reason that the disappointing economic outcomes of neoliberal reforms may be a result of the reforms themselves, rather than their supposedly half-hearted implementation by corrupt regimes. After all, if income inequality was growing in the liberal democracies as well as in authoritarian regimes like Egypt, one can hardly explain the failure of neoliberalism as the result of the authoritarian sabotage of neoliberal reforms. Indeed, the argument of this book is that the persistent economic problems of contemporary Egypt are the product of the very neoliberal policies proposed by liberal reformers.

The democratization literature tends to equate the growth of market forces with the emergence of a proto-democratic *civil society* that will push for greater democratization (Wood, 1990). Economic liberalization will result in growing affluence among a nascent middle class that will push liberalization into the political sphere, thereby leading the movement for democratization. Organizationally, this entails the development of autonomous business associations that will champion democratization in the process of reform. At a conceptual level, this interpretation presumes a kind of spillover effect in which the removal of economic constraints will carry over into a dynamic of democratization. In this sense, the market is understood to be a realm of freedom *against* a coercive state (Nitzan & Bichler, 2002, p. 65). However, the formal separation between economic and political spheres (i.e., markets and states) obscures the extent to which capitalist social property relations are composed of power relations in themselves and that states in capitalist societies play a crucial role in maintaining those power relations (more on this in Accumulation by Dispossession). The assumption that civil society represents a coherent agent of social change with a commitment to democratization glosses over the divergent interests that comprise the groups within civil society and their relationship to democracy (Overbeek, 2000, pp. 173–174; Polanyi, 1944). While all civil society actors may have an interest in strengthening the rule of law and introducing a regime of individual rights that protect them from arbitrary state power, they may not all have an interest in *democratizing* the policy-making process or redistributing power within society. In this sense, what the democratization literature conceives of as democracy may be better understood as *political liberalization* – the extension of certain civil

and political rights of *negative liberty*, but not necessarily the opportunities for participation in the political process or radical redistribu-
tions of wealth and power. In other words, political liberalization may
accommodate certain political and civil rights, but not necessarily
"bread, freedom and social justice."

In a more historical and empirical manner, other scholars have
demonstrated that, even in Europe, democratization trailed the development of capitalism by approximately a century. When democracy
was eventually institutionalized, it was in response to pressures from
below, not by the initiative of liberal-minded elites acting out the logic
of market reforms. Ruling elites were pushed to implement democratic
reforms by grassroots agitation *against* the market, often by the
working class. Therborn (1977, p. 3) points out that in nineteenth and
early twentieth century Europe and North America, "prevailing bourgeois opinion held that democracy and capitalism (or private property)
were incompatible." Far from initiating a bold new era of democratization against the established aristocratic order, the bourgeoisies
everywhere "remained obsequious in their relations with the venerable
notables of land and office" (Mayer, 2010, p. 79). As a result, European
political institutions "were established by elites for the purpose of
preserving and extending their social and economic power, and they
were continually compromised and undermined by efforts to preserve
privilege and to forestall the acquisition of power by subordinate groups
and classes" (Halperin, 1997, p. 168). As a result, before 1945, Europe
"in common with parts of the Third World ... experienced partial
democratization and reversals of democratic rule" (Halperin, 1997,
p. 168). Even when liberal democracies were established in the twentieth century, political and business elites often sought ways to diminish
the political power of the working classes that democratization entails
by manipulating the formal institutions of democracy (Pilon, 2013).

We see a similar phenomenon in the Arab states of the Middle East in
the late nineteenth and early twentieth century under colonial rule.
Colonial powers such as Britain reproduced a colonial division of labour
between itself and Arab states by "encouraging a more general economic
development under the control of notable classes and foreign intermediaries" (Bromley, 1994, p. 107). In a comprehensive study of the state in
the Arab world, Ayubi (1995) argues that the legacy colonialism in the
Middle East is the existence of a weak bourgeoisie dependent on "com-
pradour" capitalists during the colonial period. Playing virtually no role

in the nationalist and democratic movements of the mid-century, they ultimately became dependent upon their own nation-states throughout the post-war period. This is not just a case of the missing bourgeoisie as an agent of democratization. Far from emerging as the leader of a nationalist movement for democratic independence, the Egyptian business class actively collaborated with the colonial authorities to benefit from the spoils of colonialism. As Vitalis (1995) argues in his study of Egypt in the 1930s and 1940s, the "politics of investment in Egypt was ultimately less a struggle between foreign and local capital than a conflict among local investors for access to resources and control over the rents represented by industry building" (1995, p. xii).

In light of these critiques of market forces and civil society, there is no reason to believe that economic liberalization will foster democratization. Indeed, some scholars have argued that as neoliberalism deepens it becomes increasingly authoritarian (or "post-democratic"), even in contexts where liberal democracy has been long established (Bruff, 2014; Cahill, 2014; Crouch, 2004). Bruff's (2016) conception of *authoritarian neoliberalism* is a useful corrective to the assumptions that underpin the resilient authoritarianism that has become prevalent in the scholarship of contemporary Egypt. Far from being an accidental consequence of "messy" neoliberal reforms, Bruff (2016, p. 107) argues that authoritarianism is endemic to the neoliberal experience, in the sense that "state-directed coercion insulated from democratic pressures is central to the creation and maintenance of this [neoliberal] political-economic order, defending it against impulses towards greater equality and democratization." One of the consequences of this notion of neoliberal authoritarianism is to "expand more traditional conceptualizations of authoritarianism to capture more appropriately contemporary processes" (Bruff, 2016, p. 107). Indeed, authoritarianism is not just about the exercise of arbitrary, brute force (of which there are plenty of examples in Egypt, detailed in Chapters 7 and 8); authoritarianism is also "observed in the reconfiguring of state and institutional power in an attempt to insulate certain policies and institutional practices from social and political dissent" (Bruff, 2014, p. 115). For example, in his 1996 address to the Egyptian Centre for Economic Studies, Jeffrey Sachs recommended that Egyptian reformers should not announce the reforms they seek to implement, "because that will invite opposition, and you will get antibodies all around to stop the process, and reform will never happen" (1996, p. 41). Instead, neoliberal reformers should "just do it." It is not surprising then that in the MENA region the authoritarian nature of the state continued to play a crucial role in the consolidation of neoliberalism throughout the 1990s and 2000s. When the demands of the Tahrir Square protesters evolved from political liberalization to demands for "bread, freedom and social justice," the threat to the economic interests of the dominant propertied class became apparent. Indeed, it is one of the central arguments of this book that neoliberalism in Egypt *required* the persistence of authoritarian rule and that in the initial phases of the Arab uprisings, neoliberalism was threatened by populist upheaval from below, until military rule was reinstated by General Si-Si and Egypt returned to the path of neoliberal development.

In the end, economic liberals were either blind to the dislocations caused by the neoliberal economic reforms they promoted, or they resigned themselves to the belief that such dislocations were the necessary means by which to attain the growth needed to build the affluent society they sought. However, in light of recent admissions by the IMF that neoliberal policies may have been responsible for exacerbating economic inequality and jeopardizing economic growth, this belief can no longer be seriously entertained.[7] Similarly, those espousing the belief that economic liberalization fosters democratization adhered to formalistic notions of procedural democracy that reduced democratization to the neoliberal notion of the "rule of law" and the Schumpeterian notion of elections between competing elites (Schumpeter, 1950). However, as economic policies in the liberal democracies of the West become increasingly shielded from democratic input, it becomes increasingly clear that neoliberalism – while promoting political liberalization – has only a contingent relationship with democratization proper.

Accumulation by Dispossession

Any analysis of the political economy of contemporary Egypt must proceed from an understanding of capitalist development. Far from representing a quantitative expansion of commercial or market-based activity, capitalism represents a qualitative transformation in the way

---

[7] See Ostry, Prakash and Furceri (2016). The IMF has also recently admitted that redistributive policies aimed at increasing taxes on the rich – that is, the very types of policies espoused by the *critics* of neoliberalism – will not damage the prospects for economic growth. See Elliot and Stewart (2017).

markets function (Polanyi, 1944; Wood, 2002). As Polanyi points out, the markets of pre-capitalist societies remain "embedded" in non-economic social relations – such as custom and religion – and subordinated to the goals of preserving the social order. In a similar vein, Marx and Engels characterized the economic activity of pre-capitalist societies as being oriented toward the "[c]onservation of the old modes of production in unaltered form" (1967, p. 83). Because of the embeddedness in non-economic social relations, pre-capitalist social formations are oriented toward goals unrelated to the accumulation of profit, such as the normative characteristics of social life. For example, in Greco-Roman antiquity, Marx points out, that "[w]ealth does not appear as the aim of production ... The enquiry is always about what kind of property creates the best citizens" (1964, p. 83). The importance of this observation is that traditional conceptions of property, of the land and of community often run up against the transformative nature of capitalist development in ways that tend to be highly disruptive to the inhabitants of those traditional communities.

By way of contrast, capitalism is composed of a system of social property relations in which the organization of social labour and the mobilization and distribution of resources are determined by the imperatives of profit maximization rather than by the concrete needs of a society. The "disembedding" of the market from non-economic social relationships does *not* mean, however, that capitalism is devoid of power relations; nor does the fact that workers under capitalism are juridically free mean that they are free from political forms of oppression. The state remains a crucial guarantor of capitalist property relations, often in ways that involve the use of violence and repression. In the case of societies undergoing a transition to capitalism, state-based violence and repression becomes a necessary means of expanding the market through the expropriation of small producers, and the boundaries between the coercive use of "public" power for private gain often become blurred.

The expansion of the capitalist market entailed acts of violence and coercion that are downplayed in liberal accounts of capitalist development (Hayek, 2014; Perelman, 2000; Smith, 1937).[8] However,

---

[8] For example, Hayek (2014, pp. 103–104) dismisses as "myth" the claim by Marx that "a propertyless proletariat is the result of a process of expropriation, in the course of which the masses were deprived of those possessions that formerly enabled them to earn their living independently."

Marx (1976, p. 874) argued that capitalist property relations were the historical product of conquests, enslavement, robbery, murder and other acts of violent expropriation. During the last third of the fifteenth century,

> the great feudal lords, in their defiant opposition to the king and Parliament, created an incomparably larger proletariat by forcibly driving the peasantry from the land, to which the latter had the same feudal title as the lords themselves, and by usurpation of the common lands ... The dwellings of the peasants and the cottages of the labourers were razed to the ground or doomed to decay [to make way for the sheep walks]. (Marx, 1976, p. 879)

This process of "so-called primitive accumulation" also entailed the expropriation of church estates whereby "[t]he estates of the church were to a large extent given away to rapacious royal favourites, or sold at nominal price to speculating farmers and townsmen, who drove out the old established hereditary sub-tenants in great numbers, and threw their holdings together. The legally guaranteed property of the poorer folk in a part of the church's tithes was quietly confiscated" (1976, pp. 881–882). In this sense, Marx (1976, pp. 874–875) argued that "[s]o-called primitive accumulation, therefore, is nothing else than the historical process of divorcing the producer from the means of production." This pre-history of capitalism was therefore a violent process of accumulation through the enclosures of land, the commodification of resources and the transformation of non-market forms of use-value into value. Consequently, direct producers were rendered market dependent as non-market access to the means of production and social reproduction were removed.

At the same time, capitalism is an inherently crises-ridden mode of production, as Marx and Engels argued in *The Communist Manifesto*. In contrast with pre-capitalist modes of production, characterized by crises of supply, capitalism is uniquely characterized by crises of over-accumulation, in which the increasing productivity of capital coincides with its declining profitability. Harvey calls the over-accumulation of capital a condition in which "idle capital and idle labour supply could exist side by side with no apparent way to bring these idle resources together to accomplish socially useful tasks" (Harvey, 1992, p. 180). A crisis of over-accumulation results in "idle productive capacity, a glut of commodities and an excess of inventories, surplus money capital (perhaps held as hoards), and high unemployment" (Harvey,

1992, p. 181). Since the 1970s, the advanced capitalist economies of the West have increasingly experienced such crises of over-accumulation.

This "never-ending and eternal problem" for capitalism can only be resolved temporarily, and one of the means of managing such crisis is through what Harvey refers to as a "spatial fix," in which excess capital and surplus labour are "absorbed" through processes of geographical expansion. Liberalization in the Global South (in this case Egypt), is therefore not an automatic response to the failures of import substitution industrialization (which were also tied to developments in the West), but rather a political project to transform the conditions under which Western capital can be realized in the global periphery. The implication of this "globalization project" (McMichael, 2012; see Chapter 5) is that "non-capitalist territories should be forced open not only to trade (which could be helpful) but also to permit capital to invest in profitable ventures using cheaper labour power, raw materials, low-cost land, and the like" (Harvey, 2003, p. 139).

This spatial fix can manifest itself in different strategies of capital accumulation. The first, associated with the New International Division of Labour of the 1960s, facilitated the relocation of manufacturing capital to jurisdictions in the Global South characterized by cheaper labour, lax environmental standards and untapped natural resources. This strategy is associated with the development of export processing zones and other enclaves of export-oriented industrialization. The second is related to the decline of economic nationalism in the Global South and the rise of finance capital in the West (and more recently, the Gulf Cooperation Council). It is associated with the creation of real estate and housing markets, tourism sectors and investment in construction and the materials required for such sectoral development. Given the relationship between this strategy of accumulation and existing regimes of urban and rural property rights in countries that have experienced statist forms of development associated with economic nationalism or socialism, it is accompanied by processes of dispossession that affect workers, peasants and small farmers who benefited from land reforms and protected urban housing markets in the post-colonial period.

While these two strategies of accumulation are by no means mutually exclusive, the latter strategy is most closely associated with what

I refer to as the neoliberal fraction of capital within the NDP. It is not surprising, then, that the primary beneficiaries of many key neoliberal reforms were the construction, real estate and tourism industries, all of which had strong ties to the emerging neoliberal faction within the NDP. The coherence of this group and its relationship to this particular strategy of accumulation leads to its characterization as a "fraction" of capital. The liberalization process facilitated the creation of this neo-liberal class fraction in a number of ways. First, the liberalization of urban and rural property markets opened up new opportunities for land speculation that brought construction, real estate and tourism together. Second, the privatization of state-owned enterprises enabled the acquisition of construction firms and cement and steel companies to be integrated into the financialized real estate economy. But it also enabled businessmen to buy up state assets either for the purpose of reselling at a profit or – and perhaps more important – for merely acquiring the land upon which those firms resided. In this way, privat-ization, coupled with liberalized investment laws and liberalized hous-ing and land markets, opened Egypt up to a trinity of tourism, construction and real estate development.

There is, however, another side to these strategies of capital accu-mulation that are often not recognized in mainstream economics. This other side refers to the class-based component of these accumulation strategies – what Harvey calls "accumulation by dispossession" – in which assets – labour, land, resources, state assets and services – are released from communal regulation and into the sphere of the market where "[o]veraccumulated capital can seize hold of such assets and immediately turn them to profitable use" (Harvey, 2003, p. 149). As such, these assets "become commodified, thereby "opening up . . . new territories to capitalist development and to capitalist forms of market behaviour" (2003, p. 156). Crucially, for this study, accumulation by dispossession can occur either as a way of resolving a crisis of over-accumulation in capitalist centres or it can be carried out by "deter-mined entrepreneurs and developmental states" who want to "'join the system' and seek the benefits of capital accumulation directly" (2003, p. 153). In this way, the developments on the ground in the peripheral areas of countries of the Global South – like Egypt – are related to the broader conjunctures of capital accumulation at the global level. Notable instances of accumulation by dispossession include the mass privatization of state industries in the socialist bloc after the collapse of the Soviet Union, and in China after its embrace of liberalization in the late 1970s. The crisis-ridden nationalist regimes of the Global South, such as Egypt, Syria, India, Mexico and Argentina also underwent significant processes of accumulation by dispossession under the auspices of IMF administered SAPs between the late 1970s and early 2000s. In many instances, these forms of accumulation resulted in widespread land-grabbing by global multinational corporations with the help of corrupt and authoritarian regimes. Finally, in the liberal democratic west, accumulation by dispossession assumed the form of the re-commodification of de-commodified public goods and services, a phenomenon that has only intensified since the global financial crisis.

While global capital – financial capital in particular – is increasingly mobile and free from institutional and spatial regulations, it is not the case that the state has retreated from economic life (Berberoglu, 1987, 2003; Gamble, 2009). *Disciplinary neoliberalism* is aimed at changing national constitutions, domestic labour laws, and property laws to lock in neoliberal reforms and make them difficult to reverse. At the domestic level, this has resulted in states shifting from Keynesian forms of market redistribution to neoliberal forms of market discipline (Gamble, 1988). In the case of countries like Egypt, this requires the wholesale transformation of the state and the development of practices of authoritarian neoliberalism – to be discussed at greater length in Class, State and Society in the Middle East. At the global level, the IMF, the World Bank, and now the World Trade Organization serve as "structures of harmonization of national policies" enforcing a politics of neoliberal convergence through the imposition of SAPs (Cammack, 2004; Overbeek, 2000, p. 177). As a result, neoliberalism has involved "extensive and invasive interventions in every area of social life," in the sense that it has imposed "a specific form of social and economic regulation based on the prominence of finance, international elite integration, subordination of the poor in every country and universal compliance with US interests" (Saad-Filho & Johnston, 2005, p. 4). In short, the expansion of the neoliberal project is paramount to generalizing the imperatives of the capitalist market and, in the process, creating a new set of rules and laws that sanction the newly created power of capital through increasingly disciplinary states.

Class, State and Society in the Middle East

An analysis of contemporary Egyptian capitalism requires both class analysis and a conceptualization of the state. As Marx pointed out, capitalism is a form of socioeconomic organization predicated on relations of class exploitation. Class, in this sense, is conceived as an historically constituted social relationship that is experienced as a relationship between those who either own or control resources and the means of production and those who must labour for a living.[9] In this sense, it is a relation of surplus extraction between a class of direct producers and a class of appropriators. Yet, classes are not monolithic and, as we will see in the case of Egypt, the dominant class tends to be organized along the lines of class "fractions" related to different sectors of the capitalist economy.

Through class analysis, the MENA region can be studied in the context of the development of neoliberal capitalism, and its impact on the states and social relations of the region. However, transposing Marxian conceptions of class analysis onto the Global South requires an appreciation of the specificity of the various social relations under study and their differentiation from the European context within which Marxism was developed. In particular, countries of the Global South, including those of the MENA region, are characterized by a greater role for the peasantry, for small independent producers, and for those working in informal urban labour markets (Alavi & Shanin, 1982; Bernstein, 2010; Shanin, 1972). In this way, their class composition tends to differ greatly from the so-called advanced capitalist economies of the West.

The groundwork for such class analysis in the scholarship on the Middle East and North Africa was laid by Hanna Batatu (1978, 1999) in his comprehensive studies of the evolution of the class structures of Syrian and Iraqi society throughout the nineteenth and twentieth centuries. Beinin's and Lockman's work has provided a wealth of information on the development of organized labour in the Middle East, with a particular emphasis on the tensions between state dominated trade union confederations and militant rank-and-file unionists that helps to dispel the myths of a passive Arab working class (Beinin,

---

[9] For an insightful conceptual discussion of class as an historical process and relations, see (Wood, 1995) Chapter 3.

2001, 2016a; Beinin & Lockman, 1987). Ray Bush's work has focused on the evolution of class relations in the Egyptian countryside, particularly during the context of the liberalization of land tenures (Bush, 1999, 2002). From a more explicitly political economy perspective, Hanieh's work on the regional integration of the Gulf States into the global capitalist economy and the nature of capital accumulation in the Middle East as a whole has opened up important avenues for understanding the sociopolitical conflicts of the region (Hanieh, 2011, 2013).

When examining the development of capitalism in the MENA region through class analysis, it needs to be pointed out that there tends to be greater disunity and fractiousness among the propertied classes of the region. This fractiousness results in greater instances of intra-class conflict among competing *fractions* of capital. The reform process of the 1990s and 2000s exacerbated this fractiousness, ultimately resulting in the political conflict of the immediate post-2011 period.

In *The Eighteenth Brumaire*, Marx discusses the competition between various fractions of the capitalist class in nineteenth-century France in the context of the rise of Louis Bonaparte (Marx, 1973). In this sense, class fractions refer to "divisions within a class which are rooted in the differential position occupied by certain of its sections within the relations of production" (Göran Therborn, 1978, p. 157). This notion of class fractions has carried over into the analysis of the sectoral composition of capitalist classes in twentieth century Europe by a number of neo-Marxists, including Gramsci (1971) and Poulantzas (1973).[10]

More recently, Gramscian scholars working within international political economy have used the notion of class fractions in the context of neoliberal globalization. According to Van der Pijl (1989, p. 11), a class fraction is a group of economic actors within the propertied class that are "unified around a common economic and social function in the process of capital accumulation and sharing particular ideological propensities organically related to those functions." It is through organizing over a long period that a certain fraction gains dominance over others and plays a leading role in devising accumulation strategies

---

[10] For a critique of the Poulantzian conceptualization of class fraction, see Clarke (1978).

at the level of the state. While corporate elite networks facilitate the dominance of one fraction over other fractions of the capitalist class, "[a]ny formulation of the general capitalist interest is, however, always formulated from the perspective of what is only a section or 'fraction' of total capital, a fraction that has temporarily achieved a leading position within the capitalist class" (Apeldoorn, 2002, p. 26).

Within the context of Western capitalism, the relevant fractions of capital are often conceptualized in accordance with their sectoral location in the economy and their integration into the global economy (i.e., a functional and geographical differentiation). On the one hand, industrial or productive capital is differentiated from financial or money capital in relationship to their economic function. At a different level, national capital that is oriented toward the domestic market is differentiated from transnational capital that is oriented toward the export market. According to this formulation, national capital has different economic interests than transnational capital, and industrial capital has diverging interests from those of finance capital. Before the internationalization of capital, domestically oriented industrial capital was central to the development strategies of states in the MENA region and was "more embedded within society and its institutions, laws, regulations" (Apeldoorn, 2002, pp. 28–29). Given that its fate was "more directly tied to the fate of the populations who live in the spaces where industrial capital is located, and of the states that exercise political rule within those spaces," it was "oriented towards the principle of social protection" (Apeldoorn, 2002, p. 28). Managers of state-owned industries played a crucial role in carrying out development strategies and producing for the domestic market and supporting policies of economic nationalism, such as subsidies on basic goods. This fraction of capital was instrumental in guiding state policy in this phase.

By way of contrast, finance or money capital is disembedded from the society within which it operates; it is "abstracted from the production process" and comes to "express the power of capitalist property *outside of* and *external to* any specific process of commodity production" (Harvey, 1982, p. 284). As a result, the orientation of finance capital "tends to be organised around what Polanyi called the principle of economic liberalism," or what we are calling here, neoliberalism (Apeldoorn, 2002, p. 28).

While finance capital favours policies that reduce barriers to export markets, domestically oriented productive capital may feel threatened by the relaxation of trade barriers. This is where tensions can develop between the different fractions of capital. It is possible for economic reforms that benefit transnational financial capital to weaken domestically oriented fractions of productive capital. However, it is also possible for industrial capital, oriented toward the domestic market, to develop strategies of survival by establishing networks with finance capital. In this latter case, it is useful to recognize Chesnais' (2016) distinction between *financial capital* and *finance capital*. The former refers to "the simultaneous and intertwined concentration and centralization of money capital, industrial capital and merchant or commercial capital as an outcome of domestic and transnational concentration through mergers and acquisitions," and financial capital, which refers to "concentrated money capital operating in financial markets" (Chesnais, 2016, p. 5).

The strength of a hegemonic fraction of capital depends on the success of its dominant accumulation strategy. If transnational finance experiences a crisis, a window may open for a different fraction of capital to step up and determine a new strategy for accumulation. Under the hegemony of a new fraction of capital, accumulation strategies might be reformulated to reduce social tensions. However, global capitalism is a dynamic phenomenon, and the liberalization of trade and finance has repercussions on the configuration of class fractions. In this sense, Chesnais's conceptualization of financial capital – and its implications for the constitution of a hegemonic class fraction or power bloc becomes important. Chesnais (2016, p. 8) argues that, in "the context of the liberalization and globalization of capital, a merging of finance capital as 'process' *and* as 'power' has progressively taken place, leading effectively to the formation within states of a single power bloc." This process of competing and evolving class fractions can perhaps help us to understand the character of elite competition in Egypt during the period of economic liberalization.

In the context of Egypt, these fractions of capital tend to be organized into different political formations and business associations. National productive capital is organized through the Federation of Egyptian Industry (FEI). Formed in 1922, the FEI served to foster the development of an indigenous class of industrial capitalists. Under Nasser, the organization was subordinated to the developmental state by way of the Ministry of Supply and the Ministry of Trade and Industry to facilitate an industrial policy conducive to economic nationalism. During this period, the FEI president was appointed by the Ministry of Industry, the rationale being that the grassroots election of the presidency by the various member chambers would result in the dominance of one or two sectors of the economy. By contrast, the appointment of the presidency by the Minister of Industry sought to overcome these sectoral divisions in favour of a national economic vision. In the commercial sectors of the economy, the Federation of Egyptian Chambers of Commerce served a similar function and shared a similar organizational structure that subordinated it to the Ministries of Supply, Trade and Economy. Both organizations were oriented toward the import substitution industrialization developmental policy of the Nasser regime and therefore representative of national fractions of Egyptian capital.[11]

As a nationally based institution tasked with the security of the nation, the military – as an economic actor – has played an important role as a fraction of national capital in Egypt's post-war history. The most important conjuncture in the development of the military's expanding role in the economy was the 1980s when Egypt was integrated into the global economy. Through the Armed Forces Land Projects Agency, the military entered into joint ventures with private capital in agriculture and food production, port maintenance, urban planning, tourism, hotels and luxury housing, furniture, ship manufacturing and repair, technology and electronics and textile production. The expansion of the army's role in the domestic economy went hand in hand with its expansion in the political economy of the MENA region and the global economy. This period also tested the army's power when it faced competition by the newly emerging neoliberal class fraction around Mubarak. This expansion of the military's economic and political power reflects the evolution of the military as a fraction of the ruling class. With the historical legacy of one of the most significant Arab armies, the Egyptian military has experienced a process of fundamental socioeconomic transformation that has enabled it to accumulate power vis-à-vis other fractions of the dominant class.

The transnational, financialized fraction of capital, referred to as *neoliberals* in this book, is "composed of a tiny grande bourgeoisie

---

[11] For a more detailed discussion of both the EFI and the FECC, see Fahmy (2002), Soliman (1998), and Bianchi (1985, 1989).

intimately integrated into Western capital," whose interests and "dynamism rests essentially on the (rapid) accumulation of capital through service activity rather than through the exploitation of land or labor" (Farsoun, 1997, p. 25). Organizationally, this fraction of capital is represented by several private business organizations that emerged outside of the official state-dominated FEI and Federation of Egyptian Chambers of Commerce. The most important indigenous business association emerging out of the private sector is the Egyptian Businessmen's Association, which was formed in 1982 with the financial support of the Egyptian-American Businessmen's committee. More than one-half of its membership is clustered around construction, consulting and advertising, and tourism and transportation, reflecting the fact that "most of the investments of Egyptian businessmen are in consumer rather than productive sectors of the economy" (Fahmy, 2002, p. 170).

Alongside the Egyptian Businessmen's Association are three important joint business organizations that bring together Egyptian and American capital. The Egyptian-American Businessmen's Association was created in 1975 through an agreement between Nixon and Sadat; the American Chamber of Commerce was formed in 1982 under Mubarak, after a visit to Washington, DC, by Sadat just before his assassination; and the Egyptian-American Presidential Council, established in 1995 by an initiative between Mubarak and then U.S. Vice President Al Gore. These associations tied emerging Egyptian private sector business interests to American capital and played a prominent role in driving the liberalization process in the 1990s. For example, the American Chamber of Commerce was the official representative of the Egyptian private sector during the negotiations with the IMF and World Bank in the late 1980s. Other, less prominent Egyptian business associations partnered with international capital and forged ties to the neoliberal government of 2004 included the Egyptian-British Business Association and Egyptian-Dutch Business Association. Perhaps more significantly, the Egyptian-American Presidential Council, composed of equal proportions of Egyptian and American business representatives, sought to bring together the prominent Egyptian millionaires and the president of the FEI and bring them onboard the liberalization process. Controversially, the council strongly advocated for the elimination of subsidizes and the wholesale privatization of the entire Egyptian economy – policy proposals that were in line with the conditions of the loan agreement signed between Egypt and the IMF in 1991.

Finally, Islamist capital is organized in the ranks of the Muslim Brotherhood, which has financial links to states in the Persian Gulf. The socioeconomic profile of the Brotherhood as a class fraction is rather complex. On the one hand, the traditional leadership comes from the ranks of the large landowning class that was threatened by Nasser. On the other hand, it also enjoys support among private sector actors, including traders, and small and mid-sized manufacturers. By 1980, eight out of the eighteen families who dominated Egypt's private sector belonged to the Brotherhood, and their businesses constituted approximately 40 percent of private sector enterprises. The growth of this Islamist fraction of capital was facilitated by the creation of Islamic investment companies that were linked to the *nouveau riche* rather than to the older, elitist Brotherhood. In this sense, it does not fit neatly into the typology of class fractions as elaborated; rather, it seems to straddle both the domestic and transnational and the productive and financial categories. The ways in which the Brotherhood articulates this complexity and the form it has taken in contemporary Egypt will be discussed in greater detail in Chapter 6.

State-led industrialization empowered nationally oriented capitalists while marginalizing the merchants, traders and small business owners that formed the support base of Islamist organizations like the Muslim Brotherhood. As a formally banned organization, the Brotherhood was unable to form a legitimate business association to represent the interests of its members to the state. The Brotherhood persevered through charity work and by establishing economic ties with relevant Gulf States, Qatar in particular. In the current era of neoliberalism, where structural adjustment policies pursued by a financialized transnationalist propertied class fraction oversaw the dismantling of the statist model of nationalist industrialization, space has opened up for the emergence of the Muslim Brotherhood as a class fraction. Despite residual claims to being the stewards of an Islamic "moral economy" (Dalacoura, 2016), the Muslim Brotherhood has accommodated itself to neoliberal capitalism as a fraction of Egyptian capital vying for dominance within the state (Gerges, 2012). After the collapse of the Mubarak regime in 2011, the Muslim Brotherhood formed the Egyptian Business Development Association in an attempt to establish itself among the formal business community.

The ultimate goal of the competition between various fractions of capital is control of the Egyptian state. Within the Marxist tradition, the state "is never a neutral or passive mediator" (Therborn, 1978, p. 181), but rather plays a central role in the reproduction of social relations and is deeply implicated in the relations of exploitation, domination and rule. Against the proponents of pluralism (Dahl, 1961, 1973), therefore, the Marxist tradition insists that the capitalist state disproportionately represents the interests of capital against the interests of workers and social movements. Questions regarding the specific relationship between the state and the capitalist class resulted in the so-called state debate of the 1970s. The debate examined whether the state's role in the reproduction of capitalist social relations was the result of the "instrumentalist" relationship between the capitalist class and the state elite, or the structural dependence of the state upon the processes of capital accumulation (Miliband, 1969, 1970, 1973; Poulantzas, 1969, 1973, 1976). By the end of the 1970s, the Marxian position posited the "relative autonomy" of the state from capital as a means of acknowledging the structural dependence of the state on capital while recognizing the contested nature of the state apparatus itself (Esping-Andersen, 1976). This relative autonomy position came at a time when a reinvigorated Weberian position sought to reassert the autonomy of the state vis-à-vis capital, in a context defined by the increasing assertiveness – and political success – of capitalist business associations (Evans, Rueschemeyer & Skocpol, 1985; Nordlinger, 1982).[12]

Most of these debates on the state take the institutionally developed capitalist states of the West as a starting point. In particular, Weberian approaches emphasize the importance of bureaucratic rationality and administrative capacity. The administrative and institutional development of these states date back to the early modern period and continued throughout the nineteenth century (Anderson, 1974; Mooers, 1991; Wood, 1991). This process of bureaucratic and administrative development – in particular, the development of systems of public finance, public administration and judicial oversight – accelerated as a result of the two world wars (Halperin, 2004).

---

[12] For two substantive critiques of the statist approach, see Cammack (1989, 1990). For a discussion of the employers' offensive of the 1980s, see Hyman and Elger (1981) and Pontusson and Swenson (1996).

However, the states of the Global South – and the Middle East in particular – are the product of Western colonialism and have experienced processes of formation different to the states of Europe.[13] As the arbitrary product of colonial powers, the territorial integrity of such states was contested by competing centres of power in the post-independence period. The seizure of state power by revolutionary nationalist movements in Egypt, Algeria, Libya, Syria and Iraq, introduced ambitious projects of nationalist economic development, industrialization and political modernization. While the drive toward modernization and industrialization took the form of statist authoritarianism, the political institutions and administrative capacities of the Middle Eastern state remained weak and underdeveloped, as the old colonial apparatuses were abolished, and post-colonial elites struggled to consolidate their new institutions. In contrast with the charges of *oriental despotism* levelled at post-colonial Middle Eastern states by orientalist scholars (Wittfogel, 1959), this authoritarian tendency was a symptom of the institutional *weakness* of Middle Eastern states rather than an indication of their strength (Ayubi, 1995; Migdal, 1988; Owen, 2004).

In fact, the European notion of oriental despotism – applied in broad-brush fashion to almost all states of the East – is rooted in the propensity of authoritarian rulers to redistribute the surplus to the popular classes to maintain social order and preserve traditional socioeconomic hierarchies. These authoritarian legacies have led liberal critics to lament the inability or unwillingness of Middle Eastern states to respect the rule of law and effectively enforce the rights of private property.[14] Chaudhry (1994, p. 3) argues that states in the Global South lack the administrative capacities to "regulate, define, and enforce property rights" and to "dispense law." Despite their strong appearance, their capacity to tax is "strictly circumscribed." This becomes a problem because to "successfully make the 'transition' to a market economy, these capacities become absolutely necessary." In a similar vein, De Soto (2001, p. 33) argues that states cannot effectively

---

[13] For a provocative treatment of the subject that treats European states as equally subject to institutional underdevelopment and colonial interference, see Halperin (1997).

[14] Such critiques can be traced all the way back to James Harrington's seventeenth-century critique of the Ottoman state, which he characterized as an "empire of men" rather than an "empire of laws." See Harrington (1992, p. 20).

act on behalf of capital in the absence of formal property rights and proper legal institutions. It is the tendency of authoritarian states to arbitrarily redistribute the wealth of society and violate the rights of private property that is the primary obstacle to capitalist development, not authoritarianism per se.

Recent developments in the MENA region constitute an integral part of the expansion of capitalism as a global system. The rise of a global neoliberal orthodoxy has facilitated the rapid transformation of social relations in the region over the past three and a half decades. Neoliberal globalization began to take hold in the region during the 1980s and the 1990s through a series of SAPs implemented in response to the crisis of Arab statism in the mid-1980s. As in the liberal democracies of the West, the emerging neoliberal orthodoxy in the MENA region did not entail a retreat of the state from the economy. Rather, the international financial institutions charged with global economic governance advocated a new role for the state. The World Bank outlines this new role in detail in its 1997 *World Development Report* called *The State in a Changing World*, in which it advocated a shift from the planned economies of the era of 'Third Worldism" to the free markets of the post-Cold War period (World Bank, 1997). This new role required states to provide infrastructure for private investors, to strengthen judicial institutions with the goal of enforcing the rights of private property, to promote of business friendly environments for the growth of private firms, to allow the unrestricted repatriation of profits, and to substantially open up the economy to the private sector.

This new role was only new, however, in cases where post-colonial states had engaged in paternalistic forms of statist economic development and social protection, such as in many Middle Eastern countries. The capitalist democracies of the West had long institutionalized property-based legal regimes and have a long record of enabling private sector development. In the MENA region, however, securing the absolute right of private property required a different kind of interventionist state that could legislate and act on behalf of capital rather than in the interest of Arab socialism or economic nationalism. In short, the World Bank was advocating for the creation of institutionally robust capitalist states in parts of the Global South where statist forms of industrialization once dominated.

For the World Bank the ideal state is a state that actively reproduces capitalist social relations by ensuring that the short-term interests of capitalists do not undermine the system of capital accumulation. The report points out that while "[s]tate dominated development has failed ... so will stateless development." Against the strictures of classical liberalism, the World Bank now recognizes that "[d]evelopment without an effective state is impossible" (World Bank, 1997, p. 25). The bank is advocating a larger role for the state in *"protecting and correcting markets"* (Panitch, 1998, p. 15). It could also be said that the bank is advocating a larger role for the state in *creating* markets in the first place. The state accomplishes this developmental role by maintaining a degree of relative autonomy from capitalists and their particularistic interests. To do so, the state requires the legal, bureaucratic and coercive apparatuses that can guarantee the continuation of the capitalist system regardless of who or what party is in power. Only by doing so will Middle Eastern states establish the "politically organized and legally defined stability, regularity and predictability in its social arrangements" that capitalism requires (Wood, 2002, p. 178).

For the proponents of liberalization, the task of a peripheral capitalist state is to overcome conflicts among elites and to institutionalize "a culture of the market" (Chaudhry, 1994, p. 7). The former task requires the creation of "alternative institutional mechanisms for resolving conflicts and the revitalization, creation, or legalization of corporate groups in civil society" (Chaudhry, 1994, p. 7). The latter task requires promoting and legitimizing self-interest as the motivating factor behind economic activity. Thus, the final prerequisite entails the redefinition of legal rights of individuals, which would replace precapitalist, communitarian notions of rights. These changes entail struggles over land, resources and space and involves local communities, workers, peasants and the unemployed against more powerful, organized groups of landlords and capitalists. As a result, this has been perhaps the most important and most contentious aspect of the transition to a market economy. De Soto (2001, p. 35) argues that the creation of capitalist property relations is "nothing short of a revolutionary process" as it is not merely providing deeds of ownership, but rather a process of linking property and social relations together in a web of market interdependence.

This takes us back to the process of accumulation by dispossession. In places like Egypt, Tunisia and Morocco, accumulation by dispossession was well underway by the mid-1990s. The privatization of state-owned enterprises, the deregulation of urban housing markets and the privatization of agricultural land subjected workers and peasants to increasing precariousness. This process of accumulation by dispossession entailed the "commodification and privatization of land and the forceful expulsion of peasant populations, conversion of various forms of property rights … into exclusive private property rights, suppression of rights to the commons; commodification of labour power and the suppression of alternative, indigenous, forms of production and consumption" (Harvey, 2003, p. 74).

From Dispossession to Resistance to Revolt

To insist on the compatibility of neoliberal capitalism and authoritarianism is not, however, to suggest that the authoritarian state remains a monolithic and all-powerful entity looming over a passive, subject population. Despite the tendency of scholars of authoritarianism to view the region as one "frozen in time and space, with passivity becoming tautological to an Arab characteristic," the Middle East, and contemporary Egypt in particular, remains a highly contentious political space, as the events of 2011 demonstrate (Gerges, 2015, p. 10). The uprisings in Tahrir Square did not erupt out of the nothing. Resistance to the kind of accumulation by dispossession discussed in this book was building over the course of the 1990s and 2000s. While numerous books have sought to analyse the "movements of the squares" as a form of "contentious politics" against the tendency of the theorists of authoritarianism to downplay the agency of Arab civil society, this book focuses on the resistance of those who, for the most part, have been written out of the Arab uprisings narrative: the workers, the peasants and the small tenant farmers. Conspicuously absent from both Gerges' (2015) and Lynch's (2014) collections is a recognition of the contentious politics between class actors in the Middle East. While Lynch's book contains one chapter on labour movements in the Middle East, neither study focuses on the struggles between tenant farmers and landlords in the context of agrarian transformation.[15] In this sense, the contentious politics dealt with in this

---

[15] This is despite the fact that Tarrow's (2011) work, from which the current wave of contentious politics is derived, discusses the phenomenon of the spontaneous peasant-based land occupation.

book are rooted in the experience of dispossession by essentially class-based actors. Arguably, the first and most articulate 'theorist' of contentious politics was Marx himself, with his insistence on the impact that class conflict has on shaping the contours of history.

This contentious politics occupies a broad spectrum of resistance. Some of this resistance assumes the conventional forms of working-class agitation: strikes, sit-ins, protests and violent confrontation with security forces. In the Egyptian context, the struggle of workers is compounded by the fact that they are struggling against their employers, the regime and the leadership of the official trade union movement, which, over time, has become integrated into the state apparatus. Thus, the resistance of workers includes the struggle to form independent working-class organizations such as free trade unions.

The resistance of the small producers of rural Egypt tends to be more disorganized, spontaneous and dispersed. As the cooperatives of the Nasserist era became integrated into the neoliberal project of agrarian transformation, the collective locus of rural life underwent a dramatic transformation. No longer vehicles of peasant organization against the depredations of landlords, the cooperatives became another institution of authoritarian neoliberalism, compelling the small producers of rural Egypt to voice their dissent in new and less organized ways as they faced the forces of dispossession.

Such forms of contentious politics and spontaneous resistance calls to mind the types of resistance engaged in by the artisans, plebeians and dispossessed peasants of early industrializing England, chronicled so vividly by E. P. Thompson (1963), or the rural protests and the 'primitive rebels' that formed the subject of the work of Hobsbawm (1971; 1969) and Rudé (1995). Hobsbawm (1971, p. 2) acknowledged the "undetermined, ambiguous or even ostensibly 'conservative' character of such movements" in the absence of any well-articulated ideology. This recalls Polanyi's earlier depiction of a "countermovement" against the expansion of the market, characterized as a "reaction against a dislocation which attacked the fabric of society, and which would have destroyed the very organization of production that the market had called into being" (Polanyi, 1944, p. 136). In a contemporary Middle Eastern context, Asef Bayat has written about the "nonmovements" that have emerged to help shape the contours of Arab society. Nonmovements "are the shared contentious practices of a large number of fragmented people whose similar but disconnected claims produce important social change in their own lives and society at large, even though such practices are rarely guided by an ideology, recognizable leadership, or organization" (Bayat, 2017, p. 106). While Polanyi's countermovement brought together working class and landed class actors – including members of the landed aristocracy – as "those most immediately affected by the deleterious action of the market" (Polanyi, 1944, p. 138), Bayet's nonmovement is populated solely by the "dispossessed," of the "quiet, pervasive, and enduring encroachment of the poor people on the propertied, the powerful, and the public in their quest for survival and bettering their lives" (Bayat, 2017, p. 106).

Sources

My intention in this book is to capture the contested process of political and economic change by bringing in the views and experiences of not only the elite, but also those of the peasants and workers as Egypt experienced deeper economic integration beginning in the 1990s. In this regard, qualitative approaches to political economy more adequately convey these contested processes than do the economic statistics provided by official statistics. The aim of the qualitative research component is to gain an in-depth understanding of how workers and peasants experienced the process of change that was triggered by the liberalization of land and housing markets across the country.

The research for this book is based on extensive fieldwork conducted in Egypt between 2005 and 2008 that consisted of extensive interviews with workers, peasants, government policy makers and representatives of the Muslim Brotherhood. These unstructured interviews were conducted over a period of four years (2005–8) in thirteen out of a total of twenty-seven Egyptian governorates, including Cairo. These interviews offer a window into how social agents experienced the changes in social relations that occurred as part of the strategy of accumulation by dispossession. The interviews also shed light on how these social agents, coming from different class backgrounds, interpreted the nature of the social change and how they viewed the role of the state and how they reacted to policies that changed their social status and the extent of control they exercised over their lives and communities.

These interviews are supplemented by an extensive analysis of a wide variety of official documentation produced between 1990 and

2010 by the Egyptian government and Egyptian state institutions, Egyptian businesses and international financial institutions like the IMF and the World Bank. Research of this documentation entailed archival work at the Centre d'Etudes et de Documentation et Juridiques in Cairo as well as the Social Research Centre of the American University in Cairo. Other official documentation was accessed in the archives at L'institute du Monde Arabe in Paris, France. These included Arabic, French and English language sources.

Structure of the Book

This book is not about the causes of the Arab Uprisings that deposed Mubarak in the early months of 2011. Rather, this book is about the broader historical changes underway in the contemporary political economy of Egypt. Suffice it to say that these changes provided fertile ground for the rising wave of discontent that ultimately brought down the regime in January 2011. However, how these dramatic socioeconomic changes related to the outbreak of the Arab uprisings in Egypt is no doubt a complex issue that must form the subject of its own study.

The book is organized into three sections. Chapter 1 provides a conceptual and historical background for the period of economic liberalization. They explore the processes of state and class formation through an examination of the Egyptian state and economy in the post-colonial period (1952), and the ways in which new class fractions emerged as a result of various economic models pursued by Egypt's post-colonial leaders (Nasserism, Sadat, and Mubarak). Chapter 2 examines the political economy of Egypt from the creation of the developmentalist state under Gamal Abdel Nasser to the rise of the market economy under Anwar Sadat. The chapter situates the shifts in Egyptian political economy within the context of global economic changes, shifting regional alignments and emerging class struggles. Chapter 3 – Mubarak and the Neoliberal Turn – charts the rise to power of a neoliberal class fraction that is closely associated with the policies of economic liberalization and state transformation. The chapter explores the accumulation strategies of this class fraction and the legal, institutional and economic reforms of the state that facilitated the accumulation of capital during these two decades.

Chapter 4 explores the evolution of the military as an increasingly cohesive class-based organization with aspirations to consolidate its economic and institutional power. Similarly, Chapter 5 examines the emergence of the Brotherhood as a politically marginalized organization rooted in a contradictory social base with historical grievances against both the state-oriented industrialists of the Nasserist period and the neoliberals of the Mubarak era. With ties to Qatari capital, the Brotherhood ultimately attempts to make peace with the emerging neoliberal order in the years before the uprisings. The chapter traces the Brotherhood's attempts to establish their influence within the economy in the late 1970s and early 1980s, despite their political marginalization from official state institutions.

The final chapters examine the 'contentious politics' of liberal reform (Gerges, 2015). Chapter 6 examines the impact of neoliberal reforms on workers over the course of the 1990s and early 2000s and chronicles the struggles of Egyptian workers – both inside and outside the official trade union movement – against the ongoing transformations of the labor market. Chapter 7 examines the states' sustained assault on the customary rights of the peasantry and on the traditional social relations that constituted the Egyptian socioeconomic order. As the most blatant instance of accumulation by dispossession, peasants experienced increased levels of exploitation and economic insecurity as their tenure rights were exterminated and as they became subject to state sanctioned expropriation. Finally, Chapter 8 explains the significance of this study for an understanding of the uprisings in Egypt and Mubarak's subsequent deposition in January 2011.

2 | The Developmentalist State and the Market Economy
From Nasser to Sadat

From Independence to Arab Socialism

While Egypt was granted formal independence from British colonial rule in 1922, it remained tied to British imperial interests. Despite some agitation from nationalists, the urban economy was linked to the export of cotton and failed to develop industries that could absorb rural surplus labour. Throughout this period, Egyptian society was dominated by the ruling family and a small group of landed families that owned most of the agricultural land of the country, while most peasants and small farmers lived in impoverished conditions. The dominance of the cotton-producing fraction of the landed class and the cotton-exporting bourgeoisie signified a general continuity with nineteenth-century social property relations.

Egyptian society was marked by gross inequalities during this period. By the late 1940s, 20 percent of cultivated land was owned by 0.1 percent of the population, and 13 percent of cultivable land was held by small, nearly landless landowners who comprised 75 percent of the landholding population (Bush, 2009, pp. 52–53). By 1950, 60 percent of the rural population was landless (Beinin, 2001, p. 118). The political and economic systems were dominated by an alliance of landowners and industrialists who had benefited from British colonial rule. Industrialization remained limited in scope, because only consumer goods industries linked to the export sector, such as food processing and textiles production, had been developed. Only 3.6 percent of Egyptian firms employed ten or more workers (Beinin & Lockman, 1987, p. 263). This "contradictory and uneven development" resulted in the creation of a fragmented and heterogeneous working class characterized by "a large number of workers employed in very small enterprises producing labour-intensive and capital-poor conditions where the distinction between employer and employee was often not very sharp," and a large number of workers employed in "large-scale mass production industries" (Beinin & Lockman, 1987, p. 265). As a result, a large number of workers toiled in conditions resembling Lipietz's notion of "primitive Taylorization" (1987, p. 74): low wage, labour-intensive work lacking basic labour rights, "designed to extort as much surplus-value as possible," while "no attempt is made to reproduce the labour force on any regular basis" (Lipietz, 1987, p. 76).

The landowners and industrialists expanded their share of wealth during World War II, either through monopoly pricing or through joint ventures with various European powers. However, no long-term vision for economic development, social justice or redistribution of wealth was conceived by the ruling class.

The period between 1945 and 1952 was a turbulent one as the gap between the rich and the poor increased, leaving many without the means to a decent livelihood. The continued presence of the British and the collaboration of the Egyptian elite with them mobilized public protest in support of an anti-imperialist struggle. In 1952 an organized faction within the military – the Free Officers – came to power in a coup with the intent of ridding Egypt of both the descendants of Muhammad Ali's dynasty as well as the lingering British political and military presence.

In 1952, a group of radical Free Officers within the army lead a coup against King Farouk and began to implement a revolutionary process of social, economic and political change. Ideologically speaking, the Free Officers represented a heterogeneous group composed of nationalists, technocrats and socialists. The technocrats believed that science and technology, coupled with proactive bureaucratic intervention and planning, could resolve Egypt's developmental problems. The nationalists wanted the public sector to take the lead in building state capitalism by fostering the growth of specific sectors of the economy and providing resources to the private sector. The socialists believed in the need to include the popular classes in the process of economic development. The fourth group was associated with the traditional ruling classes and supported the development of the private sector and wanted to distance Egypt from the Soviet Union and the Eastern Bloc. As the revolution unfolded, it was impossible for these groups to reach an agreement on a grand strategy for economic development and the means to carry out such a program. Sadowski captured the irreconcilable characteristics and ideologies of the Free Officers when he wrote that, [the Free Officers] were an unusually diverse and cacophonous group, which included Marxists and Muslim fundamentalists, partisans of existing civilian parties and advocates of military rule, socialists and free traders, admirers of the West and violent anti-imperialists. Beyond their operational plan for the coup itself, the only thing they had found time to agree on was the need to free Egypt from the deadening monarchy of Farouq and the landowning elite that supported him. (Sadowski, 1991, p. 55)

Given their diverse ideological background, and consistent with the specificities of Arab socialism, the Free Officers kept an open door to private sector participation in the economy and demonstrated their good will by passing laws in support of private investment in the early years of the revolution. The regime abolished the need for 51 percent Egyptian ownership of industrial enterprises, enabled the repatriation of a portion of the profits over a given time period and enabled full foreign ownership of new industries (Farah, 2009, pp. 32–33). The new regime even clamped down on trade unions and outlawed strike action to increase productivity.

Despite such incentives, private capital showed little interest in cooperating with the new regime and engaged in a prolonged investment strike to derail the revolution. As a result, private gross investment levels decreased from E£112 million in 1950 to E£39 million in 1956, with most of the investment occurring in unregulated sectors such as urban real estate and construction (Farah, 2009, p. 33). The unwillingness of the private sector to respond to the regime's investment incentives forced the regime to launch a program of nationalization in 1956 to acquire the necessary capital for industrial investment. The major challenge in this period was the nationalization of the Suez Canal. After the United States declined to aid the building of the High Aswan Dam, the regime decided to nationalize the canal and use its revenues to support industrialization. This move was not welcomed by Britain and France, who had controlled the canal since the late nineteenth century. Israel also feared that it might lose access to the canal after its nationalization and joined France and Britain in what became known as the Suez War of 1956. Subsequently, the Soviet Union built the High Dam using Soviet equipment and technical skills.

Nasser's nationalism was inextricably linked to the politics of decolonization. By the late 1950s, he would become a champion of pan-Arabism, lending support to other Arab nations – like Algeria, Iraq and Palestine – seeking liberation from their colonial oppressors. In 1958, this pan-Arabism led to the merger of Egypt and Syria into the ill-fated United Arab Republic. As Cold War tensions grew, Egypt turned increasingly to the Soviet Union for aid, culminating in Nasser's eventual embrace of Arab socialism as a radical extension of his Arab nationalism.[1]

Nasser differentiated Arab socialism from Marxism-Leninism in several ways. First, Arab socialists did not believe "that dictatorship should pass from one class to another." Rather, Nasser believed that Arab socialists were "converting a state of reactionary 'bourgeois' dictatorship into one of the democracy of the whole people." Unlike Marxism, which lumps property owners together based on their private ownership of property, the Nasserist regime distinguished "between exploiting and non-exploiting private ownership." Nasser was "opposed only to the former" but sought to encourage the latter and argued that "[o]ur socialism ... believes in private ownership of agricultural land within the framework of a co-operative system" (Nasser cited in Salama & Ahmed, 1972, pp. 76–77).

Nasser also distinguished Arab socialism from Marxism-Leninism by emphasizing a non-violent transition to a post-revolutionary Egypt. Arab socialism assigned to the ruling class a role in industrialization, the maintenance of some form of "progressive" private property, the organization of agriculture through cooperatives rather than through wholesale nationalization and limiting the role of the state to that of a provider of social welfare. Private ownership was not abolished, but was assigned a subordinate role to the public sector. This was due to Nasser's belief that the state could serve as "the community's servant" entrusted with protecting the interests of Egyptian society without any bias towards any class or group. In other words, the state could belong to the "whole people and not any class" (Salama & Ahmed, 1972, p. 69).

Upholding the principles of Arab socialism entailed creating a "socialist, cooperative and democratic society" through the formation of the Arab Socialist Union (ASU) in 1962. The ASU proved more effective at organizing mass politics than its predecessors, the Liberation Rally and the National Union. Membership of the ASU, which was open to all citizens except capitalists and landlords, had reached 5 million by 1954.

---

[1] For an insightful account of Nasser's role in the geopolitics of this period, see Prashad (2008).

The regime's goal was to establish cooperation among workers, the army, peasants and students (Hopwood, 1982, p. 91).

What held these different revolutionary tendencies together was a commitment to "statism" (or "*étatism*"), which is defined as a developmental model that ascribes a dominant role for the state in the economy (Cooper, 1982; Vitalis, 1995; Wahba, 1994). Statism, however, is a notoriously ambiguous concept. As a political project that prescribes a series of policies – as opposed to a theoretical concept describing the autonomy of the state – and it lacks a precise definition and tends to incorporate competing, and often contradictory, political claims and ideologies, such as nationalism and socialism. The French notion of *dirigisme*, in which the state "compensated for the relatively weak role played by private entrepreneurs by developing a powerful capacity to intervene in the economy," is instructive in this case (Kesselman, 1992, p. 153). Both the Gaullists on the right and the Communist Party on the far left supported *dirigisme* in the post-war period. The difference in the Egyptian case is that the Nasserist regime was unable to build up the kind of administrative capacity necessary to successfully implement a sustainable statist project over the longer term. Up to a point, both nationalists attempting to build "state capitalism" and socialists attempting a transition towards socialism can collaborate on such a statist project. Statism, therefore, is fundamentally a contested phenomenon in which different social forces seek to use the state to implement different development projects. This was also true in the Egyptian case of Nasserism, where nationalists and socialists collaborated on a project of anti-imperialism and import substitution industrialization (ISI).

However, when it came to policies regarding broader issues of class politics and the redistribution of wealth, the contradictory tendencies within statism tended to become more prominent. The commitment to egalitarianism distinguished the socialists from the nationalists. This goal was promoted through the provision of public goods and services, and a number of other policies designed to redistribute the wealth of society. Such measures included free education; health care; affordable housing, by way of rent controls and public housing projects; mass employment in the public sector; price and wage controls; and consumer goods subsidies. Workers benefited from a higher minimum wage, fewer work hours per week, paid holidays, compulsory social insurance, protection from illegal dismissal and the ability to participate on the boards of companies. Ultimately, any assessment of the nature of statism needs to take into account the class basis of the social forces driving forward and benefiting from statist policies and institutional arrangements. This also was the case with Egypt.

Important Substitution Industrialization

After the failed attempt to court foreign investment, the Revolutionary Command Council began to articulate a program of ISI intended to develop a domestic, Egyptian bourgeoisie with the help of the state. By 1953, the Revolutionary Command Council began planning for an initial three-year transitional phase. As a result, the state "extended its regulatory and proprietary grip to vast areas of the economy" (Waterbury, 1983, p. 233).[2] The main architect of statism during these years was Aziz Sidqi, the "father of Egyptian industry," who began his career as an advisor to the prime minister's office and worked his way up to the post of Minister of Industry in 1956, when Egypt embraced economic nationalism. Under Sidqi, the state assumed control over various sectors of the economy, including heavy industry, construction, railways, and petroleum and petrochemicals.

This shift towards public sector control challenged the economic power that had become concentrated in the private sector. The regime dismantled monopolies and, in 1955, amended the Company Law limiting "the number of firms for which individuals could serve as directors (six) or managing directors (two)" and it imposed a mandatory retirement age of sixty for company directors. These decrees "affected some 200 businessmen from families who had steered the economy for over two generations" (Vitalis, 1995, p. 209).

This nationalist phase of Egypt's post-colonial development reflected the regime's desire for modernization, social justice and state building, but it did not amount to a coherent blueprint for the development of policy. Rather, the regime's policies were the result of trial and error and its goals were constantly being re-articulated within a dramatically changing geopolitical context (Prashad, 2008).

---

[2] While Wahba (1994) and others (F. Ibrahim & Ibrahim, 2003; Issawi, 1963; Zaalouk, 1989) argue that Nasser's economic policies were an extension of previous policies, Vitalis (1995, pp. 207–208) claims otherwise, arguing that, under Nasser and the Free Officers' rule, the state took on a very different role.

The shift to a more socialist development model occurred in 1961 as the West took an increasingly punitive position towards Egypt due to its economic nationalism. A six-point program was implemented with the aim of eradicating imperialism, abolishing feudalism, eliminating monopoly capital, pursuing social justice, building a strong national army and establishing democracy. The model entailed the development of heavy industry and infrastructure supported by agricultural revenues, the import of capital inputs and progressive social policies. Under its direction, a series of radical reforms extended state control over the financial sector and various industries, such as banks, insurance companies, transport, heavy industry, textiles, sugar refineries, foodstuffs, public works, construction, hotels, department stores, cinemas, theatres, newspapers and publishing houses. Enterprises that were not covered by the nationalization law were forced to convert 50 percent of their shares into public property while individuals were allowed shares of no more than E£10,000. Egyptians earning income in excess of E£10,000 were subjected to 90 percent tax rates (Waterbury, 1983, p. 225).

Egypt's first five-year plan was implemented in 1961 and intended to double national income in ten years. Under this plan, the public sector expanded significantly, accounting for 90 percent of all non-agricultural domestic output, 45 percent of domestic savings and 90 percent of gross domestic capital formation by 1965 (Farah, 2009, p. 35). The labour force grew from 6 million to 7.3 million over the five-year period (Farah, 2009). Socioeconomic rights and benefits were extended to workers and unions were legalized and granted collective bargaining rights (albeit with important qualifications, to be discussed in Chapter 6). The ASU defended workers against unfair dismissals, especially in nationalized industries. Workers began to enjoy a shorter working week, higher minimum wages, sick pay, holidays and social insurance and were able to sit on the boards of companies and participate in management decisions and profit-sharing schemes (Waterbury, 1983).

Agrarian Reform

The revolutionary process also resulted in a substantive agrarian reform program launched in 1952. The first phase of agrarian reform, occurring between 1952 and 1961, was more nationalist in its orientation. The goal of this phase was to break the power of the landed class and organize agriculture in a manner that would support ISI. There was no plan, however, to nationalize the agricultural sector or expropriate the landed classes. The justification for land reform came from a history of exploitation in the Egyptian countryside, supported by colonial powers. Peasants were subjected to exorbitant rents without any protection by the state, and a small minority of landowners, including members of the royal family, owned millions of feddans[3] alongside millions of peasants who were either landless or whose plots were insufficient for subsistence farming. By the 1940s,

44 percent of rural families were totally landless and had to work either on large estates or as migrant labourers. Landless peasants faced three brutal options: to join the sharecroppers on a large plantation, to join the casual labourers who maintained the canals and irrigation works, or starvation. For each member of the elite who owned fifty feddans or more, there were literally a hundred families who were completely landless. (Sadowski, 1991, p. 55)

The concentration of land decreased not only the number of small farmers but also the number of big landlords. The latter shrunk further from 14,000 (owning two million feddans) at the turn of the century to 12,000 (owning 2.6 million feddans) by 1950 (Ibrahim, 1994, p. 22). This concentration of land took place in the context of rising cotton prices and high rents. By 1952, 20 percent of the land was owned by 2,000 owners, while two million peasants and small farmers owned only 13 percent of the land (Hopwood, 1982, p. 125).[4]

The Ministry of Agrarian Reform was created to carry out the redistribution of land. There were three dimensions to the agrarian reform. First, a ceiling was introduced that limited land ownership to 200 feddans in 1952 and 100 feddans in 1961. The second aspect of the reform fixed the terms of leases in an attempt to alleviate the exploitative landlord-tenant relationship. The third aspect involved organizing the redistributed lands through agricultural cooperatives.

The state carried out the confiscation of the estates of the larger landowners and abolished private *waqfs* and *hikr* land titles to

---

[3] One feddan = 1.038 acres.
[4] Salama and Ahmed (1972, pp. 8–9) point out that "some ninety great landowners had estates each worth more than two million pounds."

undermine the power of the religious authorities.[5] Individuals whose lands were confiscated, with the exception of the members of the Royal family, were offered indemnity in the form of state bonds redeemable in 30 years at three percent interest.[6] The value of the indemnity was equivalent to ten times the land rent or seven times the basic land tax (Al-Barawy, 1972, p. 73).

The second phase, beginning in 1961, represented a more radical, socialist phase of agrarian reform, a "revolution within a revolution" (Roussillon, 1998, p. 344). In this phase, the stock of land for redistribution expanded through a number of measures. The first was the confiscation of foreigners' lands and the prohibition of foreign landownership of any kind. The second occurred through a sharp reduction in the maximum amount of land individuals and families could legally own. By 1969, an individual could own only a maximum of 50 feddans, whereas a family could have 100 feddans. Other measures, such as allowing small farmers to pay only one-quarter of the value of the land sold to them in 40 annual interest-free instalments, sought to alleviate the financial plight of smallholders (Ziadeh, 1978, pp. 269–270). This second phase also targeted landholders who had registered excess land (more than 100 feddans) under their relatives or children's names, in the attempt to amass large landholdings (Roussillon, 1998, p. 345).

Excess land was taken over by the state for redistribution to the landless and smallholding peasants. Agricultural workers were given the right to organize and defend themselves through cooperatives, and agricultural rents were fixed at seven times the basic land tax. By 1970, there were three million members of the cooperatives (Sadowski, 1991, p. 60).[7] To eliminate sub-letting, land was to be let only to a person who personally tilled it. Furthermore, peasants were provided with protection against the arbitrary powers of landlords by making leases for a period of no less than 3 years and required them to be in written form to avoid the unfair appropriation of peasant land by the

---

[5] *Waqf* land consists of property set aside for charitable or religious purposes and is usually administered by the Ministry of *Waqf*. *Hikr* refers to property rented out on long leases through advanced lump sum payments.

[6] The total area of land that was owned by the Royal family alone totaled 59,539 feddans (Al-Barawy, 1972, p. 73).

[7] By 1967, there were 4,865 Agricultural Cooperative Societies, with a membership of 2,724,677 and a total capital of E£2,775,776 (Al-Barawy, 1972, p. 124).

landlords. In the case of sharecropping, the landlord could not take more than 50 percent of the produce while all expenses had "to be apportioned equally between the sharecropper and the landlord." Landlords and tenants were required to "register their leases at the cooperative of their village for the purpose of ensuring security of the tenancy" (Ziadeh, 1978, pp. 270–271). The lessor shared in both the profit and the loss as partners, while the lease terminated on the death of the lessee. The agrarian program and rent control laws of the Free Officers affected 75 percent of cultivated land (Ansari, 1986, p. 79).

Another aspect of the agrarian reform was the organization of peasants into agricultural cooperatives. Between 1952 and 1970, 817,500 feddans of land were sold to about 342,000 landless peasants, which at the time represented about 9 percent of all rural families (Fahmy, 2002, p. 202; F. Ibrahim & Ibrahim, 2003, p. 115). The redistributed land was to be paid for over 30 years, and recipients of the new land had to join agricultural cooperatives. The state also distributed agricultural inputs such as seeds, fertilizer, and pesticides to 5,000 cooperatives and made available credit at fixed rates. The marketing and transporting of crops, especially cotton and sugar, also fell under the state's jurisdiction.

After 1961, the regime sought to achieve a greater balance between agriculture and industry. The state subsidized peasants by paying them higher prices than the level of international markets. Prices were controlled on basic foodstuffs to help workers. Sadowski (1991, pp. 68–70) argues that whatever the Nasserist regime took out of the rural economy, it put as much back into it.[8]

Workers and Peasants

The agrarian reforms had a major impact on Egyptian society. More than 50 percent of the population was engaged in agricultural labour during Nasser's time. Rural inequality was reduced as land ceilings reduced the number of large estates and land was redistributed to peasants and small farmers. The greatest impact of was on the largest and smallest landholders, with the latter securing rights to property and the former having stringent limitations imposed on their ability to accumulate land. The number of smallholders with less than five

---

[8] For a similar assessment, see Salama and Ahmed (1972, p. 77).

feddans increased by 13 percent and the proportion of land they owned increased by 74 percent. On the other end of the spectrum, the largest estates with more than 200 feddans disappeared completely (Bush, 2002, p. 10).

The reform of agricultural credit cooperatives also played an important role in restoring the rights of peasants to the land. For the first time in Egypt's history, almost one million feddans of agricultural land was released for redistribution to the peasantry (Zaalouk, 1989, p. 26) In short, Nasser's period was a unique period in Egyptian history in the sense that the rights of peasants and workers were not only recognized but enshrined in the constitution. Despite opposition from conservative forces, Nasser and the Free Officers made significant changes to the socioeconomic and political landscape of rural Egypt.

Peasants were not the only class that benefited from Nasser's revolutionary policies. Urban workers also experienced significant gains. Economically speaking, workers experienced a greater degree of economic security, particularly those working in the expanding public sector. The provision of public housing and the implementation of rent control policies significantly lowered their costs of living. In 1954 the regime established the Public Housing and Construction Company to construct housing units for low-income earners that were leased to low-income groups at a nominal rent of E£2 to E£3 per month (Hanna, 1985, p. 197). In 1956, a comprehensive policy paper commissioned by the government was published, marking a watershed in the regime's approach to the housing problem.[9] The plan was part of the regime's industrial policy and emphasized a comprehensive approach to the provision of public housing for workers (Abu Lughod, 1971, pp. 230–231).

Various forms of rent control comprised the other main pillar of the Free Officers' housing policy. As with the provision of public housing, the regime's initial approach to the rental market was relatively modest. In conjunction with the reform of rural tenancies implemented through the agrarian reform program, legislation transforming the nature of urban tenancies was passed. The first set of reforms introduced a series of rent reductions between 1952 and 1961. This

---

[9] As part of the government's infrastructural development plan, 5.5 million square meters of Cairo's street system were paved between 1952 and 1958 (Abu Lughod, 1971, pp. 142, 160).

measure was followed by a more assertive approach implemented through a rent control law passed in 1962. Public sector committees that determined rents based on construction and land costs were formed. During the remainder of the 1960s, the government continued its policy of rent reduction and rent control as a measure of making housing affordable for workers and civil servants. In 1965, rents were reduced by 20–35 percent, depending on the age of the building. Rent reductions were offered to most urban dwellers and by 1965, the Cairo governorate had constructed 15,000 low-income housing units (Bayad, 1979, p. 140; Soliman, 2004, pp. 48–49). By 1968 rents became "symbolic payment," for example, E£1 per room in low-income housing, and E£2 in medium-cost housing.

All private housing became subject to rent control under the Nasserist regime. Rent control was framed as a socioeconomic right to secure residency for lower income Egyptians. As a result of these laws, tenants obtained the right to transfer their contracts to their children with fixed rents. In this sense, Hanna (1985) and Hill (1999) characterize Nasserist rent control laws as a new form of property right for workers and peasants. For working class Egyptians, it was "preferable to be a tenant" because rent controls enabled tenants to pass on their fixed rents to heirs and close relatives, giving tenants a de facto "share in property rights" (Harik, 1998, p. 61).[10]

Politically, workers and peasants also enjoyed significant gains. Arab socialism sought an end to exploitation and promoted of economic justice and equal opportunities for all through a democratic dialogue among the popular social forces – peasants, workers, soldiers, intellectuals and national capital. The rights enshrined in the constitution of 1956 included social and economic rights and made the state responsible for upholding those rights. Other rights included civil rights and personal freedoms. Economic activity was to be organized in ways that benefited the general population rather than the elite, and the natural resources of the country were to become the property of the state.

These rights were strengthened and expanded in *Al Mithaq al-Watany* (the National Charter of May 1962), which had the goal of "socialist transformation" in Egypt. Through the charter, workers and peasants had their rights recognized by the state and had representation in all areas of government. They could occupy 50 percent of the

---

[10] For more on rent control benefits to workers, see McCall (1988, pp. 162–163).

seats of the National Assembly and were guaranteed representation in village councils. Other concrete rights for workers included profit sharing and participation in management decision making. Workers were to receive 25 percent of the annual total profits through different schemes including cash hand-outs, housing and social benefits. Nasser was also aware of the growing and unaccountable power of the bureaucracy and therefore warned about the emergence of a "feudal bureaucracy" (Salama & Ahmed, 1972).

The Contradictions and Limits of Arab Socialism

However, the revolution was not without its problems and contradictions. One of the biggest obstacles to the revolutionary transformation of Egyptian society was the lack of state capacity to implement the necessary reforms. The state's reach was limited to the main urban centres. Its control over cotton exporting companies and the fertilizer and pesticide factories only gave it the power of taxation over certain economic activities. Regulating the agricultural sector, however, remained out of reach. This administrative weakness was apparent in the way public sector contracts were handed out to the private sector. Similarly, a lack of public sector accountability allowed room for collaboration between public sector managers and the private sector. This resulted not only in a brain drain, but also in illegal resource transfers from the public to the private sector and to the black market. Even in the cities, various levels of government maintained their autonomy. As a result, policies designed in Cairo were often never implemented outside of the major urban areas.

As a consequence of this lack of state capacity, the power of the big landlords persisted despite the fact that most revolutionary reforms were aimed at attacking their institutional and informal power. While many landlords had excess land confiscated and redistributed to the peasantry, they were allowed to retain their deeds to the land, thereby enabling them to easily reclaim their lands in the 1970s under Sadat. Other landlords were allowed to sell their land and pursue new opportunities in the construction and real estate sectors and enabling medium farmers to accumulate their land. Finally, the reforms did not affect the inheritance of landed property.

The persistence of landlord power subsequently exacerbated the state's administrative weakness, as landlords were able to co-opt local government authorities by bringing them into their circles of patronage. Abuses of land reform were neither reported to the government nor confronted at the village level. In 1966, the village of Kamshish became the focal point of land reform violations when it was revealed that the head of the Al-Fiqqi family not only held hundreds of feddans, but had ordered the murder of an activist who had tried to investigate how they managed to circumvent the agrarian reforms. It was after this affair that the regime put together the Higher Committee for the Liquidation of Feudalism (HCLF). To the dismay of the regime, the HCLF "quickly determined that these violations were not confined to Kamshish but were common across Egypt." The committee estimated that "each province had twenty to thirty families whose members either evaded the agrarian reforms, controlled the village administration and party organs, or exercised oppressive influence" (cited in Sadowski, 1991, pp. 78–79).

The weakness of the regime's administrative capacity and its lack of control over rural Egypt – particularly in Lower Egypt – coupled with the lingering power of the landlords provided the perfect environment for medium landowners to prosper. By 1965, 4 years after Nasser's radical shift in economic policy and a new round of land confiscations, close to one-third of Egypt's cultivable land was still controlled by 5.2 percent of landowners (Ayubi, 1995, p. 200). Close to 70,000 farmers owning more than 10 feddans emerged as the counterpart of the old landed elite in rural Egypt (Sadowski, 1991, p. 75). This group played an important role in controlling the rural economy and politics – largely through their domination of the provincial councils and the cooperatives – and thus shaped the outcome of state policies in most parts of Egypt.

Numerous factors facilitated the rise of these medium-sized farmers. First, they operated outside of the state cooperatives, which allowed them to shift their crop patterns to growing high-value crops and livestock. Although they remained outside the agricultural cooperatives, these affluent farmers benefited from the public resources made available to the cooperatives with the help of corrupt local officials.[11] As a result, rich farmers profited by exploiting the cooperative system as well as through methods of diversification and the mechanization of agriculture. This newly emerging class, while benefitting from the

---

[11] For more on this, see Sadowski (1991).

revolution, had no loyalty to its goals, and would become an important base of conservative support for Sadat during the 1970s (Ansari, 1986).

These internal challenges and contradictions were exacerbated by economic crises. In the context of prolonged investment strikes by Egyptian capital, and the high cost of war in Yemen and Israel, economic growth failed to sustain the high levels of public spending that the progressive social policies of the revolution demanded. A lack of economic growth, combined with a growing trade deficit from ISI and the withdrawal of U.S. aid, forced Egypt to turn to the conservative Gulf States for credit. Borrowing conditions set by the Gulf States included the removal of state controls over investors and guarantees against nationalization. After 1967, Nasser announced that he was ready to "denationalize certain enterprises and expand the opportunities for the private sector. . . . He authorized de-sequestration of some lands and enterprises (movie theatres, department stores), thus re-legitimizing private economic activity" (Sadowski, 1991, p. 103). The defeat by Israel accelerated the crisis of the regime, as it emboldened conservative and Islamic forces in Egyptian society. By July 26, 1967, barely a month after the defeat in the war with Israel, Nasser's regime was forced to issue a de-sequestration law that returned properties that were sequestered by the HCLF. This meant that cases under HCLF investigation for sequestration declined from 334 to 25 and the amount of land for sequestration decreased from 55,000 feddans to 3,100 feddans (Ansari, 1986, p. 143).

At the same time, the regime began to lose the support of workers and peasants due to the corruption of state officials and the persistence of the power of the landed classes. Over time, these landed interests struck alliances with the centre-right elements among the Free Officers and thus began influencing state policy in their favour. The loss of support among workers and peasants was especially dramatic because the regime had effectively destroyed all independent progressive organizations that could help to democratize the state and society. Paradoxically, Nasser was more successful in crushing the left and the communists than he was in uprooting the conservative landed classes in rural Egypt. While Nasser "stood against the rightward pull [of Egyptian politics] . . . he always stood as an individual and never as the representative of an organized left-wing with real political power (Johnson, 1973, pp. 3–4)." Thus, despite the commitment to democratization, the regime never successfully nurtured a democratic movement that would act as its political base, and the balance of class forces began to shift away from Nasserism towards the conservatism of the Sadat regime.

On top of these internal contradictions, several external events conspired to bring down the Nasserist revolution. The failed union with Syria in the form of the United Arab Republic of 1958–1961, the costly war in Yemen from 1962 to 1967, and finally the disastrous Arab-Israeli War of 1967, all undermined the political legitimacy of the Nasserite regime. In particular, the Arab-Israeli war drained public resources and strained public subsidies, resulting in significant retrenchment and a gradual renewal of the private sector. The state increasingly relied on private credit sources to support public sector investment and production, which resulted in rising inflation and declining consumption. It also made Egypt dependent on politically unsympathetic foreign creditors such as the Gulf States.

The Nasser era represented a unique period in the history of modern Egypt where, for the first time, the propertied classes faced a serious challenge from those who controlled the state and the interests of workers and peasants formed the core of state's policies. Despite this, however, the deep-seated power of the landed classes remained entrenched, enabling them to reassert their power and reclaim their privileges under the rule of Nasser's successor, Anwar Sadat.

Economic Liberalization under Anwar Sadat

Anwar Sadat, described as "more rightist than most" of the Free Officers, became the President of Egypt in October 1970 and remained in power until his death in October 1981 (Cooper, 1982, p. 66). Sadat cut ties with the Soviet Union and established closer ties with the United States. As early as in 1971, Sadat began purging pro-Soviet members of the state and expelled Soviet military advisers from Egypt to secure the financial aid of the United States. Conservative oil regimes such as Saudi Arabia rewarded Egypt's shift of alliances in favour of the West by sending in aid, especially after the War of 1973.

In economic terms, Sadat's rule marked a significant shift away from the statism of Nasser as he opened the door for a larger role for the private sector in the economy. The *infitah,* or liberalization, of the Egyptian economy was a response both to the economic crisis of the late 1960s as well as to the regional shift towards a free market.

In an attempt to revive the Egyptian economy, Sadat encouraged foreign investors to take a bigger role.

In September 1971, Sadat announced a program for the reorganization of the state, the essence of which was to repeal Nasserist policies and facilitate a larger role for the private sector in the economy (Cooper, 1982, p. 75). Early attempts at liberalization were met with resistance by public sector workers and in response Sadat began consolidating his power by purging state institutions of Nasserist elements and replacing them with more conservative appointees sympathetic to his economic policies. Within a period of three months, Sadat made 1,237 new political appointments, notable among which were 25 new governors, 125 new secretaries and undersecretaries of the ASU in the districts, 625 members of the Popular Local Government, all of whom guaranteed support for Sadat and his policies in the coming years (Cooper, 1982, p. 77). The October War of 1973 with Israel bolstered Sadat's reputation and provided the right political environment for him to introduce his policies of *infitah*. Hoping for a generous flow of Arab investment as a sign of gratitude for the War, Sadat opened up the economy to private foreign investment.

The fundamentals of Sadat's *infitah* policy were presented to the People's Assembly in April 1974. Impressed by the export-led economic growth model of the East Asian "tigers" (Taiwan, Singapore and Korea), supporters argued that a more outward looking approach to economic development would enable Egypt to achieve higher levels of economic growth. Despite the developmentalism that lay behind the success of the Asian Tigers, the core of Sadat's *infitah* policy was a classic free market argument: foreign investment and technology combined with Egypt's comparative advantage of cheap resources and cheap labour will spur economic development. With this guiding formula, Sadat implemented policies aimed at revitalizing the private sector and transforming the role of the public sector.

In his attempt to attract foreign and Arab investment, Sadat provided guarantees against the nationalization, confiscation and sequestration of capital and property. Investor guarantees and privileges included the repatriation of profits, tax exemptions from 5 to 8 years and customs exemptions for imports geared towards production. Priority was given to investors who were self-sufficient in foreign exchange, promoted Egyptian exports and imported advanced technology and modern management techniques. According to the law, an investment project was considered part of the private sector even if it was conducted as a public/private partnership in which the public sector firm owned the majority of shares. In addition, no sector of the economy was shielded from foreign private investment, as had been the case under Nasser. Economic sectors such as textiles, chemicals, minerals, and basic metals that were traditionally reserved for the public sector were now open to foreign investment.

Two years after *infitah*, foreign and domestic private investment was concentrated in finance, services, tourism and real estate, exposing the speculative nature of investment.[12] By the end of 1976, only 66 projects had begun with a capital value of E£36 million and 3,450 employees (Waterbury, 1983, p. 132). This lacklustre response by foreign investors was interpreted by the government as the result of rigid regulations on private sector activity, prompting the government to further reduce restrictions on profit repatriations and remove the requirements for firms' self-sufficiency in foreign exchange. This "made it possible for foreign investors to purchase foreign exchange with local currency, to sell products locally for foreign exchange, and to purchase hard currency in the "parallel money market" that had first been set up to help the Egyptian private sector meet its foreign exchange needs" (Waterbury, 1983, p. 133).[13] Similar rights and incentives were extended to Egyptian investors as well, the only caveat being that, unlike foreign investors, they did not have guarantees against nationalization.

While the public sector was still considered to be the dominant economic sector responsible for carrying out the development plan, its main role was to provide essential services to both Egyptian and foreign private investors. *Infitah* also sought to revitalize the public sector through competition with the private sector and by engaging in public/private partnerships with foreign capital. In practice, this meant that the public sector was deprived of guaranteed public investment and was forced to respond to market imperatives and generate its own revenues. At the same time, Sadat reduced democratic oversight in the public sector by dismantling public organizations (*mu'assasat 'amma*) that functioned as public holding companies under Nasser. The *mu'assassat* were not simply bureaucratic apparatuses; they coordinated,

---

[12] In general, Arab investment concentrated in real estate and tourism and non-Arab investors invested in petroleum, banking and pharmaceuticals.

[13] See Wahba (1994, pp. 190–191).

planned and provided oversight for industrial activities. In effect, the state no longer made decisions regarding wages, profit distribution, credit or the organization of the public sector firms. These decisions were handed over to private firms.

Access to foreign aid was conditional on firm competitiveness, which led to a high degree of rivalry between government ministries and departments. As such, the private sector gained leverage in shaping the public sector. In this process, private investors organized themselves into a national association to more effectively represent the needs of business within the state. For instance, in 1975, the Egyptian Businessmen's Association (*Jam'iyyat rijal al-a'mal al-misriyyin*) was founded, consisting of ex-ministers and officials, board members of major banks and public sector companies, representing a wide array of interests including the state bourgeoisie, domestic private investors and international investors.[14]

The state bourgeoisie played an important role in linking the public sector to international capital by facilitating investment in tourism, finance, trade and real estate. Another notable outcome of joint ventures with the private sector was the transfer of assets from the public to the private sector. Public sector firms lacking foreign exchange often used their real estate as equity in these projects. Besides physical assets, public sector firms also lost skilled workers to the private sector through joint ventures given the absence of labour regulations and salary caps in the private sector under *infitah*.

However, *infitah* did not succeed in privatizing any notable state-owned enterprises due to a lack of private sector demand and trade union opposition. Investors often opted for joint ventures and state subsidies for inputs such as energy and raw materials. While public sector firms avoided being privatized, they were no longer bound by the Employment Guarantee Program and no longer acted as an employer of post-graduates as it had under Nasser. Thus, under Sadat, public sector expansion was limited to the top levels of the bureaucracy and the state's coercive apparatus.[15]

---

[14] The term *state bourgeoisie* refers to the heads of public sector companies who, under Sadat's reforms, were compelled to adopt profit-maximizing strategies in partnership with the private sector. See Ayubi (1991b).

[15] According to Ayubi (1991b, p. 268), "In only three years from 1977 to 1980/81, employment in the bureaucratic machine increased from 1,911,000 to 2,474,000, i.e. by 29.6 percent or some 10 percent per annum."

Infitah freed up the private sector to engage in finance, heavy industry and foreign trade, areas of the economy that were heavily regulated under Nasser. Thus, by the mid to late 1970s, a whole host of joint ventures had begun. The successful ones tended to be large projects that were joint ventures with foreign capital in textiles, food processing, chemicals and metallurgy. By 1977, a total of 693 joint ventures had been approved (Waterbury, 1983, p. 172).

However, not all private sector firms were winning. For instance, around 300 textile and knitwear firms that existed under Nasser and exported to the Soviet Union were losing because of changes in diplomatic and trade relations with the Soviet Union and the flooding of the Egyptian market by cheap Asian goods. The winners of *infitah* included three groups. The first group was characterized as crony capitalists or compradors engaged in the "own-exchange system,"[16] which primarily catered to middle class demand for luxury goods. This group imported goods and acted as middlemen between foreign firms and the Egyptian government. Waterbury (1983) argues that this particular group of importers – who he refers to as *munfatihun* – succeeded in consolidating their power due to *infitah*. The second group were the *muqawalun*, who contracted out their services to the state. Their gains surged as Sadat implemented his first Five Year Plan between 1976 and 1981. During this period, 40 percent of all public investment, amounting to E£700 million, went into construction projects. Of this, 80 percent went to private construction firms (Waterbury, 1983, p. 182). The rebuilding of the Canal Zone cities and the New Towns Project of Sadat opened up vast opportunities for contracting out and sub-contracting to the private sector and the siphoning off of public sector materials into the black market. The individual who personified the construction sector and gained the most under Sadat was Ahmad Osman, the president of the Arab Contractors and Sadat's Minister of Housing and Reconstruction. His company employed 50,000 workers and his operations reached beyond Egypt. Under Nasser, Osman's domestic business was nationalized but he was

---

[16] The own-exchange system was started in the early 1970s, but was discontinued in 1973. The system was initiated to facilitate and expedite the import of raw materials for the private sector. However, the system facilitated the import of consumer luxury goods. Nonetheless, Sadat revived the system in March 1974 "in order to satisfy the needs of the masses" (Sadat cited in Wahba, 1994, p. 191). See also Waterbury (1983, pp. 176–178).

free in his international operations. Under Sadat, Osman served as a "food security" adviser and promoted joint agri-business ventures such as the Pepsi Cola Citrus project in Ismailia.

A third group that benefited from *infitah* included those who took advantage of the relaxation of urban property regulations. This group included professionals, state officials and private investors. Landlords collected huge amounts in "key money" (*khiliw rigl*) and rent from their furnished apartments.[17] At the other end of the spectrum were the property developers who bypassed building codes and regulations and became wealthy overnight.

To make Egypt attractive for foreign investors, the regime also dismantled the socialist-inspired labour laws that protected workers' wages and benefits. According to the October Paper of 1974, wages were to be determined by market forces. In defence of his labour policy, Sadat argued that regulations limited the market for the highly skilled labour necessary to attain higher levels of productivity. The regime also believed that if workers had greater freedom of movement, they would contribute the remittances earned through migrant labour to the Egyptian economy. To this end, Sadat's regime eliminated exit visas in 1974, allowing workers to migrate to oil-rich Arab countries such as the Gulf States. Worker remittances increased from E£84 million in 1970 to E£2,860 million in 1980 and played an important role in paying off the external debt while increasing the demand for imports (Waterbury, 1983, p. 30).

While the regime managed to encourage outward labour migration to the Gulf States, *infitah* policies failed to produce employment for those remaining in Egypt.[18] Capital-intensive investment relying on labour-saving technology only contributed to the problems of unemployment. By the end of 1978, there were only 13,553 workers in 191 functioning investment projects. Even these numbers are suspect due to the "reclassification of public sector partners to joint ventures in

---

[17] Hanna (1985, pp. 201–208) defines key money as "an illegal sum of money outside the rental contract paid to the landlord" and which is considered as the difference between market rents and controlled rents. Although it appeared in the 1940s, this practice was criminalized under Nasser. However, in the 1970s key money increased dramatically.

[18] Aulas (1982, p. 14) notes that, "By the time of the 1976 census, 1.4 million Egyptians were counted as overseas, including 600,000 workers, or nearly five percent of the active population."

the private sector" (Waterbury, 1983, p. 143). *Infitah* produced a decade of "jobless growth," whereby the application of labour-saving technology in almost all fields where international capital was involved reduced the demand for labour (Ikram, 2006, pp. 215–217).[19]

Public sector workers involved in potential joint ventures expressed their opposition by using their unions to block them. Workers claimed that joint ventures with international capital would result in the liquidation of their factories and turn them into assembly plants for large international firms. Their fears were justified as these outcomes often followed. In general, public sector workers feared the loss of the gains they made during the 1960s, such as the right to organize, the right to bargain for wages, employment protection and other social security benefits. Economic liberalization meant that public sector workers were not immune from attacks on their wages, benefits and work conditions. As it happened, a *fatwa* was issued in 1976 stating that workers' union representatives need no longer be elected by workers, but could instead be appointed by management, leading to a process of trade union centralization and co-optation that will be discussed in greater detail in Chapter 6. This soon became the practice in public sector banks, while spreading to other sectors of the economy.

Infitah resulted in the growth of commercial interests associated with domestic and foreign trade. Approximately two thirds of the capital generated between 1974 and 1976 was commercial capital (Cooper, 1982, pp. 109–110). This growth in commerce was linked to the relaxation on imports of technology and equipment. Tax incentives and repatriation policies also facilitated the expansion of commerce and banking. The foreign exchange gained through remittances was absorbed in the purchase of luxury consumer goods or in real estate, cars and electronics. There was a boom in urban property development, construction, financial services, food processing, textiles, tourism and petroleum.

Sadat's *infitah* policy also radically reshaped the agricultural sector by transforming agrarian property relations. His policy sought to create a larger role for agri-business by promoting high value-added cash crops for export, with the hope of making agriculture more productive and profitable. In 1975, public investment in agriculture

---

[19] For similar arguments regarding the capital-intensive nature of Egypt's jobless growth, see Fergany (1998), Radwan (1997), Karshenas (1994).

was reduced to 6 percent of the total budget, down from 20 percent in 1965 (Sadowski, 1991, p. 71). Private investors were encouraged to fill the gap left by the public sector. To facilitate this process, the regime passed laws that deregulated the land market, liberalized rents and gave landlords the freedom to determine the type of rents – cash or in kind – they wanted tenants to pay.

The development of agri-business transferred arable land from small farmers to large commercial owners – both domestic and international – who shifted the pattern of agricultural production towards the export market and away from production for the domestic market. In contrast with Nasser, who redistributed land to peasants and small farmers, Sadat redistributed reclaimed lands to private developers, public sector workers, agricultural engineers, university students, military families and veterans, all with the goal of strengthening his base of support. More important, the state provided guarantees to private property ownership by registering title deeds to redistributed lands. While the types of deeds varied, the upshot was that there were no regulations to prevent property owners from accumulating or developing their plots as they saw fit.

During the 1950s and 1960s, Nasser's regime had sequestered property from wealthy individuals to fulfil the goals of the Revolution. Sequestered property was placed under the control of the state until a decision was reached regarding the return to its original owner, its redistribution to peasants and small farmers or its nationalization. Sadat called for the "removal of all obstacles to a speedy settlement of all outstanding claims" for the families who had lost their property to Nasser's sequestration laws (Hill, 1999, p. 132). Under Sadat, sequestered properties were restored and former landlords were compensated (in cash or in kind).[20] As early as 1971, 800 proprietors saw their land returned to them (Forte, 1978, p. 276; Zaalouk, 1989, p. 57). The case of Kamshish Village demonstrated the nature of social change from Nasser to Sadat. The ruling elite of Kamshish village – the Fiqqis – had their lands sequestered in 1961. The land was later distributed among 200 small farmers (out of a total of 576) in the village. Under Sadat the Fiqqis recovered their land and received further compensation for their "maltreatment" by the HCLF (Ansari,

---

[20] With a total offer of $10 million, Sadat also compensated Americans who had lost their property during the nationalizations of Nasser (Forte, 1978, p. 276).

1986, pp. 19–49). Estimates vary, but the properties of between 400 and 5,000 landlords were restored accounting for a grand total of 635,000 feddans (Tignor, 1990, p. 462).[21]

The second important change in property relations was the outcome of Sadat's attack on the Agrarian Reforms of 1952. In 1976, Sadat destroyed agricultural cooperatives and, by extension, peasant security in land. He transferred the resources and capital of the cooperatives into the Principal Bank for Development and Agricultural Credit, whose main office was located in Cairo. Once he had created this centralized credit agency for agriculture, he encouraged agri-business to develop and reclaim land across Egypt.

In the second half of the 1970s, the regime imported as much as 40 percent of Egypt's food requirements, 78 percent of which was wheat. Critics of Nasserist rule linked the rising food imports and agricultural decline to the restrictions that had been placed on producers. It was argued that because of pro-tenant policies, landlords had no incentives to improve their lands. These critics called for a "balance between tenants and landlords" by reversing the agrarian reforms (Ansari, 1986, p. 189). As a result, the ceiling on land ownership was abolished on the pretence that caps on landownership prevented the establishment of large estates and the development of capital-intensive agriculture.[22] Removing the limitations on landownership indeed facilitated the rise of large estates and the emergence of rich farmers who moved away from field crops – broad beans, lentils, peanuts, sesame, soya and potatoes – and invested in fruits and vegetables for export. The returns on export produce were substantively higher than for field crops. The area covering orchards expanded from 64,000

---

[21] In August 1974, 22,000 feddans, including 5,000 feddans of orchards, were to be returned to their original owners. In September 1974, another 1,700 feddans, including 700 feddans of orchards in the Sharqiyya governorate, were returned to 86 owners. In total, 147,000 feddans were returned to their former owners, land that was redistributed among small farmers by the Ministry of Agrarian Reform. The government paid compensation for 17,000 feddans of land, which the ministry had redistributed with full ownership rights to 7,500 families (Ansari, 1986, pp. 182–183).

[22] Ansari (1986) argues that, contrary to the claims by critics of agrarian reform, it was the small producers of field crops bore the brunt of agricultural restrictions – even under Nasser – because they relied on the state for inputs and for the prices of their produce. Rich farmers had elected to stay out of agricultural cooperatives and were thus not affected by prices or restrictions placed by the state.

feddans in 1952 to 313,000 feddans in 1976; by 1977, they became free of tax. The area dedicated to vegetable production had increased from 625,000 feddans in 1966 to 913,000 feddans in 1976 (Ansari, 1986, p. 190).

Under Sadat, hundreds of corporate managers opposed to privatization were purged from public sector enterprises and replaced by successors who, despite their rhetorical commitment to public sector stewardship, "showed an alarming penchant for steering their enterprises into controversial joint ventures with foreign firms and then popping up on the local boards of those same corporations" (Bianchi, 1985, p. 149). Under this new leadership, the Federation of Egyptian Industry pushed for the elimination of worker participation in management, abolition of worker profit-sharing schemes and a weakening of job security. At the same time, it advocated for public subsidies and government incentives that sought to facilitate a "decisive shift in the balance of investment and power in Egypt's mixed economy in favour of private manufacturers" (Bianchi, 1985, p. 149). Despite these developments, many private sector actors grew increasingly dissatisfied with the Federation of Egyptian Industry and sought alternative forms of interest representation in new business associations such as the Egyptian Businessmen Association.

Class, Property and State Power

The policy of *infitah* was biased in favour of the propertied classes. Even prior to *infitah*, the regime sought to restore property to the urban and rural elite and establish its political base of support. Under Nasser, sequestration was "predominantly used to dispossess the wealthy classes"; under Sadat, it became "the means for suppressing political rivals, including the working class" and the peasantry (Ansari, 1986, pp. 183–184). By changing property relations, Sadat had two broader goals in mind: to end the political isolation of the propertied class and to gain the trust of foreign and especially Arab investors.

One of Sadat's main contributions to reshaping Egypt was the extension of state power into parts of Egypt where the state previously did not have much control. This was accomplished through the dismantling, in 1978, of the ASU and its replacement by the National Democratic Party (NDP) that, from its conception until 2011, was the party of the ruling class and over time became more effective in organizing the various conservative and landed interests in Egyptian society. While the Local Government Law of 1975 was presented as a step towards decentralization and democratization, it strengthened the power of the central government and took away the power of local popular councils at the village level. This regressive step was accomplished by purging the ASU – which had granted peasants and workers representation at every level of the state – of radical elements while increasing the number of conservative representatives. By purging left-wing forces, Sadat not only gutted the ASU, he also increased the power of appointed officials at every level of the Egyptian state. The executive village councils, representing the central government and appointed at the village level, were empowered to veto the power of the popular councils. This not only watered down the representation of peasants and workers in decision-making processes, but it also increased the opportunity for corruption and collusion whereby local council members were bought off by the powerful local elite.

The political networks created in rural Egypt ensured that a majority of the votes would be cast in favour of the NDP. These networks were maintained by rewarding loyal villages with government resources and withholding resources from rebellious villages where support for the NDP was low. Provincial governors – appointed by Sadat – tended to identify with the ruling party. The NDP also became an important vehicle through which businessmen, contractors, traders, speculators and rural magnates voiced their interests and determined policy outcomes.[23]

Indeed, the launch of *infitah* in 1974 marked the beginning of a long process of consolidating and institutionalizing the rights of private property. In 1971, Sadat adopted a new constitution that contained several articles establishing the sanctity of private property and the limits of the state's power over it. Private property was protected from confiscation and sequestration by the state. Property owners were fully compensated by the state in cases where private property was violated for the purpose of the public interest and in accordance with the law.

---

[23] Sadat also lifted the "Political Isolation Decrees," which prevented the rural propertied class from participating in political life under Nasser. This class would come to form a strong interest group fighting against Nasserist policies.

The importance of these constitutional changes was that, while Nasser had allowed private property to exist as long as it did not subject anyone to exploitation, Sadat elevated the sanctity of private property over the concerns of social justice.

This institutionalization of private property rights came about mostly due to court rulings that assessed the constitutionality of laws passed under Nasser. The Supreme Constitutional Court, which was enshrined as an independent judicial body in the 1971 Constitution, played an active role in asserting the rights of private property through the reversal of Nasserist policies. The outcome of Supreme Constitutional Court rulings empowered the propertied classes, whether in rural or urban Egypt, at the expense of peasants and workers.

The final assertion of the right of private property was due to two different court rulings. The first ruling upheld the right of private property and accused Nasser of violating his own constitution through his policy of sequestration. Consequently, the court rendered Nasser's appropriation of lands over the limits set by the regime unconstitutional. The court emphasized that "the Constitution's call for 'social solidarity, self-sufficiency and just distribution which bridges the gaps of classes' does not allow the violation of other principles of the constitution such as protecting private property," which it argued Law 104/1964 allowed for (Hill, 1999, pp. 130–132). The second ruling in 1979 nullified any legislation that limited the restoration of property on the grounds that "such limitation was tantamount to confiscation" (Ansari, 1986, pp. 182–183).

Crisis and Conflict: The Outcomes of *Infitah*

While policies of *infitah* intended to increase the flow of foreign investment to Egypt, the results remained less than impressive. Growth averaged 6.7 percent per year and per capita income increased by an average of 4.3 percent per year between 1971 and 1980 (World Bank, 2018f). This was an improvement on the 5 percent average annual growth rate and the 2.3 percent average annual increase in per capita growth that occurred between 1961 and 1970. However, this improvement was due less to *infitah* than to the increase in oil production in the Sinai region, rents from the Suez Canal, the billions of dollars in remittances from Egyptian migrant workers working in the Gulf oil industries during the OPEC crisis years and the growth of the tourism industry (Economist Intelligence Unit, 1988, p. 13; Rutherford, 2008, p. 135).[24] Even then, public sector investment made up the bulk of this investment. Between 1975 and 1983, public sector investment amounted to 26 percent of the gross domestic product (GDP), while the share of domestic private investment stood at 4.6 percent of GDP and that of foreign private investment was a meagre 3.4 percent, mostly from oil companies (El-Ghonemy, 2003, p. 79).

Infitah also failed to resolve Egypt's negative balance of trade. Egypt's trade deficit rose from 4.6 percent of GDP in 1970 to 18.6 percent in 1979 (World Bank, 2018c). According to Aulas, Egypt's external debt "increased on an average of 28 percent per year under Sadat, compared to 13 percent over the previous ten years" (1982, p. 8). Debt servicing accounted for 10 percent of GDP (Cooper, 1982, pp. 106–107). Sadat's response to this escalating economic crisis was another generous gesture towards the private sector (foreign and domestic) to pull the economy out of the crisis. However, to avoid an escalation of the social conflict and possible social disorder, he continued to borrow and support price subsidies, leading to a dramatic rise in external debt, from 23.6 percent of Gross National Income in 1970 to 87.3 percent in 1979 (reaching a high of 90.6 percent in 1978) (World Bank, 2018d).

The cost of living also began to rise under Sadat's *infitah* program. By 1974, inflation rose to 10 percent (World Bank, 2018k). Real wages began to fall due to this inflation. Sadat's regime responded by increasing the minimum wage (four times), maintaining subsidies on basic goods and exempting small farmers and low-income earners from paying taxes. These measures did not succeed in arresting inflation or its impact on those with fixed incomes. Between 1974 and 1979, inflation averaged 10.6 percent with 1977 being the worst year. In January 1975, the workers of Helwan Steel Complex protested the government's refusal to consider the demands of their union. The workers of Misr Spinning and Weaving Company in Mahalla al-Kubra organized a 3-day strike, winning a wage increase for all public sector production workers in the country. In August, textile workers in

---

[24] After the 1973 war with Israel, Egypt had gained its oil fields in the Sinai Peninsula and oil production resumed soon after. At the same time, the value of remittances had increased from U.S.$189 million in 1974 to U.S.$2,855 million in 1981. And finally, Egypt received grants and aid from conservative Arab states in return for its war with Israel.

Alexandria held a 2-week-long strike, defying a government ban on strike activity. In December, the government sequestered the funds of the General Union of the Egyptian Workers, the largest union in the country at the time. In 1975 and 1976, textile workers in Mahalla al-Kubra met violent state repression during their demonstrations demanding bonuses and minimum wages.[25] In Cairo, angry protesters attacked police precincts and ransacked the homes of officials in the worst case of domestic unrest since 1952. These strikes and protests culminated in the bread riots of January 18 and 19, 1977, in which hundreds of Egyptians were killed, easily surpassing the violence of the previous year.

By 1979, the agricultural sector had undergone radical changes as a result of Sadat's assault on small farmers. Rents had increased by as much as 100 percent. Law 65 of July 1975 increased rents to seven times the land tax, while landlords gained the right to evict tenants who failed to pay rents within a specified period of time (Ansari, 1986, pp. 91–92). These changes in tenancy relations affected 1.5 million peasants and an area of 2.5 million feddans, or around 43 percent of the cultivated land (Ansari, 1986, p. 192).

In short, the restructuring of property relations led to the rise of a class of rich farmers who enjoyed guarantees against nationalization and the sequestration of their properties. Rich farmers eventually succeeded in dominating village popular councils after Sadat changed the definition of a peasant to anyone owning less than 50 feddans (Sadowski, 1991, p. 81). The engrossment of land by large property owners resulted in a mass migration towards the cities. Between 1972 and 1979, 650,000 labourers left agriculture to find work in the cities (Roy, 1991a, pp. 559–560). While some of these workers succeeded in moving to the Gulf States to work in the construction sector, most found jobs in the booming Egyptian construction sector.

The Islamists, who openly criticized Sadat for failing to run the state and meet the needs of the people, captured this discontent. Islamists viewed Sadat and his regime as corrupt, with no ethos to serve society; their only perceived goal was to accumulate wealth. The absence of accountability within all levels of the state led to rising levels of corruption. According to Lutfi Abd al-Azim, the conservative and

---

[25] Beinin (2009a) argues that Sadat's wage increases and bonuses were in response to workers' mobilization and strike action.

pro-*infitah* editor for *al-Ahram al-Iqtisadi*, Sadat brought decadence, vulgar affluence and supported the growth of a class of *nouveau riche*. Azim argued that the majority of Egyptians now live under a "regime of 'economic apartheid' ... that deprives the majority of the essentials of life while bestowing fantastic benefits and advantages upon a tiny segment of society" (Cited in Waterbury, 1983, p. 230). In the eyes of many Islamists, Sadat was called the "'Pharaoh' who was of those who make corruption" and therefore became a legitimate target of assassination (Sadowski, 1991, p. 129). *Infitah* had sharpened class conflict and social tensions to the point that even its initial supporters no longer viewed it as a viable strategy of economic development. Instead, it polarized Egyptian society by widening social inequalities. It ultimately ended with Sadat's assassination in 1981 by Islamists who had infiltrated the lower ranks of the military.

Conclusion

During the Nasser years, attempts were made to develop a national economy as a means of gaining real independence from the West. This began with strategic nationalizations, agrarian reform and import substitution industrialization in an effort to stimulate domestic industrial development. Geopolitical developments and Cold War politics pushed Nasser closer to a non-aligned, socialist path of development. By the early 1960s, Nasser embraced "Arab socialism" and sought to strengthen the rights of peasants, vis-à-vis their landlords, and enhance the social protections enjoyed by workers. This shift was not without its limits or contradictions. While workers enjoyed higher wages, rent controlled housing and health care, they were denied the right to strike, and the trade unions often suppressed the rights of workers in the interest of the regime. On top of this, these socioeconomic benefits were limited to workers in the formal labour market, which did not encompass a majority of the working class. In the countryside, the state sought – through the cooperative movement – to extract the surplus from the peasantry to stimulate industrialization. In other words, trade unions and cooperatives became sites of contradiction between the interests of peasants and workers on the one hand, and the interests of the regime on the other.

In the 1970s, Sadat introduced at partial and highly politicized process of liberalization that sought to undo most of the progress made under Nasser and align Egypt with the United States and Saudi Arabia. By doing so, Sadat helped to shift the balance of class forces back towards the old landed classes and opened space for the emergence of commercially oriented actors in the Egyptian economy. This liberalization process was not, however, without its opponents. The decade also witnessed an upsurge in popular discontent as workers began protesting the early efforts at privatization and the popular classes protested the imposition of International Monetary Fund reforms in the infamous bread riots of 1977. Liberalization was beginning to open up cracks in the social fabric; cracks that would open into gaping fissures 30 years later.

3 | "We Need the Government to Unleash Us, the Tigers"

Mubarak and the Neoliberal Turn

People should react to market forces, not to administrative fear.

Boutros-Gali

Accumulation, Dispossession and the Transformation of the State

The technocratic language of structural reform promoted by international financial institutions (IFIs) and neoliberal reformers obscures the profound social and political content contained in these reforms (Boas & McNeill, 2004). By contrast, characterizing the structural reform movement as a process of accumulation by dispossession highlights the social and political components of economic reform and helps us to understand its deeply contested nature. Far from representing the natural development of markets, the structural reforms implemented over the past two decades represent a class-based project of market making by the state at the behest of members of the dominant class at the expense of the popular classes. This process of accumulation by dispossession is composed of several different elements.

Privatization represents the most obvious element of accumulation by dispossession. The growth of the private sector in Egypt was directly linked to the destruction of public sector companies through the process of privatization. As Harvey (2003, p. 158) points out, the effect of privatization was an "enclosure of the commons," in which assets "held by the state or in common were released into the market where overaccumulating capital could invest in them, upgrade them, and speculate in them." In many instances, this resulted in the direct transfer of resources, machinery and capacity from public sector companies to the private sector. In this context, "overaccumulating capital" refers primarily to foreign, Western-based capital backed by the International Monetary Fund (IMF). This privatization process opened up "[n]ew terrains for profitable activity" (Harvey, 2003). For

Western capital, this "helped stave off the overaccumulation problem," but for the neoliberal fraction of Egyptian capital, privatization acted as a moment of "primitive accumulation." In this case, the transfer of public services and assets to the private sphere "according to an entrepreneurial logic" has resulted in a "radical transformation in the dominant pattern of social relations and a redistribution of assets that increasingly favour[s] the upper rather than the lower classes" (Harvey, 2003, p. 159).

Second, accumulation by dispossession required the public subsidization of private accumulation. In Egypt, this process assumed the form of the availability of easy credit from public sector banks providing capitalists with the means of accumulation in the form of fictitious capital. In this case, massive loans were made available to aspiring entrepreneurs (linked to the dominant party and from within the dominant class) with no collateral and no restrictions on the volume of borrowing. On top of this, there were no legal repercussions in the event of loan defaults, thanks to an amendment to the law passed in 2004 under the so-called government of businessmen. Well-connected businessmen could borrow as much money as they wanted, with no collateral and no repercussions in the event of default. In this sense, public sector banks effectively subsidized the process of private capital accumulation by assuming the risks while accruing none of the rewards. Frustrated liberals often dismiss this as "corruption" in the service of authoritarianism. There is little recognition of how this is a problem endemic to neoliberalism.

Third, changes to the nature of tenure provided capitalists with access to cheap land that was instrumental to their accumulation strategies (Bush, 2002). This process would result in the expropriation of peasant land, to be discussed in detail in Chapter 7. As discussed in Chapter 1, this process of accumulating land by means of eliminating customary forms of tenure bears a striking resemblance to the enclosure movement discussed by Marx (1976) at the end of volume one of *Capital* as the basis of "so-called primitive accumulation." Recall that Marx referred to this process as a means of divorcing the direct producers from their means of subsistence. From a more contemporary perspective, it also bears a striking resemblance to the developments that occurred in Chiapas, Mexico, in the late 1980s, and early 1990s (Vergara-Camus, 2014), and more recently in Africa (Bryceson, 2000; Peters, 2004). This process also requires the intervention of the state. On the one level, state intervention occurs in the form of "privatisation, decollectivisation, land registration and land titling." On another level, it may require the coercive intervention of the state. While states in other parts of the Global South may have "abandoned the previous focus on expropriation" (Kay, 2000, p. 129), the Egyptian state has merely begun the process of coercive dispossession of small rural producers.

Fourth, the value of capital increased dramatically by means of the growth of capital markets that facilitated dispossession rather than reward the expansion of existing capital stock in the "real economy." For example, in 1999, the market capitalization of listed domestic companies on the Egyptian stock exchange sat at 37 percent of gross domestic product (GDP) (Azzam, 2002, p. 66). By 2006, it had increased to 87 percent of GDP and peaked at 106 percent in 2007, before succumbing to the financial crisis in 2008.[1] This growth in market capitalization outpaced the annual growth rate of gross fixed capital formation over the same period. Often this increase in value was merely the result of the transfer of public resources to various private interests through the process of privatization. Share values increased due to the perceived potential, by prospective shareholders, for further accumulation by the newly privatized firm. In the rural economy, this growth in share value could be the result of the transfer of public lands into private hands. In this case, the prospect of land development – itself dependent upon dispossession – sends positive signals to investors and drives up the share value of the prospective developing firm. Second, the prospect of mass layoffs in newly privatized – or soon to be privatized – firms was also a driving force behind the increasing value of shares in capital markets, signalling the imminent restructuring that opens up new opportunities for accumulation. Improved stock performance, therefore, encouraged further layoffs and was intrinsically bound up with the processes of dispossession. This development was not unique to Egypt, but was endemic to the neoliberal model of financialized growth during the 2000s and has continued in the wake of the global financial crisis (GFC) of 2007–2008 (La Monica, 2013).

Finally, the neoliberals organized and penetrated various organs of the state, thus ensuring their influence over the formulation of laws that affected their interests. Most of these capitalists became engaged

---

[1] World Bank indicators: Market capitalization of listed domestic companies percent of GDP).

in politics in 2005, after the formation of the Nazif government. This penetration of the state took place both at the legislative and executive levels. In the latter case, this entailed the increasing prominence of neoliberals within the cabinet and taking control of key ministries or creating new ones. This increasing influence at the level of the state enabled the neoliberal fraction to have greater influence over the restructuring of the Egyptian state. This took the form of the trans-formation of the interventionist and redistributive role of the Nasserist state – the state as an owner of assets and a redistributor of wealth – to a state that acts primarily as a facilitator of private capital accumula-tion. As Boutros-Gali, a prominent neoliberal, former IMF official and new Minister of Economy in 1997 said upon assuming office: "[W]e are trying to achieve a change in governance. We must change the concept of the state from that of a predator to that of a mediator or a facilitator. People should react to market forces, not to administrative fear" (cited in Weiss & Wurzel, 1998, p. 91). This corresponds with the prescriptions of state transformation of the *World Bank Develop-ment Report* (1997) discussed in Chapter 1.

Such a transformation often entails welfare state retrenchment in the form of cutting back on redistributive social policies or transforming existing social policy to make it more market enabling (such as work-fare). But it also entails state restructuring in the form of the weakening of, or dismantling of, ministries or departments tasked with industrial policy or other *dirigiste* forms of economic planning, and the elevation of new ministries tasked with facilitating private sector growth. To do this, the state requires fundamental administrative restructuring: an overhaul of cumbersome bureaucratic procedures, a simplification of exchange rates, the consolidation of the tax system and public finance and increased institutional support for the private sector in the econ-omy. Second, this process of state transformation entails the "expan-sion of *de facto* state intervention and regulation in the name of competitiveness and marketization" (Cerny, 1997, p. 251). The global spread of competition policy since the 1990s as a means of imposing the imperatives of market competition on economic actors is a case in point (Dabbah, 2010). Finally, the state needs to be transformed into an effective guarantor of the rights of private property. What neolib-erals refer to as "the rule of law" is identified as a crucial element for a successful shift to a free market economy because it protects private property (and the interests of private investors) and diminishes the discretionary power of public officials and the state (Hayek, 2014). Achieving this goal entails reforms that secure the independence of the judiciary from political interference and the "constitutionalizing" of the rights of property. In the words of the Egyptian government, the process of liberalization requires a "reduction of the discretionary role of the state and reducing government intervention to policies that are consistent with market economy principles" (Egypt, 2005, p. 6).

The Crisis of the 1980s

The 1980s was a decade of political and economic crisis in Egypt. The assassination of Sadat in 1981 foisted the presidency onto Hosni Mubarak and changed the political context of reform away from liberalization and towards a security clampdown against the rise of Islamic extremism. The bread riots, combined with the economic failures of *infitah*, the rise of "conspicuous consumption" and corruption among the *infitahyoun*, sparked a popular backlash against the reform process begun by Sadat. The re-introduction of the Emergency Law enabled the regime to repress the Muslim Brotherhood and to confiscate its property and its assets.[2] Within this political context, the reform movement that supported *infitah* was largely derailed until the late 1980s.

The initial phase of Mubarak's presidency was marked by a "comparative political tolerance" in which the press "enjoyed greater freedom ... than at any time since the overthrow of King Farouk in 1952" (Miller, 1984). Mubarak freed many dissidents who had been imprisoned by Sadat, and he reached out to the more moderate – i.e., non-violent – Islamist organizations. While important elements of authoritarianism remained in place – no right to strike or public demonstrations, and Emergency laws that expanded the authority of the state – the early years of his rule marked a pragmatic shift away from Sadat's more ideologically oriented authoritarian rule.

By the mid 1980s, Egypt faced a serious economic crisis. As the U.S. Federal Reserve drove up interest rates in the early 1980s, it precipitated a third-world debt crisis that hit countries that had embarked on

---

[2] The Emergency Law was introduced in 1967 in the context of the war with Israel. Sadat repealed it in 1980, but it was reinstated in 1981 by Mubarak under the pretence of combatting Islamic fundamentalist terrorism.

import substitution industrialization forms of economic development – like Egypt – particularly hard. As a result, inflation soured, peaking at 23.9 percent in 1986. In the same year, unemployment peaked at 14.7 percent (Ikram, 2006, p. 211) and growth slumped to 2.6 percent (World Bank). This deteriorating economic position resulted in a decline in real income per head, growing trade and fiscal deficits and a mounting external debt of 150 percent of GDP (Niblock & Murphy, 1993, p. 35). Debt servicing obligations between 1984 and 1987 had increased by an average of U.S.$1.7 billion per year, and total debt exceeded U.S.$40 billion by June of 1987 (Ikram, 2006, p. 56). By 1989, Egypt's debt service obligations consumed 40 percent of its foreign exchange revenues (Bromley & Bush, 1994, p. 202).

In 1985, the Egyptian government entered negotiations with the IMF over debt rescheduling and a U.S.$1 billion loan. The IMF and the World Bank expressed concern about Egypt's macroeconomic stability and proposed a series of structural reforms that would make the Egyptian economy more competitive. The IMF demanded cuts to subsidies as a means of reducing the deficit and ending price distortions, a devaluation of the exchange rate to encourage exports and reduce the trade deficit and increase interest rates to encourage foreign direct investment (FDI). The IMF argued that subsidies on cotton production, energy and food imports were distorting market prices and forcing Egypt to run budget deficits, thereby contributing to long-term public debt. Regarding the exchange rate, it was argued that the overvalued pound discouraged the production of cotton exports – Egypt's historical comparative advantage – exacerbating Egypt's trade deficit and, coupled with subsidies, channelled cotton inputs towards domestic textile production in public sector enterprises.

The government's concern with political stability resulted in a luke-warm reception of the Fund's suggested reforms. Despite the increasing integration of the Egyptian Trade Union Federation (ETUF) into the corporatist structures of the state, militant rank-and-file workers increasingly engaged in strike activity, with 1985 and 1986 signifying the high point of what Beinin (2016a) refers to as the 1984–1994 "cycle of contention." In 1986, for example, close to 40,000 textile workers in Shubra al-Khayma and Ghazl al-Mahalla went on strike (Beinin, 2016a, p. 45). Egypt had not seen such labour unrest for at least a decade. Egyptian officials were also concerned about mass rioting akin to the bloody bread riots of 1977, which were also initiated by the need to implement IMF structural reforms. In the summer of 1988, significant rioting had erupted in the Cairo suburb of Ain Shams.

With these concerns in mind, Egyptian officials informed the IMF that "considerations of domestic political stability precluded the full and immediate implementation of all the measures recommended by the Fund and World Banks staffs" (Momani, 2005, p. 17). Instead, the Egyptian government proposed a gradual unification of the exchange rate system and an incremental increase in interest rates. Energy prices would be gradually increased to world levels over a 5-year period. Subsidies on certain goods would be gradually reduced, but strategic goods like wheat, rice, sugar and cotton would be exempt from reform.

A standby agreement was eventually signed in 1987. The terms were generally favourable to Egypt, particularly given the IMF's concession on the issue of exchange rate devaluation – the issue to which the Egyptian government was perhaps most adamantly opposed.[3] The Egyptian government was also able to hold the line on bread subsidies and energy price controls. However, the program broke down in late 1987 due to Egypt's failure "to comply with the majority of the IMF terms" (Momani, 2005, p. 25).

Over the course of 1987 and 1988, Egypt came under increasing pressure from its international creditors, including the United States. The World Bank withheld U.S.$250 million in soft loans until Egypt eliminated energy subsidies and USAID withheld aid marked for the development of an energy project. The U.S. vetoed a prospective loan to Egypt from the African Development Bank destined for the development of a power plant in Cairo, and Canada and Australia began to phase out wheat exports, increasingly wary of Egypt's arrears. In September 1988, Mubarak announced publicly that he "told the IMF that this reform must be in line with our social and economic situation and the standard of living" (cited in Seddon, 1990, p. 96). This statement, accompanied by his characterization of the IMF as an "unqualified doctor who prescribes life-threatening dosages of medicine," reflected the tense state of negotiations between Egypt and the Fund (Momani, 2005, p. 27). In return, the Egyptian-born head of the IMF's Middle East department likened Egypt to "an employee who earns £100 a month but spends £122" (Seddon, 1990, p. 98).

---

[3] For an insightful account of the geopolitical considerations involved in the IMF's acceptance of Egypt's Letter of Intent, see Momani (2005, pp. 19–20).

In response to this pressure from its creditors, the Mubarak regime introduced a new investment law in 1989 (Investment Law 230/1989), which built on reforms that were introduced during Sadat's tenure. It allowed foreign companies full rights of ownership, facilitated the transfer of state land to the private sector, allowed the transfer of net profits abroad and provided guarantees against the expropriation and/ or sequestration of property or accumulated assets. Businesses benefited from tax holidays ranging from 5 to 15 years, foreign employees were exempt from paying taxes and profits were exempt from general income tax. This new Investment Law also opened up tourism, housing and construction to private investment, thereby facilitating land reclamation and the cultivation of fallow and desert lands. Desert reclamation and cultivation projects enjoyed 50-year leases and foreign capital no longer had to engage in joint ventures with Egyptian capital.

The new investment law signalled to the IMF Egypt's willingness to press forward with far reaching structural reforms. On top of this, the Egyptian government eliminated specific food subsidies to reduce the food subsidy bill by 30 percent. It also increased interest rates, but not to the level proposed by the IMF. By 1990, Mubarak "agreed the need for far-reaching reforms, but insisted on a gradualist approach" given the very real "dangers of widespread social unrest if austerity measures of the kind implied by the IMF demands are implemented" (Seddon, 1990, p. 103). The regime had already renewed the Emergency Law of 1981, but it also "recognized that invocation of the state of emergency and 'national security'" would be "inadequate to contain a major surge in popular discontent and unrest" (Seddon, 1990, p. 103).

A new round of negotiations between Egypt and the IMF saw the Mubarak regime moving closer to the IMF's demands on cutting subsidies, ending price caps and privatizing select state enterprises. The response by Egypt's creditors to its Letter of Intent with the IMF was positive. The World Bank made U.S.$165 million available in loans for Egypt's energy sector and held out the prospect of an additional U.S.$300 and U.S.$400 million in structural adjustment loans and aid to debt-stricken public sector enterprises. Finally, USAID unfroze U.S.$230 million in funding that it had initially frozen as an expression of its dissatisfaction with the slow pace of reform.

Nonetheless, Egypt and the IMF remained far apart on the key issues of currency devaluation, exchange rate reform and wholesale price liberalization. Egypt continuously insisted on a gradualist approach to reducing subsidies and raising interest rates, while holding the line on devaluing the pound and reforming the exchange rate system. As a result of Egypt's participation in the Gulf War in 1991, the United States intervened on behalf of Egypt in its ongoing dispute with the IMF. U.S. pressure was exerted on the IMF to concede to Egypt's gradualist approach to reforms. In the end, the IMF approved a new stand-by agreement with Egypt despite the fact that "reducing subsidies, limiting the budget deficit, raising energy prices particularly electricity, modifying the tax structure, and full unification and devaluation of the exchange rate were not being implemented by the Egyptian government" (Momani, 2005, p. 40). The new stand-by agreement laid the foundations for Egypt's Economic Reform and Structural Adjustment Program – a wide-ranging economic restructuring program, consisting of loans from the IMF, World Bank and African Development Bank – introduced in the latter half of 1991. This marked the "first real structural adjustment package (SAP) in the history of Egypt's relation with the Bretton Woods institutions" (Abdel Khalek, 2001, p. 44).

The Neoliberal Turn, 1991–1995

The Economic Reform and Structural Adjustment Program contained six key components. First, it promoted macroeconomic stabilization in the form of fiscal restraint, an increase in interest rates and a reform of the exchange rate. Second, it pushed for the privatization of public sector enterprises and other state-owned assets. Third, it called for price liberalization through the elimination of remaining subsidies and price caps. Fourth, it demanded trade liberalization in the form of removing tariff barriers. Fifth, it supported investment-friendly policies that ended discrimination against foreign investors, that protected foreign investors from potential expropriation and that provided investment incentives such as tax holidays in specific industrial zones. Sixth, it promoted the liberalization the financial and banking sector. Finally, it also advocated the creation of a social fund for development intended to create labour-intensive employment to reduce the impact of public sector privatization on the labour market.

While many of these proposed reforms were holdovers from the 1980s, the adoption of the Economic Reform and Structural Adjustment Program represented a break from "business as usual" in Egyptian economic policy (Richards, 2004, p. 88). For the first time, the Egyptian government was bound by international agreements with its creditors to implement sweeping reforms of its economy. Not only had it entered into a structural adjustment program with its various donors (the IMF, the World Bank and the African Development Bank), its major supporter, the United States, "made it clear that it would scale down economic aid if Egypt did not speed up its reforms" (Weiss & Wurzel, 1998, p. 114).

However, as was the case in the late 1980s, members of the ruling National Democratic Party (NDP) disagreed over the pace, scope and direction of reform and, as a result, the process remained slow for the first half of the 1990s, in contrast with the "shock therapy" occurring in parts of the former Soviet Bloc. A tenuous balance had to be struck between the structural imperatives behind the reforms, and the practical concerns regarding the political context on the ground. During this initial period from 1991 to 1993 – what Sfakianakis (2004, p. 84) calls the period of "reform stabilization" – there existed within the NDP a group of apprehensive, conservative reformers and neoliberal reformers. Since the bread riots of 1977, and the rise of violent Islamic extremism in the 1980s (providing the justification for the Emergency Law of 1981), Egypt's ruling elite had become increasingly sensitive to threats to the social order. In contrast with Sadat, Mubarak himself was "not really concerned about economic policies as long as political stability was not at stake" (Weiss & Wurzel, 1998, p. 114).

Those within the NDP who sought to accelerate the reform process included Mubarak's eldest son, Gamal, and his Western-educated, IMF- and World Bank-associated friends who played an important role in ensuring the adoption of a neoliberal economic model. Gamal was a London banker with close ties to numerous U.S.-educated, neoliberal-minded businessmen who would emerge as the main benefactors of the reform process. Gamal was also linked to the newer private sector business associations that had emerged in the late 1970s and early 1980s, particularly the exclusive Egyptian Businessmen's Association, the American Chamber of Commerce and the Egyptian-American Presidential Council. The Egyptian Businessmen's Association and the joint Egyptian-U.S. business associations played in increasingly important role in attempting to form a cohesive business coalition behind the liberalization process, viewing the older, established business associations – such as the Federation of Egyptian Industry (FEI) – as being too close to the regime. The Egyptian Junior

Business Association started in 2000, with 500 members, many whom are in real estate development.

Among Gamal's allies was Mohamed Mohieldin, a senior economist at the Egyptian Centre for Economic Studies, who became the chairman of the NDP's economic committee and later Minister of Investment. Mohieldin was the "link between private sector, ruling party and government" (Roll, 2010, p. 365). He was later appointed Egypt's representative to the World Bank. Another prominent member of this neoliberal faction is Yousef Boutros-Ghali, who worked as an economist for the IMF in the 1980s. While at the IMF, he worked on the Latin American Debt Crisis. Between 1986 and 1993, he served as advisor to the governor of the Central Bank of Egypt and was a key negotiator of the IMF standby agreement of 1991. Between 1996 and 2004, he served as Minister of State for Economic Affairs, Minister of Economy and Foreign Trade and Minister of Finance until his conviction – in absentia – on corruption charges in 2011 after the fall of the Mubarak regime. In 2008, he sat on the IMF's policy-setting committee. Finally, Rasheed Mohamed Rasheed, a mechanical engineer from Alexandria who received a business education in various prestigious U.S. universities, including Harvard, Stanford and MIT, served as the Minister of Foreign Trade and Industry from 2004 to 2011 and sat on the President's Council. Rasheed was also a former executive at Unilever who had close ties to prominent businessmen in the real estate, construction and tourism sectors and was himself a major shareholder in EFG-Hermes, an Egyptian investment bank that is active across Northern Africa. These men formed the vanguard of the neoliberal push in Egyptian politics in the early 2000s.

Gamal was also influential in the creation of the Egyptian Centre for Economic Studies, a neoliberal think tank established in 1992 whose members later filled the cabinet under Nazif. Board members included Rashid Mohamed Rashid, Mohamed Mansour, Ahmed El-Magraby, and prominent businessmen including steel magnate Ahmed Ezz, Nassef Sawiris and the textile industrialist Alaa Arafa. The Egyptian Centre for Economic Studies became an important intellectual propagator of neoliberal policy ideas over the course of the 1990s and early 2000s, and many of its members found their way into government posts or as the beneficiaries of liberalizing reforms.

Gamal's "new guard" came into constant conflict with the "old guard" within the NDP who wanted to protect public sector enterprises and those who wanted to speed up the process of privatization. Prime Minister Atef Sedqi had a history of criticizing the IMF during the fraught negotiations in the late 1980s. Other members of the old guard included the Minister of Information (and former NDP Secretary General) Safwat el-Sherif, the Minister of Parliamentary Affairs Kamal El-Shazli, the NDP Secretary General and former Minister of Agriculture and Land Reclamation Youssf Wali and the former presidential Chief of Staff Zakareya Azmi. These members of the old guard were not ideologically committed to Egyptian-style *dirigisme*, and they were definitely not Nasserists; rather, they were conservatives who worried that the pace and scale of economic reforms expected by the IMF would lead to widespread social unrest.

The FEI represented a moderating force during the liberalization process. In 1993, the Mubarak regime would appoint, for the first time in its post-war history, a prominent private sector industrialist – Farid Khamis[4] – to the presidency of the federation. Khamis had close ties to various export industries and sought to increase the FEI's autonomy from the regime by introducing more bottom-up processes of decision making. According to Soliman, the appointment of Khamis "signaled the rise of the export-oriented industrialists as the state's favorite group among the industrial capitalists" (Soliman, 1998, p. 75). Yet this shift of the FEI towards export-oriented industry did not necessarily entail a wholesale embrace of the liberalization process. Numerous Egyptian industries – even those in the private sector – remained sceptical of the benefits of exposing Egyptian industries to international competition. It continued to oppose liberalizing reforms that it felt threatened the productive sectors of the Egyptian economy.

Another important player in stalling the reform process was the leadership of the ETUF. The ETUF's relationship to the reform process was complex.[5] While the majority of the union leadership were members of the NDP, they were constantly pressured by rank-and-file opposition to the privatization process (to be discussed in Chapter 6). For example, as a member of the People's Assembly (the parliament),

---

[4] Khamis eventually fell out of favour with Mubarak and was removed from his position in 1999 and moved closer to the neoliberals.

[5] While Beinin (2009a, 2016a) and Wurzel and Weiss (1998) characterize the ETUF leadership as an arm of the state bureaucracy, Bianchi (1986) and Paczynska (2006) present a more nuanced and contested relationship between the union and the ruling party.

future ETUF President Sayyid Rashid (1992–2006) voted in favour of privatization in 1991. However, other ETUF leaders "objected to privatizing the public sector for the next decade," but they "never mobilized their members to protest" (Beinin, 2016a, p. 44).

One of the first reforms introduced by the Sedqi government was Public Sector Company Law No. 203 in the summer of 1991 (203/1991). Law 203 "shielded the public companies from direct ministerial interference," thereby paving the way for future privatizations. Public sector firms were grouped under numerous holding companies "whose government-appointed board members were expected to manage … according to market principles" (Weiss & Wurzel, 1998, p. 44). To secure trade union acceptance, the law exempted "strategic" companies or companies of a "national character" from privatization.

Financial liberalization was also introduced to supplement privatization. The Capital Market Law was passed in July 1992, eliminating preferential, state financing for public sector enterprises through the National Investment Bank. This dealt a fatal blow to what remained of the *dirigiste* development model established by Nasser because it effectively exposed public sector enterprises to market competition by forcing them to turn to the revived stock market for private sources of financing. Denied their privileged source of financing, public sector enterprises were increasingly compelled to operate along the lines of profit-oriented, private sector firms without having to be privatized. For those public sector firms that struggled to remain profitable, this process merely furthered the case – made by neoliberal reformers and international creditors – for their subsequent privatization.

To reduce outstanding budget deficits, the government implemented a number of tax reforms. In 1991, a sales tax was introduced on manufacturers, importers and specific services, and was eventually extended to retailers in 1995. During the 1992–1993 fiscal year, it brought in double the revenue of the consumption tax it had replaced. In 1993, a 20 percent tax on luxury items was also introduced in an attempt to bring some balance to Egypt's woefully inegalitarian taxation system.

The Egyptian government also began a gradual process of liberalizing trade and agriculture. Part of this process coincided with Egypt's participation in several significant multilateral trade agreements, such as the Uruguay Round of the General Agreement on Tariffs and Trade that was concluded in 1994. Between 1990 and 1991, the percentage of domestic production protected by non-tariff barriers was reduced from 76 percent to 26 percent (Weiss & Wurzel, 1998). Import tariffs and customs duties on 44 raw materials and 53 locally manufactured products were reduced by the end of 1993 and preferential tariffs for public sector enterprises were abolished completely.

Movement towards the liberalization of the agricultural sector began with the passage of Law 96/1992. The significant elements of the law liberalized agricultural rents by eliminating rent control and removing the caps on landownership, effectively enabling the concentration of land by the more affluent landowners.[6] Proponents of the reform cited the increasing fragmentation of small plots and the declining productivity in Egyptian agriculture that were attributed to the Nasserist land reforms of the 1960s. It was argued that agricultural plots were becoming so small that they could no longer sufficiently act as a means of subsistence for an average Egyptian family. Despite being passed in 1992, however, the law would not be enforced until 1997, under the Ganzouri government.

The abolition of subsidies was a major component of the Uruguay Round of the General Agreement on Tariffs and Trade. By 1993, subsidies on basic consumer goods had been reduced by 6.2% (Weiss & Wurzel, 1998, p. 60). However, the removal of subsidies remained one of the most contentious aspects of the reform movement in Egypt. First, the bread riots of 1977 were a direct response to the removal of subsidies on bread and Egyptian politicians rightly feared the consequences of such radical and rapid price liberalization. Second, the impact of price liberalization tended to be immediately felt by lower income Egyptians, in part because so many basic goods were subsidized. For example, in the early 1990s, lower income families spent up to 64% of their income on food alone (Weiss & Wurzel, 1998, p. 57). As a result, the regime wavered significantly on the removal of subsidies and price caps, often to the annoyance of the IMF. Subsidies were reduced or removed only gradually, and often in a highly targeted fashion. The 6.2 percent reduction in subsidies implemented by 1993, for example, fell far short of the IMF's proposed 40 percent reduction on consumer goods subsidies (Weiss & Wurzel, 1998, p. 53).

However, it was not just lower income Egyptians who opposed price liberalization. In 1994, Mubarak blocked a proposed increase of

---

[6] The reform marked the beginning of a systematic process of accumulation by dispossession in rural Egypt, which is discussed in greater detail in Chapter 7.

electricity rates at the request of the FEI. The opposition of the FEI was part of a concerted campaign in the same year that "estimated that the liberalization of foreign trade would destroy the national industry" (Soliman, 1998, p. 82). The campaign promoted the position that "the protection of national industry is a protection for the Egyptian consumer" (Soliman, 1998, p. 82). In this campaign, the FEI forged an alliance with opposition members in parliament. As Soliman points out, the greatest support the FEI received in parliament came "from the members of the leftist Tagamu Party and the member of the Nasserist Party" (Soliman, 1998, p. 82).

It is in this context that the Egyptian-American Presidents' Council was formed in 1995. The council was composed of 15 U.S. business representatives and 15 Egyptian business representatives and was chaired by Gamal Mubarak. The U.S. representatives came largely from the telecommunications, oil and gas and pharmaceuticals industries, while the Egyptian representatives came from Egyptian British Bank, The Ezz Group, Fine Foods Group, Nile Clothing Company and the Orientals Group (owned by Farid Khamis, the president of the FEI at the time). According to Momani (2003, p. 94), the Presidents' Council "became a new means of communicating American desires for Egyptian economic liberalization" (Momani, 2003, p. 94) to facilitate the inflow of American FDI into the country. The council, which many perceived as a de facto shadow cabinet, "worked to advance many structural economic reforms, such as helping Egypt to privatize the telecommunications, banking, customs and taxation sectors" (Momani, 2003, p. 94).

By the end of his tenure in 1996, Sedqi had little to show in the way of privatization, which was a key plank in the reform process. Only 24 of 314 companies had been privatized under Law 203 between 1991 and the end of 1995 (Weiss & Wurzel, 1998, p. 125). The Egyptian government also raised tariffs and non-tariff barriers over the same period, predominantly in response to private sector businesses fearing international competition. For example, tariffs were raised on eggs and inspection taxes were increased in 1994. The reforms to the Unified Labour Law proposed in 1995 had been delayed due to opposition from the ETUF and various opposition parties, as had reforms to company law, foreign ownership of property and the introduction of competition policy. On top of this, Mubarak continued to rule out a devaluation of the Egyptian pound.

However, despite the political setbacks regarding the reform movement, the judiciary demonstrated its willingness to push ahead in several significant rulings regarding the constitutionality of the reforms. Despite meeting opposition on the grounds that many public sector enterprises were profitable and that Law 203 on privatizations was therefore unconstitutional, the Supreme Constitutional Court sided with the government, signifying an important shift in the judiciary towards a neoliberal orientation conducive to the reform process, a shift that would continue throughout the 1990s.[7] In 1995, the Supreme Constitutional Court also played an important role in liberalizing housing markets by challenging the constitutionality of Nasser-era rent control laws. The court declared article 29 of Law 49/1977 unconstitutional, which meant that rental contracts could no longer be extended to relatives to the "third degree" by marriage as such practices would infringe "on the rights of private property of the landlord" (Moustafa, 2003, p. 911). This ruling paved the way for the passing of Law 4/1996, which ended rent control and promoted home ownership.

By the end of Sedqi's tenure in January 1996, Egypt's macroeconomic circumstances was a mixed bag. Growth declined from 5.7 percent in 1990 to 4.6 percent in 1995 and unemployment increased from 9.6 percent to 11.3 percent over the same period (ILOSTAT, 2018e; World Bank, 2018f, 2018t). While inflation dropped slightly (by one percentage point), the investment scenario in Egypt remained dismal. Gross fixed capital investment – as a percentage of GDP – was down to 19.1 percent in 1995 from 26.9 percent in 1990 (World Bank, 2018h). The bulk of this remained in the hands of the public sector, as private sector investment represented only 4.5 percent of GDP in 1995, down from 12.3 percent in 1990 (it would drop to 2.4 percent the following year) (World Bank, 2018i). In contrast, the manufacturing sector demonstrated significant growth up until 1999: its annual growth rate increased from 4.2 percent in 1994 to 9.6 percent in 1999 (World Bank, 2018l, 2018m).

The Minister of the Poor, 1996–1999

The reform process accelerated under the Premiership of Kamal El Ganzouri from January 1996 to October 1999. However, Ganzouri's

---

[7] For the profitability of Egyptian SOEs, see Ayubi (1995, p. 343).

liberalizing credentials were hardly well-established. According to Wurzel and Weiss (1998, p. 76), Ganzouri "had been considered as a long-standing supporter of central planning and the public sector who only recently emerged as a supporter of the private sector." Pressured by Egypt's pre-existing international agreements and pro-free market members of the NDP within the government, Ganzouri's government passed 36 new laws intended to promote foreign investment and economic liberalization, signifying an acceleration of the reform process. These laws encouraged "build-operate-transfer" projects, foreign bank ownership, foreign investment in real estate and the promotion of exports.

Ganzouri had inherited a stalled privatization process. By the summer of 1996, as many as 274 of 314 companies (87 percent) identified by Law 203/1991 had not yet been privatized (Weiss & Wurzel, 1998, p. 117). To accelerate the privatization process, a High Ministerial Privatisation Committee was established, including members of the Prime Minister's Office, the Public Sector Ministry and the Ministry of Finance. The purpose was to "depersonalise privatisation decisions and to relieve responsible decision makers from political pressure" (Weiss & Wurzel, 1998, p. 116). At the beginning of 1996, President Mubarak publicly voiced his support for the privatization process for the first time, arguing that it was the only way to save the Egyptian economy from indebtedness.

One of the major reforms introduced by the Ganzouri government was the liberalization of urban and rural property markets. Law 4/1996 ended rent controls and sought to encourage the creation of a private housing market that favoured landlords and private investors. Proponents of the reform argued that existing rent controls discouraged landlords from renting and refurbishing properties. The law, however, only applied to new builds, thereby exempting approximately 95 percent of existing tenancies. Ganzouri also put Law 96/1992 into force, a law passed five years previously that liberalized rural rents as a means of facilitating the privatization of agricultural land.[8] Between 1992 and October 1, 1997, rents increased to a rate 22 times the amount of tax paid by the landowner; after this date, rents were subject to market forces. The Supreme Constitutional Court also

---

[8] The details and consequences of the law are discussed in greater detail in Chapter 7.

dismantled rent control for commercial contracts in 1996 and 1997. As a result, commercial contracts were no longer inheritable by children or partners of original tenants. The changes affected more than 800,000 commercial tenants who had lost their rights for secure contracts by 1997 (Moustafa, 2003, pp. 911–912).

The government also introduced the Investment Guarantees and Incentives Law (8/1997) in the hope of attracting FDI. The new investment law addressed the issue of expropriation, containing language stipulating that "companies and establishments may not be nationalized or confiscated" (Article 8 cited in Organisation for Economic Co-operation and Development [OECD], 2007b, p. 30). The law equalized the treatment of domestic and foreign investors, created a 10-year tax holiday for projects under the Social Fund and 20-year tax holidays for projects outside of the Old Nile Valley, extended complete foreign ownership of local projects, and reduced the number of regulations on foreign investment. The law also provided permanent exemption from taxes, duties and customs in the free zones. Investors in the zones were offered full exemptions from corporate tax throughout the life of the project as well as cheap or free land to start their projects. Other incentives ranged from land reclamation in the desert, to industry and mining, air transportation and tourism.

In 1995, Egypt became a member of the World Trade Organization and committed itself to an agenda of trade liberalization. Between 1996 and 1998, the tariff range on imports was reduced from 5 percent to 70 percent to 5 percent to 40 percent (Abdel Khalek, 2001, p. 56). During the same period, Egypt became a participant in several regional, multilateral trade agreements seeking greater trade liberalization between members. In 1994, it became a member of the Common Market for Eastern and Southern Africa (COMESA), and in 1997, it became a founding member of the Greater Arab Free Trade Agreement (GAFTA). As with most "free trade" agreements, both GAFTA and COMESA committed Egypt to more than just the removal of tariffs and non-tariff barriers; it also committed Egypt to pursuing the free movement of capital and labour, tax harmonization, common standards and competition policy. While it would take a few years for the reforms associated with these agreements to be implemented, the agreements served as another mechanism by which to lock in Egypt's liberalizing trajectory.

At the same time, however, the Ganzouri government embodied the divisions within the NDP. Despite the unprecedented number of liberalizing reforms passed through parliament, his government retained certain populist policies, and he maintained control over various committees in the cabinet. In this sense, Ganzouri's premiership can be seen as an attempt to balance the antagonisms within the NDP. Deteriorating economic conditions in the wake of the East Asian crisis, and the increasingly precarious security situation after a series of terrorist attacks by Islamic extremists over the course of 1996 and 1997, signified a growing degree of discontent among the popular classes that served to caution reformers and bolster the political position of the more cautious reformers within the NDP. Growth had dropped 1.5 percent between 1997 and 1998 (World Band Indicators), and while official unemployment hovered around 8 percent, an upsurge in strike activity in 1998 – the largest since 1994/1995 and the second largest since the early 1970s – forced neoliberal reformers to ease up on the pace of reform, particularly in the areas of privatization of public sector enterprises and labour market reforms. Ganzouri was himself critical of the privatization program, which he saw as a means of enriching individuals close to the regime. By 1998, therefore, only 113 of 314 enterprises were partially privatized (Adams, 2000, p. 269). As a result, public sector jobs continued to be created at the rate of 150,000 per year under his premiership, public sector wages were increased and numerous subsidies on basic goods were retained. Under Ganzouri's premiership, the poverty rate declined from 25 percent to 21 percent, earning him the nickname "minister of the poor" (Abdel Razek, 2011).

For these reasons, the Ganzouri government came under criticism by the neoliberal faction within the NDP. Among this group, Ganzouri was still seen as a technocrat wedded to the old statist model. In particular, he was vehemently opposed by Gamal Mubarak and other neoliberal ministers in his cabinet and in the Shura Council. Ganzouri was accused of bailing out insolvent state-owned enterprises without the advice of the Ministry of Finance or even the cabinet. He cancelled the Egyptian National Railway Authority's E£1.4 billion debt and funded costly infrastructure projects, such as Toshka, the Gulf of Suez, East of Port Said, North Sinai, Aswan and the second Cairo underground project. Finally, he was accused of influencing the Central Bank to implement policies that would benefit the needs of public sector enterprises. Nonetheless, he remained untainted by the corruption that implicated other high-profile members of the NDP, such as Yousef Boutros-Ghali.

By the end of Ganzouri's tenure, Egypt's macroeconomic environment had somewhat improved. Growth had risen to 6.1 percent by the end of 1999 and unemployment and inflation had dropped down to 8 percent and 3 percent respectively, the lowest levels for both indicators throughout the decade (ILOSTAT, 2018e; World Bank, 2018k, 2018f, 2018t). Investment levels were finally rising, particularly private sector investment, which comprised 9.9 percent of GDP by the end of 1999 (World Bank, 2018i). By the end of the decade, Ganzouri had balanced the budget, kept inflation at 3.6 percent and guarded the exchange rate. However, his term in office was cut short in October of 1999 (World Bank, 2018k).

From Crisis to Consolidation, 1999–2004

The appointment of Atef Ebeid (1999–2004) as Prime Minister seemed to signal the success of the neoliberal members of the NDP. Prior to his post, Ebeid was an American-trained economist who served as Minister of the Public Business Sector under Ganzouri and played a key role in implementing the privatization program. After his term as PM he headed the Arab International Bank from 2005 to 2011. The focus of the Ebeid government was to restructure the state in ways that shielded monetary policy from political influence and to accelerate the liberalization of the financial sector. To accomplish this, Ebeid dismantled the Ministry of Economy in 2001, which was associated with the kind of interventionist industrial policy of the Egyptian statism, sending signals that the market – rather than the state – would be the primary determinant of economic activity from henceforth. The responsibilities associated with the ministry, such as fiscal and monetary policy, were transferred to the Central Bank of Egypt in 2003, which was granted autonomy from ministerial oversight by the passage of Law 88/2003, the Law of the Central Bank, Banking Sector and Money (commonly referred to as the Banking Law). Monetary policy was now shielded from political contestation. This process of shielding fiscal and monetary policy from contestation by various interest groups and stakeholders is a common feature of state restructuring in the neoliberal era.

The same Banking Law furthered the liberalization of the financial sector by reducing the role of public sector banks, increasing the role of private sector banks[9] through privatization, and by reducing public bank shares in joint venture banks. Under Sadat, liberalization of the banking system led to the emergence of private banks.[10] However, despite the emergence of these private banks, the four largest banks – National Bank of Egypt, Banque du Caire, Bank of Alexandria and Banque Misr – remained state owned and were now the target of privatization efforts. To scale back the state's presence in the financial sector, public sector banks were mandated to divest their shares in joint venture banks, reducing their maximum share at 20 percent (El Shazly, 2001).[11]

Banking deregulation allowed the entry of more private sector banks into the Egyptian market and allowed foreign partners to purchase majority shares in joint venture banks. In 1999, for example, two specialized real estate banks, Credit Foncier Egyptien and Arab Land Bank, merged into the Egyptian Arab Real Estate Bank, following on the heels of the liberalization of urban and rural property markets implemented by the previous government. As a result of these reforms, the private sector's share of domestic credit increased from 29 percent in 1990 to 54 percent in 2003 (Roll, 2010, p. 353).

The Ebeid government also sought to liberalize real estate finance and create mortgage markets. In 2003, the Mortgage Finance Law was passed 2 years after the passage of the Real Estate Financing Law[12] (148/2001) and was intended to respond to the drop in the real estate market and the subsequent decline of the construction sector in 2000. The law allowed the entry of real estate financing companies into the market, which was expected to compensate for a weak banking sector, thereby strengthening the links between the real estate, construction

---

[9] In 1961, Nasser nationalized the banks, and the financial sector remained partly regulated until the late 1980s (Economist Intelligence Unit, 1988, p. 12). Agricultural banks provided subsidized credit to agricultural producers and interest rates remained fixed.

[10] By 1984, there were 97 private banks with total deposits worth U.S.$20 billion.

[11] At the time of the reform, public sector banks owned more than 20 percent of the shares in 8 of the 23 joint venture banks.

[12] The real estate finance Law No. 148 of 2001 intended to "ease the blockage in the housing market, spur economic activity and foster several feeding industries" (The Arab Republic of Egypt, 2005, p. 15). For details of the Law, see the National Bank of Egypt (2001).

and tourism sectors with global financial capital. The law sought to enable developers to concentrate on real estate development without worrying about possible buyers, providing finances for possible consumers, and allowing the securitization of mortgages (Loza, 2004). The Mortgage Finance Law, according to the Minister of Economy and External Trade, Yousef Boutros Ghali, aimed to facilitate the purchase of residential and commercial property, as well as financing the establishment, restoration and upgrading of such property by youth, small landowners and entrepreneurs, craftsmen and others (Fahmi, 2001).

By 1999, Egypt was a member of both the COMESA and the GAFTA. Both agreements had come into force by 1998, increasing the government's commitment to trade liberalization. By 2000, duties on imports from COMESA countries were eliminated, and by 2005, tariffs on goods from GAFTA countries were abolished.

In 2003, the Ebeid government finally devalued the Egyptian pound. Devaluation had long been a key reform promoted by the IMF, only to be constantly delayed by successive Egyptian governments. Indeed, Hosni Mubarak himself was a prominent opponent of currency devaluation. As a developing country increasingly dependent on food imports, Mubarak believed – understandably – that currency devaluation would significantly drive up food prices and lead to the return of the kinds of bread riots that destabilized Egypt in the last years of Sadat's tenure. In the interest of social stability Mubarak continuously sought to defer currency liberalization to some unspecified time in the future.

The Ebeid government abandoned its fixed exchange rate system in May 2000 and moved to a managed-peg exchange rate system by January 2001. Later that year, the government began devaluing the pound more rapidly, under the belief that devaluation would benefit the growing tourism, oil and financial sectors. Critics argued that devaluing the pound would have negative impacts on firms exposed to foreign debtors, exacerbate inflation and facilitate the growth of a black market in U.S. dollars. Nonetheless, on January 28, 2003, the Ebeid government moved off the managed-peg exchange rate system and began floating the pound, a move strongly endorsed by the IMF.

In other areas of reform, Ebeid's record remained unimpressive – by neoliberal standards – despite his unwavering support for opening up the Egyptian economy. While state-dominated hotel and tourism sectors were privatized, the cotton industry remained under public sector control, civil service reform and bank privatizations were put on hold and the privatization of the insurance companies had not yet begun. Overall, the record of privatizations was underwhelming. According to the United Nations Conference on Trade and Development (UNCTAD) (2005, p. 5), privatizations "had been slower than expected until 2003." Between 1999 and 2003, privatization transactions had fallen 16 percent from the previous 6 years – even Gourzani, the so-called "minister of the poor" had a better record of privatization. Receipts from privatizations had also fallen by almost 30 percent (UNCTAD, 2005, p. 5). Labour reforms also failed to meet expectations. While the Unified Labour Code was finally reformed in 2003 after almost a decade of delays, it still exempted large swathes of the public sector (to be discussed in detail in Chapter 6) from its remit, to the disappointment of neoliberals and the various IFIs supporting the reform process. In fact, total public sector employment increased between 2001 and 2004 (International Labour Organization, 2018c). Regarding investment, the government had also yet to implement a unified law on investment.

By the end of Ebeid's tenure, Egypt had actually fallen in the World competitiveness rankings from the 40th position in 1999, to the 62nd position in 2004 (UNCTAD, 2005, p. 4). Indeed, under Ebeid's premiership, growth continued to decline, from a high of 6.1 percent in 1999 to 2.4 percent in 2002,[13] and private sector investment dropped from 9.9 percent in 1999 to 7.6 percent in 2004 (World Bank, 2018f, 2018i). Unemployment rose from 8 percent in 1999 to 11 percent in 2003 and inflation rocketed from 3 percent in 1999 to 11.2 percent in 2004 (ILOSTAT, 2018e; World Bank, 2018k). The sectoral performance of the Egyptian economy also failed to fully live up to the expectations of the neoliberal reformers. While exports rose from 15.1 percent of GDP in 1999 to 28.2 percent of GDP in 2004, this represented only a slight increase from the 27.8 percent of GDP that exports comprised in 1991 (World Bank, 2018b). Despite a long series of legislation promoting an export-oriented economy, manufacturing exports declined from 37.1 percent of merchandise exports in 1999 to 30.5 percent in 2004, signifying a failure of the government's policy to promote exports through the establishment of free trade zones and incentives offered to the private sector. Indeed, the value added of both the agricultural and

---

[13] Although it increased to 4.1 percent in 2004, it was too little and too late to save Ebeid.

the manufacturing sectors remained static over the course of Ebeid's term in office.[14] This poor economic performance and his lacklustre record on neoliberal reforms meant that Ebeid's days as prime minister were numbered. In this context, the shift to an emphasis on financial services and real estate development may signify recognition of this failure and represent a change in the nature of the interests and accumulation strategies of the dominant fraction of the capitalist class in Egypt.

The Government of Businessmen, 2004–2011

The new government of Prime Minister Ahmed Nazif, established in 2004, significantly accelerated the reform process and further transformed the Egyptian state. Nazif appointed reformist economists and businessmen with neoliberal leanings to carry out his "New Economic Initiative" agenda. Instrumental in this policy shift was Gamal Mubarak, who was active in reforming the NDP through a "peaceful coup" to make more room for business voices. In 2000, Gamal was appointed to the NDP's governing body and quickly moved up the ladder to reform the party. He was appointed chair of the Policies Secretariat, which gave him the power to reform the regime through the ruling party. Gamal also brought several significant neoliberal-minded businessmen into the upper ranks of the NDP and into government. Among these were Ahmed Ezz, a capitalist bent on monopolizing the steel industry in Egypt and a strong supporter of phasing out state subsidies and privatizing public services. Ezz was appointed chairman of the NDP's secretariat for membership issues and chairman of parliament's budget and planning committee. Rashid Ahmed Rashid, a member of the executive board at Unilever, became the Minister of Foreign Trade and Industry under Nazif.[15] Mohamed Mansour, chairman of the Mansour Group conglomerate, became the Transport Minister in 2006. Ahmed El Maghraby, an executive of French tourism giant Accor, became the Minister of Tourism in 1999 and Minister of Housing in the Nazif government. Dr. Hossam Badraway, the owner and manager of Nile Badraway, one of Cairo's biggest and best

---

[14] Food, beverages and tobacco increased their share of value added between 1998 and 2004; chemicals declined and even services declined (World Bank, 2018a, 2018m).
[15] Rashid obtained several management degrees at various American universities, including Stanford, MIT and Harvard.

equipped private hospitals, and a strong proponent of privatization of the health sector, was appointed chairman of the NDP's business secretariat and the chairman of parliament's Education Committee.

This marked a radical shift from the time when bureaucrats and experts had dominated various state apparatuses from the post-WWII period up until the early 1990s. Between 1990 and 1995, eight businessmen were in the parliament; in 1995–2000, their number had increased to 37; and between 2000 and 2005, their number more than doubled to 84. By 2005 parliamentary elections, 150 seats were occupied by businessmen, including some of the crucial positions such as chairs of the Parliamentary Committees. Businessmen were now well represented in the Legislative Councils, the People's Assembly and the Shura Council.[16]

With the NDP now firmly behind the liberalization process, a new ambitious package of reforms was implemented including new investment laws to attract foreign investment, institutional and administrative reforms to transform the nature of the Egyptian state, more privatizations of public sector enterprises and the liberalization of the financial sector. The main thrust of the reform movement occurred during the first Nazif government from 2004 to 2008. As is often the case with ideologically committed neoliberal governments, the bulk of the more contentious and radical legislation was implemented in the first two years of the new government.

To begin with, the Nazif government implemented a series of administrative reforms aimed at transforming the Egyptian state. A new Ministry of Investment was established through which much of the important neoliberal reforms were conducted. The creation of this new ministry constituted a significant centralization of economic authority, because it supervised the Capital Market Authority, the Mortgage Finance Authority, the Egyptian Insurance Supervisory Authority, the privatization program, the General Authority for Investment and Free Zones (GAFI) and the Special Economic Zone Authority.[17] The Ministry of Investment also subsumed the Ministry of Public Enterprise. As such, whoever controlled the Ministry of Investment – in this case, the committed neoliberal Mohieldin – controlled much of the reform process.

---

[16] The Shura Council is the upper house of Egyptian parliament that was created in 1980. It was dissolved in 2013.

[17] The GAFI was created by Law 65/1975 and was called the General Authority for Investment of Arab Funds and the Free Zones.

GAFI was also transformed and given a "progressive" new leadership, a majority of whom come from the private sector. It now has a board of trustees composed of representatives of investors and exporters that advises GAFI on investment promotion. As a result, GAFI underwent a "smooth transition from a regulatory body to a facilitation and promotional agency" (UNCTAD, 2005, p. 9).

One of the government's main pieces of legislation was the Investment Guarantees and Incentives Law (13/2004), which abolished discrimination between foreign and domestic investors. The new law further liberalized trade through the removal of customs tariffs and other import restrictions, and opened up infrastructure projects, real estate and utilities to private, foreign investment. By 2005, "almost all Egyptian commercial activities that are open for private investment are also open to FDI" (UNCTAD, 2005, p. 4).

In 2005, the new government introduced the Protection of Competition and Prevention of Monopolistic Practices Law (3/2005) to sanction uncompetitive practices, break up trusts and prevent unfair takeovers of newly privatized public sector enterprises.[18] The enforcement of this competition policy became the jurisdiction of the newly established Egyptian Competition Protection Authority, which was run by a board of directors comprised of representatives from other government ministries, the judiciary, academia and the private sector. The adoption of competition policy signifies an important transformation of the Egyptian state, away from a *dirigiste* state that protects the public sector from market forces to a "competition state" (Cerny, 1997) that seeks to enforce market discipline on economic actors. In this sense, its stated purpose is to prevent large concentrations of ownership in the private sector and replace the economic dominance of the public sector characteristic of the old statist model.

Along with the elevation of the Ministry of Investment within the Egyptian state, political reforms were introduced that increased the economic power of the Prime Minister. Mubarak introduced Presidential Decree No. 30/2005, which transferred decision-making power to the Prime Minister over the approval of investment projects.

The Nazif government also implemented reforms intended to increase the competitiveness of the economy, enforce contracts and protect private property. A commercial court designed to resolve

---

[18] With the exception of public utilities.

business disputes more quickly was established. Alongside this investor conciliation committee, the government re-activated and gave legislative backing to the 1998 investor complaints committee. A 2005 UNCTAD report noted the 'striking feature' of the Nazif government's 'accessibility and its willingness to listen to and act upon concerns raised by investors (UNCTAD, 2005, p. 6), in comparison to its predecessors. Such reforms sought to transform the state into an "enabler of economy activity, guaranteeing competition, providing a stable macro environment, and protecting the rights of different parties" (Egypt, 2005, p. 5).

Bureaucratic reforms reduced the costs of business transactions and shortened the time required to issue licenses, thereby making it easier to do business in Egypt. The GAFI shortened the time required to start up a new company to 7 days[19] (UNCTAD, 2005, p. 4), down from up to 6 months in 1998. The government also simplified registration of property to make the real estate market appealing to investors.

The Ministry of Investment was also the driving force behind the reinvigorated privatization process. The neoliberals in the Nazif government pursued privatization with greater vigour than any previous government. When Nazif came to power, 172 state-owned enterprises remained to be privatized.[20] By way of contrast with preceding governments, the Nazif government adopted a "no sacred cows" approach to privatization, meaning that no restrictions would be imposed on FDI in the privatization process, and the government was prepared to "absorb more restructuring costs" (UNCTAD, 2005, p. 6). During the first 2 years of his term in office – July 2004 and March 2006 – 80 companies were sold off, including "some of the state's most prosperous enterprises" (Farah, 2009, pp. 45–50; Rutherford, 2008, pp. 223–224). Fifty-nine of these firms were sold over the course of 2005–2006 for a total of U.S.\$2.6 billion. The four state-owned insurance companies were next on the block slated for privatization.[21] This wave of privatization was not primarily intended to reduce public expenditures, but rather was intended to raise the revenues needed to

---

[19] UNCTAD says 3 days.
[20] Egyptian governments privatized 197 state-owned enterprises between 1993 and 2003.
[21] Three of these four companies controlled 75 percent of all investment in the insurance sector, most of which included real estate assets in areas where the value of land had soared (Abdel Razek, 2005, pp. 25–31).

pay off the domestic debt accumulated in the speculative private sector driven building frenzy of the latter half of the 1990s. As such, the privatization process ended up "subsidizing the private sector at the expense of the nation as a whole" (Farah, 2009, p. 50).

The Nazif government also introduced new financial sector reforms with the goal of transferring the assets, deposits and loans of public banks to private or joint sector banks. In 2004 the banking system comprised 63 banks, with a total asset value of E£633.4 billion, almost one-half of which belonged to the four public sector banks. Over the course of 2004, all but two of the public sector banks were privatized. Financial sector reforms also resulted in the entry of foreign financial institutions into the Egyptian economy and a growth in capital markets. Thus, by 2008, the number of banks had been decreased from 62 in 2003 to 39, and foreign ownership in the sector increased with the private sector controlling around 15 of the Egyptian banks. However, foreign financial institutions only extended loans to large-scale enterprises and ignored smaller businesses. This situation forced the government to backtrack on their plans to privatize the remaining two public sector banks to meet the needs of smaller businesses.

Financial reforms also stimulated the growth of capital markets. Between 1990 and 2000, Egypt's stock market capitalization increased from U.S.$1.8 billion to U.S.$32.8 billion (from 4 percent to 33 percent of the GDP), and the number of companies listed on the stock market grew from 573 to 1,033 over the same period (Vignal & Denis, 2006, p. 106). By 2007, Egypt's stock market capitalization rose to 106 percent of GDP and the value of stocks traded reached 59 percent of GDP in 2008, up from 45 percent 2 years earlier (World Bank, 2018n, 2018s).

What was significant about the growth of capital markets and the entry of foreign financial institutions was the transfer of ownership rights to foreign capital, thereby protecting them against expropriation (Roll, 2010, p. 366). The expansion of capital markets also reduced the power of the state over the financial sector, facilitating the prospects of capital flight. This created further pressure on the government to accommodate the needs of private investors.

By the end of Nazif's first term in office, Egypt's macroeconomic indicators reveal a substantial reversal of Ebeid's failures. Growth increased from 4.1 percent in 2004 to 7.2 percent in 2008, and unemployment dropped from 10.3 percent in 2004 to 8.7 percent in

2008 (ILOSTAT, 2018e; World Bank, 2018f). Investment levels were up, with private sector investment – at 14.4 percent of GDP – finally exceeding the levels attained *before* the implementation of the structural adjustment program in 1990 (World Bank, 2018i). Manufacturing's contribution of value-added to GDP rose from 1.7 percent in 2003 to 8 percent in 2008 (World Bank, 2018m). However, inflation peaked at 18.3 percent in 2008, resulting from a combination of price liberalizations (notably cutbacks to food subsidies) and the rising costs of food imports during the so-called global food crisis of that year (World Bank, 2018k).

Neoliberal Class Formation

Much of the scholarship on the liberalization process focuses on the instances of cronyism, and sometimes outright corruption, that accompanied its progress. Early on in the process, Sadowski (1991) described the "cronyism," whereby powerful interests in the state and economy united to maximize their share of resources through control of the market. Richards (2004, pp. 24–25) writes of a "symbiosis between government regulators and speculative entrepreneurs," resulting in "insider trading" in the construction sector, "where public land may be sold very cheaply to a friend who then resells it at its market value." Farah (2009, p. 81) argues that "[P]rivatization ... led to collusion between state bureaucrats and businessmen for the sale of public sector enterprises at prices much lower than the market." In numerous cases, "companies were sold to investors through loans provided by state banks," and "investors bought state-companies with loans backed by false guarantees and retained ownership of the companies even after they defaulted on the loans" (Farah, 2009, p. 81).

As discussed in Chapter 1, a significant number of scholars have characterized this liberalization process as being frustrated by the resilient authoritarianism of the Egyptian state (Demmelhuber, 2011; Heydemann, 2004). In this sense, corruption and cronyism is a by-product of authoritarian politics. Many of these scholars have employed network analysis to examine the ways in which the regime co-opted prominent members of Egypt's business community to foreclose any kind of democratizing opposition from arising within civil society (El Tarouty, 2016; Sfakianakis, 2004; Wurzel, 2004, 2009).

From this perspective, the authoritarian regime has actively worked to frustrate the latent democratization within the liberalization process.

There are several significant problems with this characterization of the liberalization process and the evolution of Egypt's business class. First, it downplays the extent to which corruption and cronyism was prevalent in the neoliberal transformations that took place in the liberal democracies during the 1980s and 1990s. In other words, it downplays the extent to which corruption and cronyism may be a by-product of neoliberalism itself. Second, it presumes that economic liberalization, in general, *should* foster the development of an independent business class that can challenge the authoritarian state. In doing so, it downplays the extent to which members of the Egyptian business class "buy in" to the regime, precluding the need to co-opt them. Finally, it also presumes that the "resilient authoritarianism" of Egypt's crony capitalists stifled the further liberalization of the economy. This suggests that capitalists approach liberalization with the desire to foster competitive markets. Each of these claims is problematic for the following reasons.

First, the focus on corruption downplays the extent to which ostensibly democratic states engaged in similar practices at the outset of their neoliberal transformations. For example, in the UK under Thatcher, the valuation of state-owned assets was "structured to offer considerable incentives to private capital," meaning that they were priced well below market values. Several enterprises – including water companies, railways and even auto and steel industries – owned "high-value land in prime locations that was excluded from the valuation of the enterprise" – and in many instances, "[P]rivatization and speculative gains on the property released went hand in hand" (Harvey, 2005, p. 60). The wave of privatizations of state-owned land under the more recent Conservative-Liberal Democratic coalition government (2010–2015) was likened to "asset-stripping with a political purpose" (Toynbee, 2016). This sale of state assets "at too-low prices" was deemed "doubly suspect" due to the "closeness of this government with private interests," and "the in-and-out revolving doors between ministers and business" (Toynbee, 2016). Indeed, instances of corruption in the democratic world have been on the rise since the onset of the neoliberal project (Whyte & Wiegratz, 2016). While it is perhaps the case that corruption is more endemic in countries like Egypt, it may only partly be due to the existence of authoritarianism. It may also be due to the absence of more nuanced processes of capital accumulation developed in the liberal democracies that legitimize dubious transactions that are deemed "corrupt" in less sophisticated systems of economic governance (stock buy-backs, for example). In other words, corruption seems to be endemic to neoliberalism – the difference between the corruption in emerging markets and that of advanced economies is merely one of degree, not kind.

Second, the claim that liberalization failed to empower a business class independent of the state that could challenge the authoritarianism of the regime – and presumably support the democratization process – presumes this to be the norm in instances of economic liberalization in authoritarian states. In this regard, the network analysis of the resilient authoritarianism thesis shares the same assumptions as the democratization literature it seeks to challenge. As argued in Chapter 1, the claim that economic liberalization fosters democratization at the behest of a rising business class is highly dubious. In the case of the transition to capitalism in England in the seventeenth century, the process of "liberalization" was driven forward by a fraction of the dominant aristocracy, and their challenge to the monarchy in no way resulted in the democratization of English life. As Therborn (1977), Mayer (2010) and Halperin (1997) have all convincingly demonstrated, the thrust of democratization in Europe came from outside of the capitalist class, who – far from seeking to overthrow the established political and economic order – sought to find its place within it. Why this should be any different in the case of Egypt is never considered by the proponents of resilient authoritarianism.

Finally, the claim that resilient authoritarianism stifled further liberalization presumes that the primary dynamic of liberalization is to facilitate the growth of a capitalist class that is independent of the state and to foster competition between rival capitalists as opposed to increasing the power of capital in general over the labouring classes as a whole. In support of their position, proponents of resilient authoritarianism cite the attempts by 'cronies' of the Mubarak regime (or at least of Gamal Mubarak's entourage) to monopolize the market and prevent competition by market rivals. The history of economic liberalization in Europe, however, reveals a process of creating markets embedded within non-market forms of coordination that facilitated the rise of cartels that engaged in everything from price fixing to coordinated wage setting (Streeck & Yamamura, 2001). On top of this, however, it is simply not the case that the desire of elites to preserve Egypt's authoritarian practices and institutions stifled the liberalization process. Indeed, as mentioned above, the period after 2004 represented an acceleration of the liberalization program. Privatizations increased dramatically, and labour market reforms were introduced after nearly a decade of delay. A 2007 IMF Financial Sector Assessment Program report found that "substantial progress was made since the launch of the government's 2004 financial sector reform program especially in building a more efficient banking system" (IMF, 2007, p. 16). The report also noted "equally important achievements" in the non-banking sector, including the steady expansion of the Egyptian stock market, which posted "one of the best performances in the region" (IMF, 2007, p. 55). The OECD's 2009 African Economic Outlook report characterized Egypt's strong growth (7.2 percent in 2008) as the "fruit of an ambitious market-oriented reform programme, with substantial price liberalization and privatization of state-owned enterprises" (OECD, 2009, p. 227).[22] In the eyes of the main liberalizing international institutions – the IMF and the OECD – Egypt's liberalization record was impressive between 2004 and 2008. The liberalization process slowed down beginning in 2008 as a result of an escalating strike wave in the context of a food crisis – a crisis that prompted the NDP to slow down the reform process and begin discussing policies of income maintenance and wage increases.

This is not to deny that the liberalization process was characterized by corruption, cronyism or uncompetitive market practices such as monopolization. It is merely to argue that an overemphasis on these traits – which exist in established neoliberal economies in the West as well – prevents us from focusing on the deeper shifts occurring in the Egyptian economy during this period. The transformation within Egypt's economic elite is more coherent, and the existence of corruption and the persistence of authoritarianism is less aberrant, than network analysts claim. The common thread that unites the "whales of the Nile" is their relationship to the tourism, construction and real estate sectors, all of which had strong ties to the emerging neoliberal fraction within the NDP and the more internationalized business

---

[22] The report points out that any possible slowing of the liberalization process will be the probable result of the international economic crisis.

associations like the Egyptian Businessmen's Association and the President's Council. These economic sectors closely resemble the financialized fractions of transnational capital articulated in Chapter 1. As the failures of Egypt's privatization drive and its Free Zones to stimulate the production of manufactured goods for export became apparent at the dawn of the new millennium, the importance of liberalizing housing markets and land became the lynchpin of the neoliberal accumulation strategy seized upon by those within the "networks of privilege."[23] In other words, and against the prevailing wisdom of the IFIs and neoliberal economic doctrine, the liberalization process did not empower the growth of private sector actors from outside the dominant class, but rather provided opportunities for members of the dominant class to reorient their accumulation strategies. At the centre of this new network of privilege was Gamal Mubarak. It was around him that a transnationally oriented neoliberal fraction of the Egyptian capitalist class coalesced, largely in the construction, real estate and tourism sectors.

By 2000, two of the top three sectors on the Egyptian Stock Exchange – which was growing dramatically during this period – were financial services and construction (Vignal & Denis, 2006, p. 108). By the end of 2007, the real estate, travel and leisure, and construction and materials sectors dominated the stock exchange. The Real Estate Financing and the Mortgage Finance Laws passed earlier in the decade led to a property boom that proved to be a boon to each sector. Over the course of 2007, the real estate sector's stock performance increased 113 percent, travel and leisure's grew by 90 percent, and construction and materials increased by 86 percent (Egyptian Stock Exchange, 2007, p. 9).[24]

Construction remained one of the most buoyant sectors of the economy. In 2000, the sector ranked 36th in the global construction market, with a value of U.S.\$12.71 billion. In 2000–2001, the construction sector employed 1.5 million workers and contributed 4.7 percent (E£16.56 billion) to Egypt's GDP (American Chamber of

---

[23] According to the World Bank development indicators, Egypt's manufacturing exports, as a percentage of merchandise exports, continuously declined from 1998 to 2008. During the first half of the 2000s, fuel exports comprised the largest portion of merchandise exports.

[24] The leader in the Egyptian stock market, however, was the manufacturing sector.

Commerce in Egypt, 2003). In 2001–2002, the sector's investment levels reached E£41.2 billion, representing 48.2 percent of the country's total investment. The sector's growth levels of 8.3 percent were higher than the general economic growth of 7.4 percent in this period (American Chamber of Commerce in Egypt, 2003). By 2003, the private sector's share in the construction industry increased by almost 30 percent and private sector control of cement production increased to 68 percent (American Chamber of Commerce in Egypt, 2003). During the same period, an additional 198 construction companies were established with a total investment of E£659.5 million.[25] Between 2004 and 2006, the construction sector was 'buoyant," growing by 14 percent in real terms over the course of 2005 and 2006. The OECD's 2008 African Economic Outlook report indicated that between 2006 and 2007, the construction, tourism and real estate sectors (along with manufacturing) were the main factors driving Egypt's impressive growth rate (OECD, 2008, p. 273).

This period also witnessed the increase of private investment from both domestic and foreign investors. By 2010, 83 percent of construction investment came from the private sector. The level of private investment – in Egyptian pounds – in the tourism sector increased by 102 percent between 2003 and 2010. Construction increased 500 percent during the same period, demonstrating an immunity from the GFC of 2007–2008 that negatively affected tourism investment. Real estate increased 114 percent and demonstrated a similar resilience to the GFC, being affected instead by the uprisings in 2011.[26]

Reforms favouring private investors finally succeeded in registering significant net inflows of FDI, signifying the increasing internationalization of the Egyptian economy. Between 2004 and 2006, net inflows of FDI as a percentage of GDP increased from 1.9 percent to 9.3 percent, declining to 8.9 percent in 2008 before registering a steady decline beginning in 2009 as a result of the GFC (World Bank, 2018e). In 2006, FDI "rose to unprecedented levels," positioning Egypt second behind Saudi Arabia as the top recipient of FDI among Arab countries (OECD, 2008, p. 273). Most of this foreign investment came from U.S.

---

[25] Cairo Investment Forum 2007 attended by the author.

[26] Private investment increased by 318 percent between 2003 and 2011; public sector investment increased by only 118 percent during the same period. In 2003, 53 percent of investment came from the public sector; by 2011 it had declined to 37.6 percent (Central Bank of Egypt, 2018).

and EU investors, with very little coming from other Arab countries, apart from the Gulf Cooperation Council (GCC) states. Between 2000 and 2006, American and European investment constituted 84 percent of Egypt's average annual inflows of FDI, signifying a greater integration with Western capital (OECD, 2007c, p. 15).

Despite this dominance by U.S. and European investment, flows of Arab investment increased during the mid-2000s. Between 2005 and 2007, FDI from the GCC states grew from 4.5 percent to 25 percent of Egypt's FDI (Hanieh, 2011, p. 151). The prospects of cheap land and flexible labour laws with an unrestricted international market for potential luxury homebuyers resulted in the launch of several major projects. For instance, DAMAC Properties, one of the Middle East's largest luxury property developers from Dubai, entered the Egyptian market in 2006 with a deal to develop a 320 million square metre tourism project in Gamsha Bay, on the Red Sea coast. The company also developed Park Avenue in 6th of October City to cater to upper class tourists. Another Gulf luxury real estate developer, Emmar Properties, entered the Egyptian market through its subsidiary Emmar Misr (a joint venture with the state-owned Al Nasr Housing and Development Company) and launched six projects. The company's investment in Egypt was estimated at E£43.3 billion (Economist Intelligence Unit, 2006, pp. 32–33).[27]

While Arab capital had a long history of investment in Egyptian real estate, by the mid-2000s, GCC investors were branching out into financial services.[28] By 2008, GCC firms either directly controlled or were major shareholders in 9 out of 12 of Egypt's major banks (Hanieh, 2011, p. 158). For example, Abu Dhabi Islamic Bank and

[27] In Cairo, it was engaged in building a residential area on Moqattam Hills, where apartments sold at E£4,500 per square metre. The eight villages planned to be built were not open to the public and were sold by invitation to a select citizenry. In the southwest of Cairo, Emmar Misr planned to build Cairo Gate, Egypt's largest mall, across from Smart Village where the company planned to develop 300,000 square metres into office park space for the workers and commuters of Smart Village. The company has 3.78 million square metre plot of land in the suburbs of New Cairo near the American University's new campus. On the Mediterranean coast, Emmar Misr has plans for hotels, office parks and malls close to Bibliotheca Alexandria. In the North Coast, in Sidi Abdel Rahman, the company has 6.2 million square metres of land intended to build luxury residences, hotels and shopping malls (Neumann, 2009).

[28] Prominent investors included Dubai real estate giant Emaar Properties – to build a 4 million square meter luxury residential complex in Cairo for U.S.$4 billion.

Emirates International owned 51% of the shares in Egypt's National Bank for Development. Al Watani Bank, one of Egypt's most success-ful private banks, was bought by the National Bank of Kuwait. Even EFG-Hermes, Egypt's largest investment and private equity firm, was majority controlled by the Abu Dhabi Investment Authority and the Dubai Financial Group (Hanieh, 2011, p. 158).[29]

In the post banking reform period, closer ties between the Egyptian real estate sector and the private banking sector was exemplified in the merger of the French bank, Credit Agricole and Mansour and Magh-raby Investment Development in 2006 (Roll, 2010, p. 359). With the establishment of Credit Agricole Egypt, the Bank expanded its activ-ities in the field of mortgage financing to support the business interests of the El Mansour and El Maghraby families in the real estate and construction sectors. The relationship between the private sector and government officials demonstrated a new era in the formation of "networks of privilege" (Heydemann, 2004) between the private sector, government officials, bureaucrats and capitalists. Another example will demonstrate this relationship further. In 2001, Mansour and Maghraby Investment Development had become an important shareholder in EFG-Hermes, the Egyptian investment bank. In 2004, Rashid Mohammed Rashid joined the two families becoming a major shareholder in EFG-Hermes.

The rise of these sectors of the Egyptian economy were closely linked to prominent Egyptian capitalists with close ties to the Nazif govern-ment. Members of this government included Mohamed Mansour (Minister of Transport) and Ahmed El-Maghraby (Minister of Tour-ism and later Minister of Housing). Mansour and Maghraby were joint owners of Mansour and Maghraby Investment Development. With Rashid Mohammed Rashid (Minister of Industry), Mansour and Maghraby played an important role in implementing the reforms that boosted the financial profile of the Egyptian investment bank EFG-Hermes, of which all three men were major shareholders. By the end of 2005, the bank's share price "was nearly 20 times higher than it had been in mid-2004" (Roll, 2010, p. 361). Mansour and El Magh-raby had also established financial ties with French finance capital (Crédit Agricole) to acquire the Egyptian American Bank, leading to the creation of Crédit Agricole Egypt. With the establishment of Crédit

---

[29] The Dubai Investment Group holds 25 percent of the shares in EFG-Hermes.

Agricole Egypt, the Bank expanded its activities in the field of mortgage financing to support the business interests of the El Mansour and El Maghraby families in the real estate and construction sectors.

Mansour and El Maghraby also owned Palm Hills Development, a development company founded in 2005. Benefiting from the liberalization of urban and rural property markets as well as financial reforms, the company became the second largest real estate developer in just six years. Its total land bank stood at over 48.3 million square metres by 2008 while the Company's market value was E£19.5 billion in March 2008. Mubarak's other son, Alaa, held E£49,535,000 worth of shares in Palm Hills Development (El-Karanshawi, 2011).

Another prominent player in Egypt's real estate, construction and tourism-based strategy of accumulation was Ahmed Bahgat. Bahgat made his fortune in the United States in the mid-1980s and began cultivating stronger ties with the Mubarak regime upon his return to Egypt.[30] Having established numerous businesses in the manufacture of consumer goods, he began to move into real estate in the 1990s as Egypt began liberalizing. One of his largest projects was called Dreamland, a development project in Cairo's new, emerging suburbs consisting of almost 2,000 acres of residential buildings and recreational, entertainment, shopping and sporting facilities. Bahgat had acquired the public land needed for the development below market value and with the aid of loans secured through state banks.

The Sawiris family – Naguib, Samih and Nassef – are the sons of Onsi Sawiris, the founder of Orascom Construction Industry.[31] By the 1990s, Orascom branched out into telecommunications and media and controlled a dozen subsidiaries, including Egypt's largest and second largest private construction and cement manufacturing firms, as well as

---

[30] El Tarouty cites the Bahgat case as an example of the regime "co-opting" businessmen. She argues that the regime's refusal to allow Bahgat to leave the country until he paid his debts to the state banks is an example of "authoritarian clientelism" that was used to pressure Bahgat to support the regime during the 2011 uprisings. However, as she points out, it was Bahgat that initially approached Mubarak – suggesting that, rather than being co-opted, he "bought in." The coercion she says was used against Bahgat by the regime amounted to pursuing past debts owed to state banks, which seems to be a reasonable move by any public authority.

[31] Onsi had established his first construction company in 1950, only to have it nationalized under Nasser, prompting a 12-year, self-imposed exile in Libya. Upon his return to Egypt in the late 1970s, he founded Orascom.

the country's largest tourism development projects. They were facilitated in this endeavour by access to cheap credit from state banks. In this regard, Sfakianakis characterizes the Sawiris as "the quintessential cronies that rose to new riches as a result of their connections with bureaucrats and politicians" (2004, p. 91). In the late 1990s, Naguib established Orascom Telecom, after buying the state-owned mobile phone company sold off during the privatization drive. In 1998, Samih Sawiris formed Orascom Hotels and Development, which now owns 115.9 million square meters of land in seven different countries. As a fully diversified tourism and real estate developer, Orascom Hotels and Development specializes in the development of entirely self-sufficient cities composed of hotels, marinas, golf courses, shopping centres and restaurants. Nassif, the youngest brother, became the head of Orascom Construction and sat on the board of the Egyptian Centre for Economic Studies.[32]

In 2005, Orascom Development Holding was tasked with implementing the government's National Housing Project. The National Housing Project had an estimated budget of E£25 billion and a target of 85,000 housing units annually until 2011. To realize the National Housing Project, the government sold state land below market values to Orascom on the condition that they would produce low-income housing.

By the end of 2008, Sawiris firms "had an aggregated market capitalization of more than E£90bn (U.S.$16.3bn) which corresponded to 19 percent of total market capitalization" (Roll, 2010, p. 359). Far from being pawns of the Mubarak regime, the Sawiris had attained a market power that made them independent of the regime's power. Such was the economic power of the Sawiris family that the Mubarak regime – dependent on the family's investment – "was not in a position to turn against it" (El Tarouty, 2016, p. 97).[33] The Sawiris increased their power against the regime by taking advantage of Egypt's capital market reforms to establish a Swiss company called Orascom Development Holding AG, which it used to acquire most of the shares of Orascom Hotels and Development (one of their tourism companies) through a share swap. They established a secondary listing for Orascom

[32] Orascom also had deep ties with the World Bank and the Pentagon.
[33] While El Tarouty claims that, despite their wealth and power, the Sawiris were also dependent on the regime, her account of the family suggests otherwise.

Hotels and Development on the Egyptian exchange, but for all intent and purpose, the holding company enjoyed Swiss nationality that protected its assets for any potential expropriation by the Egyptian state (Roll, 2010, p. 366). It needs pointing out that, despite this, none of the Sawiris became emboldened supporters of democratization. In fact, it was only after the fall of the Mubarak regime that Naguib Sawiris established the Free Egyptians' Party, which purportedly supports secularism and democracy in Egypt. However, the party soon became rife with internal accusations of anti-democratic practices and tolerance of former NDP members. In 2014, it supported Si-Si in the presidential elections.

Other established construction and development firms also sought to reap the spoils of liberalization. A primary example was the Talat Mustafa Group, founded by the late Talat Mustafa. The conglomerate was divided into several different branches: construction, agriculture and real estate. The eldest son, Tarek Talat Mustafa, played an important role in the NDP's Policies Committee until 2011 and was former head of the parliament's housing committee. Tarek's brother Hisham headed up the real estate branch and served as the Deputy Chairman of the Shura Council's Economic Committee and sat as a member of the ruling NDP's Supreme Policies Council until his murder conviction in 2008. By 2007, the Talat Mustafa Group was the biggest real estate developer in Egypt with a land bank boasting 50 million square meters of land. Its projects included Al Rehab City (more than 9.9 million square metres of land) and Madinaty (33 million square metres) and numerous resorts and hotels under the Four Seasons management group (Denis, 2006, pp. 54–55; England, 2007). The company's board of directors included former Central Bank of Egypt experts as well as members of the Bin Laden family of Saudi Arabia.

Not only new companies began forming, but the shift in economic strategy and the privatization of public sector construction firms offered unlimited opportunities for the private sector. Ahmed Ezz took advantage of the privatization of public sector enterprises to acquire profitable steel companies at nominal prices, by which he became one of the most successful private sector capitalists in Egypt. In the early 1990s, he owned three small factories that made steel and ceramics (El Ezz Steel Rebar, El Ezz for Flat Steel and el Gawhra for Porcelain and Ceramic Products). In 2000, he acquired 30 percent of the Alexandria

National Iron and Steel Company in Al Dekheila, a successful public steel company that was privatized by the government (El Tarouty, 2016, pp. 62–63). He later acquired 55 percent of the company, now renamed Ezz Al Dekheila. By 2005, he was an influential member of the NDP's policy committee, which enabled him to influence the passage of an amendment to Law 3 of 2005 on the Protection of Competition and the Prohibition of Monopolistic Practices that protected his monopoly (El Tarouty, 2016, p. 66). By the late 2000s, it was alleged that Ezz controlled 58 percent of the steel market in Egypt – an effective monopoly – leading former speaker of the Parliament, Fathy Sorour to claim that Ezz is "more powerful [than the president] and he represents a dangerous power and disobeys the President" (El Madany, 2009; El Tarouty, 2016, p. 67). Ezz's main competitor in the steel market would eventually come from the military, and he would ultimately be charged and convicted of money laundering by the Supreme Council of the Armed Forces government that assumed power after the deposition of Mubarak in February 2011.

Finally, Gamal Mubarak and members of his family were key architects and beneficiaries of Egypt's embrace of neoliberalism during the 2000s. Between 2003 and 2011, Gamal Mubarak made more than a 1.1 million percent rate of return on his initial capital investment of U.S.\$1750 in EFG Hermes Holding company, located in the British Virgin Islands – a notorious tax haven. For every dollar invested, he earned U.S.\$11,884 (Diab, 2016b). Gamal was eventually arrested on charges of corruption by the Supreme Council of the Armed Forces government.

The rise to prominence of this neoliberal class fraction coincided with a dramatic concentration of wealth and rising inequality. At the level of the firm, the Egyptian economy became dominated by a smaller number of large firms. Although in 2008, market capitalization in relation to GDP was 60 percent higher than it had been 5 years previous, this rise was associated with a smaller number of private sector companies, which stood at 380 in contrast with 978 five years earlier (Roll, 2010, p. 355). Among some of the main beneficiaries of credit from the banking sector were large-scale capitalists in real estate and construction. According to an Egyptian banking sector analyst, Salwa El-Antari, 343 clients received 42 percent of the overall credit facilities allocated to the private sector, while 28 clients among these secured 13 percent of the overall credit (Roll, 2010, p. 356). Similarly, records of the Banque du Caire indicate that in the first half of the 2000s, "46 businessmen held nearly 74 percent of the bank's loan portfolio" (Roll, 2010, p. 356). The steel magnate, Ahmed Ezz was a major beneficiary of bank credit in the 1990s and after. In the 1990s, Ezz was heavily indebted to the public sector banks. After the reform of the banking sector in the post 2000 period, Ezz continued to enjoy easy access to large-scale credit facilities.[34]

This concentration of wealth was reflected in the rising number of millionaires in Egyptian society. This growth of multi-millionaires has occurred *within* the top 0.04 percent of income earners (Ahram Online, 2013). By these measures, the levels of wealth inequality have grown significantly, as an increasing amount of landed property and urban property has been accumulated by the wealthy. Measured in terms of the GINI coefficient, Egypt's wealth inequality stood at 67.8 percent in 2010. By 2017, it had risen to 91.7 percent (Credit Suisse, 2010, 2017). Not surprisingly, this concentration of wealth at the top end of the class structure was accompanied by rising levels of poverty among the lower urban and rural classes, laying the foundation for the rise of popular unrest that would characterize Egyptian society from the mid-2000s to the uprisings of 2011.

Conclusion

Over the course of the 1990s and the 2000s, Egypt embarked on a process of liberalization that, while contested, resulted in a dramatic transformation of the Egyptian economy as well as the composition and accumulation strategies of the dominant class fraction of Egyptian capital. This fraction, growing in prominence within the NDP, rooted its accumulation strategies in the transnationalized and financialized circuits of capital taking hold in specific sectors of the economy: notably finance, real estate, tourism and construction. Against the claims of scholars of authoritarian resilience, the individuals associated with this class fraction had no interest in democratizing Egyptian

---

[34] It is ironic that the banking reform of the 2000 was initiated to deal with the non-performing loans of the public sector banks. In 2004, the Central Bank established a non-performing loan unit. An examination of more than 5,000 loan default cases indicated that 250 of the default cases exceeded E£50 million (Roll, 2010, p. 357).

society and even less interest in ensuring that markets remained "free" and open to competition as postulated by neoliberal economic doctrine. Rather, this class fraction was intent on transforming the authoritarian structures of the Egyptian state to accelerate the neoliberal transformation of the Egyptian economy and shield it from both popular pressures from below and from conservative, redistributive pressures from above.

4 | "We Feed the Nation"
The Military as a Fraction of Capital

The Military as a Class Fraction

The post-colonial period was a unique historical context for the rise of the military in the Arab world. At the time, scholars and politicians "considered the military to be a powerful corporate interest group, a vanguard of the middle class, and sometimes the most modernity-oriented group in society" (Grawert, 2016, p. 4). In countries such as Iraq, Syria, Algeria, Libya and Egypt, the military became an essential actor in the construction of the post-colonial social, economic and political order. In doing so, it assumed numerous different, yet reinforcing roles. First, the militaries of the Arab world often challenged the power of the older, landed classes that benefited from colonialism. In this regard, they acted as vehicles of social mobility, mostly for men from the lower middle classes. In some notable instances, even the sons of lower class men could rise through the ranks to achieve social mobility. For example, Nasser was the son of a postal worker, Ben Bella of Algeria was the son of a farmer, Gaddafi from Libya was the son of a goatherd and Saddam Hussein was born a bastard into a family of shepherds. Given the importance of the military as an institution of social mobility, the popular classes tended to perceive it as a progressive force in the post-colonial era, an image that the military itself perpetuated (Ayubi, 1995; Picard, 1988).

Second, the military was also integral to instilling and promoting the notions of citizenship and secular identity essential to securing the unity and legitimacy of the post-colonial state. In this sense, they represented important national – and national*ist* – institutions seeking to transcend tribal, ethnic and religious identities that tended to fragment Arab societies. This made them crucial actors in the nation-building projects that followed independence in the post-war period.

Finally, Arab militaries also acted as agents of industrialization and economic modernization. In the absence of an indigenous, national

110

bourgeoisie, the fledgling Arab states relied heavily on the military to carry out statist economic planning and the management of public sector enterprises. Trimberger (1978) referred to this as a form of "revolution from above," similar – albeit less successfully – to the late industrializing projects of Germany and Japan in the nineteenth century (Gerschenkron, 1962). As a result, the military's legitimacy rested just as much on its effective role in carrying out nationalizations, fostering industrialization, redistributing land and creating jobs through the expansion of the public sector as it did on defending the country from external threats (Abdel Malek, 1968; Ayubi, 1995). In the immediate post-colonial period, the military managed to institutionalize its prestigious position in society as Arab citizens continued to view the institution with high levels of respect given its role in changing the balance of class power through the implementation of land reform and state-led industrialization programs.

In light of these roles, military interventions in politics and society were commonplace in many Arab states after independence from colonial rule due to "an urgent need for authority in countries where the state was still embryonic and the public services defective" (Picard, 1988, p. 117). The Middle East and North Africa region witnessed approximately 55 coups or attempted coups between 1940 and 1980 (Abul-Magd, 2017, p. 16). The armies of Iraq, Syria and Egypt became increasingly involved in the political and economic spheres. Yet the nature of their economic activity was often masked in secrecy (Mitchell, 1991a; Owen, 2002; Picard, 1988).

Despite this historical role, much of the scholarship on the military in the Arab world has focused primarily on its political role – namely, its role in establishing and preserving authoritarianism. Democratization theorists have long argued that keeping the military out of politics is crucial for developing and safeguarding democracy, and that military intervention in politics undermines the role of democratic institutions in facilitating peaceful political competition among the elite (Diamond, 1997; Kechichian & Nazimek, 1997; Stacher, 2012). While recognizing that the military has traditionally been the only effective force to modernize Arab society (Huntington, 1968; Janowitz, 1977; Trimberger, 1978), democratization scholars feared that the military may decide not to retreat to the barracks, thus contributing to the rise of authoritarianism and the undermining of democracy (Cook, 2007; Diamond, 1997; Droz-Vincent, 2009; Janowitz, 1988; Jaraba, 2014).

While these contributions shed some light on the political role of the military in post-colonial societies, they fail to take account of the evolution of the military as part of the process of state and class formation in the Arab World. The development of the military in post-colonial states like Egypt needs to be situated within the context of capitalist development, where the military emerges as an important actor fulfilling the tasks of economic development, and in the process evolves and develops its own class interests and a unique class position – as well as autonomous institutional power it can exercise over the state. Far from being a rigid institution supporting a static authoritarian state, the militaries of the Middle East have never been "fixed or stable" institutions, rather, they "necessarily, change over time" (Owen, 2002, p. 200).

This point is central to understanding the evolution of the Egyptian military's relationship with the state in the post-colonial era. The Egyptian military has evolved into a dynamic class-based organization with interests that change over time and that seeks to secure those interests, either in competition or in collaboration with other fractions of the ruling class. Such an approach examines the military within the broader context of state formation, a process conditioned by internal as well as external factors and relationships with other classes and precludes treating the military merely as part of the "deep state" or "shadow state."[1] Such an approach requires the identification of the linkages and processes that transform the military into a fraction of the ruling class over time, and this necessitates a discussion of how the development of capitalism transformed the military and its class position vis-à-vis other classes and within the state.

It needs pointing out, however, that the military is not a monolithic class-based organization. Rather, its hierarchy has come to mirror the primary class divide between the propertied and the propertyless in Egyptian society. Most of its 450,000 personnel are conscripts and low-ranking officers with little or no property or economic opportunities. At the top of the hierarchy, however, sits tens of thousands of elite officers who "live as a class apart, with their own social clubs, hotels, hospitals, parks and other benefits financed by the state" (Hubbard,

---

[1] The military's economic role is often characterized as part of a "deep state" or "parallel state" engaged in "the grey economy," suggesting that the military is working outside of, and against, the capitalist economy (Levinson & Bradley, 2013; Momani, 2013; Tadros, 2012).

2018). While Egypt is not unique in this regard – the militaries of the liberal democratic world are also comprised of elite, high-ranking career officers and working-class foot-soldiers – it differs from its Western counterparts in the extent to which its officer class has been able to pursue its emerging class interests through military owned industries and enterprises.

Prior to the internationalization of capital associated with globalization, domestically oriented industrial capital was central to the development strategies of post-colonial states. As discussed in Chapter 2, newly independent post-colonial states like Egypt embarked on strategies of import substitution industrialization to create a national economy and break its dependence on foreign capital. Public sector managers played a crucial role in carrying out development strategies and catering to the needs of the domestic population. This domestically oriented industrial fraction of capital – usually rooted in the growing public sector – was instrumental in guiding state policy in this phase. Given its access to technology and skilled labour (often in the form of engineers) the militaries of the Arab world played a crucial role in this process of development. In the case of Egypt, the Ministry of Defence and the Ministry of Military Production (MoMP) were key institutions in facilitating Egypt's import substitution industrialization development project.

Under the hegemony of finance capital in the 1980s, economies underwent extensive processes of liberalization, and statist development strategies were abandoned in favour of market-led, export-oriented development strategies. While finance capital favours policies that decrease barriers to export markets, domestically oriented industrial capital may feel threatened by exposure to international competition that accompanies the relaxation of trade barriers. This is where tensions can develop between the different fractions of capital. It is possible for economic reforms that benefit transnational financial capital to weaken domestically oriented fractions of industrial capital. In this case, tensions may emerge between transnational capital and the more domestically oriented militaries of the region. However, it is also possible for industrial capital, oriented towards the domestic market, to develop strategies of survival by establishing networks with finance capital, that is, to adapt to the emerging neoliberal order through processes of financialization. In the case of Egypt, the military proved especially adept at adapting to the neoliberal order, particularly over the course of the 2000s.

Politics also plays an important role in determining the ability of the Arab militaries to adapt and survive. The strength of a hegemonic fraction of capital is dependent upon the success of its dominant accumulation strategy as well as its political legitimacy. If transnational finance experiences a crisis – which it did in Egypt between 2008 and 2011 – a window may open for a different fraction of capital to step up and determine a new strategy of accumulation. Under the hegemony of a new fraction of capital, accumulation strategies may be reformulated to reduce social tensions. In this sense, the different phases of development in Egypt posed different opportunities and challenges to the military as a fraction of its capitalist class.

In this context, the Egyptian military has evolved into a dominant fraction of the Egyptian capitalist class since its initial formation in 1952. The first phase of the military's development corresponds with the period of statism under Gamal Abdel Nasser that lasted until 1967. The second phase corresponds with Anwar Sadat's "corrective revolution," which lasted until the end of his rule and opened up the Egyptian economy for foreign capital. The third and crucial phase began in 1981 and lasted until 1991, a decade during which in the military significantly expanded its economic activity. The 1990s witnessed some setbacks for the military as the neoliberal elite associated with Gamal Mubarak attempted to sideline the military and establish its hegemony within the Egyptian ruling class. However, this neoliberal fraction entered a period of political and economic crisis in the context of the food crisis and growing strike waves of 2008 that weakened its legitimacy. Since the January 25th revolution, the Egyptian military has reasserted its influence and subordinated other fractions to its hegemonic position in the Egyptian state.

From Nationalist Revolution to *Infitah*

The Military under Nasser

Between 1952 and 1967, the military was one of the strongest institutional elements within Egypt's political system. In 1952, the Egyptian monarchy was overthrown in a military coup initiated by a group within the military calling themselves the Free Officers, headed by the charismatic Nasser. The coup turned into a revolution intent on abolishing feudalism and modernizing Egypt's social and economic order by pursuing social justice and implementing a program of national industrialization. The intersection of economic modernization, social transformation, and national security institutionalized the unique role of the military in post-revolutionary Egypt. Social justice required the abolition of "feudalism," which brought the Free Officers into conflict with the landed aristocracy of the *ancien régime*. Economic modernization entailed the repression of labour militancy and the persecution of the radical left. Finally, national security – as it was expressed in Nasser's ideal of non-alignment – entailed self-sufficiency, both in terms of economic development (e.g., national energy projects, control over infrastructure) and military production.[2]

In this sense, the Egyptian military became a crucial agent in a kind of "revolution from above" (Trimberger, 1978) that resulted in the implementation of redistributive land reforms and nationalist forms of import substitution industrialization. Indeed, one of the first acts of the Free Officers was to implement the Agrarian Reforms that would set a cap on landownership and redistribute the surplus to the peasantry. However, attracting foreign capital preceded the program of land reform. Like many countries attempting to establish a national economy, the Free Officers had no initial intentions of engaging in widespread nationalizations or moving towards socialism (Beinin, 1989). Rather, they were intent on attracting foreign investment and encouraging private capital accumulation. Shortly after coming to power, the new regime increased the threshold of foreign ownership – from 49 percent to 51 percent – allowed under Egyptian law. The new regime was particularly keen to attract U.S. foreign investment and granted an oil concession to the Colorado Oil Company in 1954. Economic incentives were not the only way the regime sought to attract foreign investment. The Free Officers also clamped down on the radical left – comprised largely of the Egyptian Communist Party – and its influence on the labour movement. As discussed in Chapter 6, the regime established a highly authoritarian form of corporatist industrial relations to ensure the subjection and pacification of the Egyptian working class and imprisoned scores of communist trade unionists (Beinin & Lockman, 1987).

---

[2] This latter issue became important in the context of unacceptable U.S. conditions placed on arms sales to the new regime. This drove the regime to turn to the Soviet Union, which supplied cheap armaments in exchange for cotton.

As was common even among the capitalist economies of the West during the early post-war period, the new regime engaged in nationalized production in certain strategic industries, such as iron and steel production, railways and transportation, and utilities. In 1954, the regime established the Iron and Steel Company at Helwan. It also established Egyptian State Railways to assume control of railway development and created a National Production Council to provide capital for industrialization projects. The purpose here was not to substitute public investment for private investment, but rather to facilitate private capital accumulation through the production of state supported capital inputs – such as iron, steel and electricity – and the provision of subsidized shipping costs for the transportation of goods. The Free Officers also established the MoMP in 1954 with the aim of attaining self-sufficiency in arms production. Firms like Maadi and Helwan Engineering Industries – also created in 1954 to produce pistols, grenade launchers and machine guns, and metal components for heavy ammunition – were creatures of the MoMP. While the Ministry was eventually abolished by Nasser, it was revived by Sadat in 1971.

As Nasser's desire for economic independence and his commitment to non-alignment brought him into increasing conflict with the capitalist states of the West, the new regime found it increasingly difficult to attract foreign investment. The nationalization of the Suez Canal Company in 1956 – and the ensuing conflict with the United Kingdom and France – alienated Egypt from the Western camp of the emerging Cold War. While the United States condemned the ensuing British, French and Israeli attack on Egypt, it nonetheless denied the new regime a loan required to finance the proposed development of the Aswan high dam, a project that would expand agricultural and industrial production in the country and was therefore crucial for national economic development.

At the same time, Egyptian capital engaged in a prolonged capital strike to protest the regime's attacks on its class privileges (Abdel Malek, 1968). Between 1950 and 1956, private gross investment declined from £E112 million to just £E39 million, with most of the investment occurring in unregulated sectors such as urban real estate and construction (Farah, 2009, p. 33). In this context, concerns regarding national security in a region caught between Cold War superpowers were increasingly integrated into the project of economic nationalism. As such, the military began to play an increasingly important role in Nasser's developmentalist project. This was evidenced in the role it played in the construction of massive development projects, such as the creation of the Aswan dam in the early 1960s, with the help of the Soviet Union.

Over the course of the Nasser period, the size and power of the Egyptian military grew dramatically. Between 1952 and 1955, military spending increased from 4.9 percent of GNP to 5.7 percent. As Egypt became increasingly embroiled in regional conflicts – first with Yemen and then with Israel – military spending ballooned to 12.7 percent of GNP by 1967 (Abul-Magd, 2017, p. 67). The number of officers integrated into the state apparatus also increased. In 1961, just over one-half of all government ministers in 1961 had a military background, and by 1962, army officers occupied almost two thirds of the administrative positions within the state bureaucracy (Abul-Magd, 2017, p. 43; Picard, 1988, p. 125).

Despite its role in Nasser's statist development project, the military elite were never committed socialists. As Abul-Magd (2017) points out, the vast majority of high-ranking officers were non-ideological pragmatists who demonstrated a remarkable ability to adapt to changes in the broader context of Egyptian politics and remained loyal to their own institution. As Ali Sabri – the left-wing Prime Minister and head of the Arab Socialist Union during Nasser's socialist phase in the 1960s – mentioned at the time, the military has no ideology, it merely has "rightist self-interests" (Abul-Magd, 2017, p. 63). The political and economic power of the military expanded under the command of Abd al-Hakim 'Amir, field marshal, minister of war, commander in chief and deputy supreme commander. The extent of this growth enhanced the autonomy of the military from the Arab Socialist Union and gave rise to "duality of power" within the Egyptian state between Nasser and 'Amir (Abul-Magd, 2017, p. 62).

Military factories attained a degree of economic autonomy from the larger socialist economy in which they functioned. They implemented capitalist practices such as promoting workers based on productivity gains, they were exempt from full employment and job creation practices, and they were uninhibited from implementing innovations intended to increase manufacturing speed. In military factories, workers were not represented on the management boards, they were prohibited from unionizing and they were unable to affiliate to the Arab Socialist

Union. Military factories engaged in civilian production – such as refrigerators and heaters – also did not follow the planning directives of the state and they refused to coordinate with the Ministry of Industry and other state-owned enterprises.

The military's political role waned dramatically after its defeat in the 1967 war with Israel. The defeat was associated with the failings of 'Amir, who was eventually arrested for allegedly plotting a coup against Nasser and who died under mysterious circumstances in the autumn of that year. The defeat by Israel also ultimately shifted the balance of power among the political classes away from the military towards the old propertied class who threw its support behind Sadat after Nasser's death in 1971.

The Military under Sadat

Sadat oversaw the de-politicization of the military and the demilitarization of the cabinet (Cooper, 1982). According to Abul-Magd (2016, pp. 26–27), Sadat "marginalized the officers in politics" and "reduced their economic influence" in the economy. Seeking to reduce its political influence, Sadat frequently rotated the military's top officers and replaced retired officers with civilian administrators. The proportion of governors appointed from the military declined to 9 percent by 1980 (Abul-Magd, 2016, p. 27). By the end of the 1970s, only 7.5 percent of government ministers had military backgrounds (Cooper, 1982, p. 208; Picard, 1988; Springborg, 1987). Sadat also reduced its size and cut its budget. While military expenditures understandably increased in the first few years of Sadat's tenure – peaking in 1973 during the Arab-Israeli war – they dropped considerably by 1974. The numbers tend to vary, but all convey a similar downward trajectory. According to Abul-Magd (2017, p. 251), military expenditures declined from 31 percent of GNP in 1973 to 22.8 percent in 1976 and 1977.[3] According to the World Bank, military expenditures decreased from 16.7 percent of gross domestic product in 1974 to 5.8 percent in 1980 (World Bank, 2018p). As a percentage of central government expenditures, military spending dropped from either 40.4 percent in 1977 and 1978 to 19.7 percent in 1980 and 1981 (Abul-Magd, 2017, p. 251), or from 30.9 percent in 1977 to 18.1 percent in 1981 (World Bank, 2018p).

---

[3] Abul-Magd has no data for this metric after 1977.

At the same time, Sadat encouraged the military to engage in the *infitah* economy by expanding the capabilities of the arms industry to minimize the military's alienation from the regime. As Sadat cut the military's budget, the regime devised new strategies to ensure the military's economic self-sufficiency. As Sadat reoriented Egypt away from the Soviet Union and towards the US and the Gulf monarchies, he brought the military closer to Western and Gulf capital and U.S. arms suppliers. In 1975, for example, Sadat established the Arab Organization for Industrialization (AOI) with the financial backing of Saudi Arabia, Qatar and the United Emirates to attract Arab capital and Western technical assistance for the manufacture of weapons in Egypt.[4] The AOI forged partnerships with multinational corporations in Europe, Asia and North America for the production of aircraft, automobiles, subway coaches, computers, helicopter engines, armoured vehicles, munitions and fighter jets. The AOI is not subject to the Central Auditing Authority and its budget is not subject to Parliamentary scrutiny (Väyrynen, 1979). Over the course of the 1980s, 1990s and 2000s, it has grown to represent one of the main pillars of the Egyptian economy – amounting to approximately 11 percent of gross domestic product. By 2012, the AOI owned 12 factories with 16,000 workers (Halawa, 2012). Military-run businesses established in this period enjoyed exemptions from taxation and business restrictions and enjoyed privileged access to state resources, such as credit. Thus, while diminishing its political power, Sadat increased the economic power and autonomy of the army and forged long-standing relationships between it and the private sector.

In 1979, Sadat created the National Service Projects Organization (NSPO) "to use surplus military labour and equipment for civilian projects ... such as consumer goods, construction, agriculture, energy and water" (NSPO, 2018). The goal of the NSPO was to enable the military to achieve "self-sufficiency in some of the requirements necessary" for its operations, to absorb surplus military labour into the civilian economy (as Egypt made peace with Israel), and to carry out the state's developmental plans (NSPO, 2018). In the early years, the NSPO's activity was limited to chemicals and mining. By the late 1990s, it had dramatically expanded its activity into other spheres of the civilian economy and would become a key institution in expanding

---

[4] For more on the activities of the AOI, see AOI (2018).

the military's business interests (discussed in the section, The Military and Economic Liberalization).

An important part of this arrangement was to enable to military to adapt to peacetime conditions without experiencing any serious retrenchment of its institutional resources. The notion of self-sufficiency was really a euphemism for enabling the military to secure and expand its financial autonomy from the state. This would enable Sadat to continue demilitarizing the state while ensuring his regime remained insulated from any prospective coups. The unintended consequences of Sadat's actions would loom large over the future of Egyptian politics. By the 1980s, the military was beginning to evolve into a fraction of Egyptian capital.

The Military under Mubarak

Some scholars argue that the military's power has declined since the close of the Nasser era and the rise of the NDP under Sadat. Focusing on the military's formal presence in the Egyptian state, Kandil (2012, p. 146) argues that "Sadat's policies during the seventies pushed the military to the point of oblivion and downgraded its political influence."[5] Beginning in the 1980s, it is argued, the military saw itself eclipsed by the growth of internal security forces created to act as a counterbalance to insulate the regime from prospective coups. Such a position, however, conflates the military's power and influence with its formal role in the Egyptian political system. As Ayubi (1995, p. 263) argues, the military elite no longer had to occupy top positions in the state as the military's institutional interests were increasingly being realized in the economy in a fashion that made it increasingly autonomous from the regime.

Far from experiencing a decline, the military saw both its economic *and* political influence grow as Egypt liberalized under Mubarak in the 1980s, becoming what Springborg (1989, p. 107) describes as "an almost entirely autonomous enclave of middle-class modernity in an increasingly impoverished and marginalized Third World economy" (Cook, 2007; Picard, 1988; Springborg, 2014; Stacher, 2012). Indeed, Abul-Magd (2017, Chapter 3) identifies the 1980s as the period in which the military did the most to expand its civilian economic power,

---

[5] For a more substantive engagement with Kandil's argument, see Joya (2018).

creating a veritable business empire alongside both the public sector and the private sector.

Politically, Mubarak secured the interests of the military through a process of "incentive based military acquiescence," which prevented any attempted coups during his 30-year rule (Nassif, 2013). For example, Mubarak re-integrated the military into the Egyptian state at the level of the governorates, reversing the process of demilitarized administration introduced by Sadat. Former military officers and commanders filled positions in various governorates as both governors and deputy governors, and served in leadership positions at the local government levels such as heads of cities and boroughs, as well as in key administrative departments as senior bureaucrats, such as welfare, health and education (Abdelrahman, 2015, p. 24; Harb, 2003; Nassif, 2013, pp. 518–519). The gradual decentralization of power initiated under Mubarak meant that these political offices had gained greater political significance. These new offices – and the powers delegated to them – enabled former officers to align themselves with the interests in the growing real estate sectors to enrich themselves. The most notable example in the 1990s and 2000s, is the role that former officers turned governors played in collaborating with the Ministry of Housing to facilitate the transfer of public lands to the private sector and accumulate wealth for themselves in the process (Abdelrahman, 2015; Joya, 2013; Nassif, 2013, p. 518).

The military's economic role also expanded dramatically under the leadership of Field Marshal Abdel Halim Abu Ghazala who served as Defence Minister between 1981 and 1989. With his close ties to the U.S. military and corporate world, Abu Ghazala managed to secure resources for the military by expanding its role in the civilian economy and striving to achieve self-sufficiency in military production capabilities. From having privileged access to public lands under the pretext of national security, to playing a central role in the country's agriculture, to furthering the goals of food security, the military continued to develop various departments that allowed it to engage in different aspects of the country's economy, launching 300 civilian projects between 1980 and 1987 (CIA, 1987). The military's advantages included access to advanced technologies for their industries, a unique privilege among all Arab armies (Ayubi, 1995). U.S. loans and military aid enabled the military to become one of the most important customers for U.S. weapons, which in turn paved the way for the establishment of

American subsidiaries in Egypt. Additionally, the Egyptian military established links with other global weapons industries such as France's Aerospatiale, and offered assembly plants for multinational corporations such as the Benha Electronics factory (CIA, 1987).

Over the course of the 1980s, the military conducted its economic activities through four organizations: the NSPO and the AOI; the Ministry of Defence and the MoMP; and the Armed Forces Land Projects Agency (AFLPA). According to Abul-Magd (2017), the military justified its expansion into the civilian economy in terms of achieving economic self-sufficiency, but also in nationalist-populist terms of ensuring the welfare of the lower classes through the provision of goods and infrastructure below market prices. These organizations have expanded the reach of the military into all areas of the economy, including land development and agriculture, port construction and management, marine transportation, industrial production and research and development infrastructure. Within these organizations, the military has engaged in joint ventures with domestic, regional and international capital including the United States, France, the United Kingdom, Italy, Germany, Japan, Brazil, Spain, the United Arab Emirates, Kuwait, Saudi Arabia, China and Turkey.

As the earliest productive military organization incorporated into the Ministry of Defence, the MoMP undertakes national development goals in the areas of housing, healthcare, roads, seaports, educational facilities, and water provision.[6] At the beginning of the 1980s, the MoMP had 15 factories employing 70,000 workers producing $240 million worth of goods. Over the course of the 1980s, the MoMP expanded its activity into the production of medical and surgical instruments, sewing machines, agricultural machines, cooking pots, television sets, gas ovens, refrigerators, semi-automatic bakery lines, electric meters, infrastructure for transportation such as large merchant ships, and armaments, including warships, battle tanks, explosives, machine guns, ammunition, bombs and small arms. Through joint ventures with Gulf capital, this branch of the military also engages in housing production for low-income Egyptians.

Under Abu Ghazala, the AOI established seven factories employing 18,000 workers, producing $100 million worth of production in 1981.

---

[6] For a detailed list of Ministry of Defense, projects in each of these areas see Ministry of Defense (2018).

By 1982, arms exports were the second largest source of export revenue (Abul-Magd, 2017, p. 90). Over the course of the 1980s, the AOI produced French jets, Chinese fighters, Brazilian training jets, British helicopters, missiles, aircraft engines, guns and ammunition and more (Paul, 1983). Through the National Organization for Military Production (which is a branch of the MoMP) and the AOI, Egypt became capable of meeting 60 percent of its military needs and began exporting military products to regional markets. During the Iran-Iraq war, Egypt's arms sales reached $1 billion in 1983 alone (Springborg, 1989, pp. 108, 111). By the end of the 1980s, General Motors established subsidiaries through the Nasr Car Company while military-led infrastructure developments paved the way for U.S. cars on Egyptian roads. Developing these capabilities would not have been possible without the state subsidies on energy and manufacturing inputs, the exemptions from tax laws and the revenue secrecy that military industries enjoy.

Under Mubarak, Abu Ghazala transformed the NSPO into a vehicle for producing civilian goods and services in a gradually liberalizing economy.[7] During this time, Abu Ghazala expanded the NSPO by reforming its internal statutes through a ministerial decree. He granted it a legal personality to enable it to behave like a corporation and establish a wide array of companies in partnership with private capital, whether foreign or domestic. He also insulated its budget from that of the Ministry of Defence, thereby securing its financial autonomy from the regime. The NSPO is now divided into five different sectors or "fields": agriculture and food industry, industrial, engineering, services and mining. Within these different fields, the NSPO engaged in everything from agriculture and food production, port maintenance, urban planning, tourism, hotels and luxury housing, furniture manufacturing, ship manufacturing and repair, technology and electronics and textile production.[8]

Indeed, the most prominent example where the military began consolidating its power was in the agricultural sector. With the help of USAID, state subsidies, military research and skilled conscript labour, the Egyptian military – through the NSPO – launched a program to achieve "food security" through the Food Security Division in 1982

---

[7] For more on past projects and goals of the NSPO, see NSPO (2018).
[8] See the government of Egypt website (GOE, 2018) for more details.

(CIA, 1987; Mitchell, 1991b, p. 99; Sadowski, 1991). The Food Security Division engaged in a long-term project of land reclamation to develop intensive agriculture in field crops and fruit, turning it into the "single largest agro-industrial organization in Egypt," consisting of dairy plants, poultry farms, egg production, fish farms, slaughter-houses, and so on (Springborg, 1989, p. 112). The NSPO developed cattle ranching for milk production, producing approximately 9,000 tons of milk products per year. By 1983, the NSPO was producing a quarter of Egypt's daily bread consumption, and by 1988, it had 2,600 bakery plants (Abul-Magd, 2017, p. 95). In 1986, the military's activities in the agricultural sector expanded into fruits and vegetables as the 6 October Agro-Industrial Complex was launched with the ability to grow produce in plastic houses over thousands of feddans of land. This foray into food security corresponded with the military's claim of carrying out the developmentalist vision of the state, because its industrial food production was oriented to the domestic market to "feed the nation" and alleviate the growing problem of dependence on food imports. According to the NSPO, as of 2018, approximately 14,600 feddans of land "have been reclaimed and cultivated with field crops and fruit in El-Nubaria, El-Tal El-Kebir, wadi El-mullak, Shobra she-hab by the use of the modern techniques of irrigation" and green house farming (NSPO, 2018).

The AFLPA was set up in 1981 to administer the management and sale of military-owned lands.[9] Initially, the agency would receive compensation from the state for the sale of vacated state lands. Compensation was given to defray the costs of relocating military infrastructure. However, a 1982 presidential decree issued by Mubarak broadened the scope of the organization, enabling it to undertake all administrative, commercial, financial services and activities" required to attain its objectives(Abul-Magd, 2017, p. 102). However, the AFLPA's authority also extended to non-military lands. A 1981 law gave the Minister of Defence the authority over the classification of desert land. This authority was strengthened in 1986 by a ministerial decree issued by Defence Minister Ghazala, giving the military the right to approve industrial and agricultural projects on desert land. A 1990 Presidential decree further authorized the AFLPA to sell state land that

---

[9] The AFLPA was initially established by Sadat in 1981 under a different name.

was occupied by civilians on the basis of *Wadi al Yad* – that is, without legal title.[10]

By the late 1980s, the military was one of two dominant actors in the economy alongside the numerous public sector enterprises that comprised the Egyptian economy (Picard, 1988, p. 138). During this time, the military's "alliance with public and private sector enterprises and its proliferation of arms industries" created "a class of military, and military-dependent, *munfatihun*" (Springborg, 1989, pp. 109–110). As a result of these developments, a symbiotic relationship appeared to have emerged between the private sector and the military through procurement contracts to the private sector worth millions of dollars, while the military benefited from "access to advanced technologies found in the private sector" (Springborg, 1989, p. 117).

However, the military's increasing insertion into the (slowly) liberalizing Egyptian economy was conducted in the frame of nationalism and developmentalism. While Abul-Magd (2017) dismisses the military's state developmentalist mission as self-serving rhetoric, her own account demonstrates that the military engaged in the production and distribution of "de-commodified" goods and services for segments of the lower classes in ways that acted as forms of social protection. Under Abu Ghazala, the military "expanded services for the around seventy thousand workers and employees in Abu Za'bal, Shubra, Helwan, and Maadi, including housing, health care, transportation, and day care for children of female employees" (Abul-Magd, 2017, p. 101). This type of economic activity represents a kind of conservative paternalism reminiscent of the corporatist or Bismarkian welfare states of Continental Europe (Esping-Andersen, 1990). Such paternalism intends to provide a degree of social protection that ensures social order and solidifies the authority of the military as a national institution, often against the regime itself.

In this way, the military sought to resolve or contain the unfolding contradictions of class polarization within an increasingly liberalizing economy in the interest of national unity. On the one hand, through its provision of cheap foodstuffs and de-commodified goods and services

---

[10] It engages in joint ventures with the private sector by using military land as capital. Its areas of activity included numerous significant land development projects, including the New Valley Project, the recent Suez Canal expansion and the construction of the new administrative capital outside of Cairo.

for the lower classes, the military sought to ameliorate the negative consequences of economic polarization and pre-empt the growth of any social discontent. On the other hand, it sought to meet the consumerist desires of the growing upper middle classes by producing cars, building shopping malls and constructing luxury resorts. As the Egyptian economy entered a phase of neoliberal structural adjustment in the 1990s, the military's ability to manage such contradictions would be put to the test.

The Military and Economic Liberalization

Liberalization radically reoriented the strategies of capital accumulation in Egypt. The public sector was no longer the engine of growth and the domestic market was no longer the primary target of government policy pertaining to production and consumption. Export-oriented agricultural and industrial production by private sector firms, under the rubric of global finance, became the dominant accumulation strategy of Egyptian capital in the context of Economic Reform and Structural Adjustment Programme. In terms of the domestic market, the government promoted tourism and real estate development as two of the most important sectors for growth. This marked a significant shift away from what Beinin (2016b, p. 17) refers to as "peripheral Keynesianism" of the pre-liberal era. The interests of the neoliberal fraction now hegemonic in the NDP were being elevated as the dominant strategy of capital accumulation in the country (De Smet, 2016; Roccu, 2013).

These developments raised the prospects for conflict between military and civilian economic interests. By the early 1990s, the military industrial complex was effectively operating "outside the control of the government's general accounting organization" and was "run by men powerful enough to negotiate joint ventures with foreign companies and to make their own arrangements for the sale of their products to other Arab regimes" (Owen, 2002, pp. 204–205). At the same time, the privileged status of the military was increasingly being called into question. Not only had peace been secured with Israel two decades earlier, the Cold War was ending, meaning the military had to find new ways to justify its huge state budgets. By 1991, the military's budget accounted for between 10 percent and 14 percent of government expenditures – not including the hidden expenditures traditionally associated with the Egyptian military (Abul-Magd, 2017, p. 251; World Bank, 2018o).[11]

On top of this, pressure from the World Bank, the IMF and the United States placed severe constraints on the military's ability to retain the accumulation strategies it employed in the 1980s. Growing the private sector was the primary intention of the Washington Consensus that was defining the mandate of the international financial institutions during the late 1980s. In 1989, the World Bank (1990) expressed its hope that the resources of developing countries would be "increasingly allocated to more productive purposes" due to the "changing political climate of the 1990s." It argued that military budgets comprised – on average – 20 percent of the budgets of developing countries, and that in a context of increasing austerity, these expenditures had been ring-fenced, becoming "a prime source of external debt." As an international financial institution, the Bank noted that it was "important to place military spending decisions on the same footing as other fiscal decisions" and encouraged states to "explore ways to bring military spending into better balance with development priorities" (World Bank, 1990, p. 16). In April 1991, the Development Committee of the IMF met in Washington to discuss – among other matters – the reduction of excessive military expenditures among debtor nations (IMF, 1991b, p. 128). By October, the IMF issued a statement suggesting that while judgements regarding the appropriate level of military expenditures required to assure [national] security, were a sovereign prerogative of national governments," such expenditures "can have an important bearing on a member's fiscal policy and external position," and that "information about such expenditures may be necessary to permit a full and internally consistent assessment of the member's economic position and policies" (IMF, 1991a, p. 85). The United States also sought to push the military out of the economy. In a 2008 diplomatic cable published by Wikileaks, then U.S. Ambassador to Egypt Margaret Scobey summarized decades of American policy when she indicated in her assessment of the military that "[w]e [the United States] see the military's role in the economy as a force that generally stifles free market reform by increasing direct government involvement in the markets" (Scobey, 2008).

---

[11] This already represented a decrease from 22 percent in 1985.

The military now found itself on the defensive in terms of being able to take for granted its privileged status in the Egyptian state, most notably the presence of senior military figures in successive cabinets. As such, prominent military figures found themselves being pushed out of government: fewer and fewer officers were appointed to cabinet as more and more businessmen entered the People's Assembly. While Mubarak's cabinets included former members of the military throughout the 1990s, neoliberal businessmen affiliated with Gamal Mubarak came to dominate the cabinet of Prime Minister Ahmed Nazif after 2004, and this arrangement continued until the uprisings of 2011.

Such a scenario raised fears, within the regime, of provoking a coup. To pre-empt such a threat, Mubarak attempted to "coup proof" the regime by appointing more retired generals to the governorates and appointed officers to senior bureaucratic positions. As mentioned, Sadat began a process of demilitarizing the Egyptian state by reducing the number of retired generals appointed to the governorates. While the nine border governorates have traditionally been held by generals due to their strategic significance, non-border governorates were increasingly granted to civilian governors close to the regime beginning in the 1970s. While Mubarak carried on this practice of appointing more civilians to govern the provinces, he began to reverse this trend in the 1990s. In 1987, he reduced the number of military governors to eight; 10 years later, eleven governors came from the military. By 2011, one-half of the governorates were ruled by former generals, leading Abul-Magd (2017) to refer to the Egypt of the 2000s as the "republic of retired generals."

On the one hand, this change in civil-military relations did result in a decline in the military's political status, as Kandil (2012) has argued. By the mid-2000s, Egyptian military analysts and insiders spoke of disgruntled middling officers on salaries falling below those enjoyed by private sector managers. These same officers expressed disdain for Defence Minister Tantawi, claiming that he was more loyal to Mubarak – and hence, to the regime – than to the military and was intent on running the institution into the ground (Scobey, 2008).

In contrast, these changes positioned the generals to take advantage of the liberalization of land tenures during this period. A 1995 Prime Ministerial Decree (2903/1995) authorized governorates to dispose of public land for real estate development, shifting power away from the New Urban Communities Authority to the governors who could now deal directly with private investors (World Bank, 2006, p. 66). Coupled with the decentralization of administrative power, the "Governor generals" were able to engage in lucrative land deals with private investors, implicating them in the types of land grabs discussed in Chapter 6.

At the same time, and to the chagrin of the international financial institutions, military spending as a percentage of government expenditures remained relatively constant over the course of the 1990s. After a slight dip in 1992, military expenditures hovered between 10 percent and 13 percent of government expenditures between 1993 and 2005 as the military turned its attention to domestic, Islamist terrorism, particularly in Upper Egypt (World Bank, 2018o). It was not until the formation of the government of businessmen under Nazif in 2004 that any progress was made in cutting military expenditures to any significant degree, with the largest cuts occurring in 2005–2006 (Figure 1).

Nonetheless, prominent military officers also attempted to slow down the process of economic liberalization – particularly privatizations – if only to protect their own industries and business interests. The generals initially opposed the process of privatization, believing that it would primarily benefit the fraction of civilian neoliberals coalescing around Gamal Mubarak, which it was intended to do. By the 1990s, private

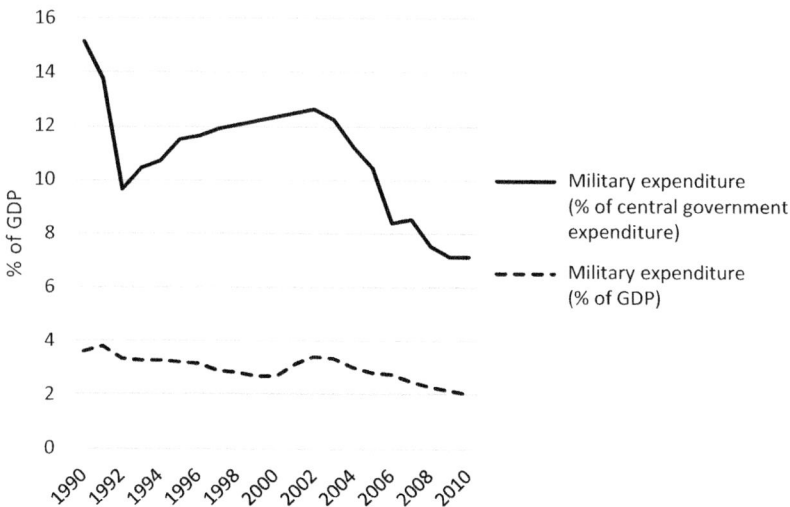

Figure 1 *Military expenditures, 1990–2010.*
Source: World Bank (2018p)

sector firms accounted for over 70 percent of the non-hydrocarbon economy in sectors such as trade, manufacturing, hospitality, transportation, communication as well as tourism and construction.

The military eventually developed a strategy to work with the private sector to secure its own interests during this time of change. As civilian capitalists close to the regime acquired numerous state-owned industries during the privatization process – such as telecom, oil and natural gas – the military began exploring ways to take advantage of its vast land holdings. This required institutionalizing their interests in ways that would enable them to be de facto partners in any sale of state lands for development purposes by effectively controlling the various state authorities established to administer the sale and development of public land.

At the beginning of the liberalization process, the regime established new administrative authorities mandated to administer the distribution of state lands and the types of development projects associated with those lands. The Tourism Development Authority, the New Urban Communities Authority and the General Authority for Reconstruction Projects and Agricultural Development were created in 1991. On the one hand, these new administrative institutions were intended to bolster the institutional authority of the Egyptian government to implement structural reforms. However, the law that created these new bodies also required that they "coordinate" with the Ministry of Defence before selling any state land to private interests. This requirement effectively situated the military in a privileged position over the eventual privatization of state lands.

The military's privileged access to state land proved immensely profitable and became the basis of investment in other economic activities, often in the private sector. Through its control over broadly designated military land, it was able to insert itself into emerging tourism, housing and agricultural markets, as well taking advantage of growing demand for natural resources. As land became increasingly valuable after the liberalization of tenures in 1996, the military began accumulating land across the country, often displacing residents under the pretext of national security goals. The military owned some prime real estate along the coasts, which were used to develop numerous luxury resorts and villas. Resorts and villas were built in Sidi Krayr near Alexandria and Ayn Sokhna near Suez, and five-star hotels were constructed on military land in Alexandria, Aswan, Fayyum and Marsa Matruh.

Through the AFLPA, the military also used its control over land to involve itself in the construction of housing and shopping malls for the upper and middle classes in newer communities in the Greater Cairo area, such as Nasr City, Helwan and 6th of October City. Apartment complexes and new urban communities have been developed to suit the tastes of privileged Egyptians and often include exclusive social clubs and high-end shopping malls. This type of luxury accommodation cost around E£400,000 for 86 square metres in places like Nasr City just after the uprisings.

One of the biggest land reclamation projects that involved the military in forging business partnerships with private investors was the New Valley Project (often referred to as the Toshka project) inaugurated in January 1997 in Upper Egypt. Once fully operational, Toshka was expected to resolve the problems of food scarcity and urban overcrowding by creating an alternate delta parallel to the Upper Nile Valley with the capacity to settle six million people and providing between 800,000 and 2.2 million feddans of land for cultivation. The land upon which Toshka was to be developed was state land "owned" by the military as "strategic" land. The infrastructure for the project was provided by the government and investment came from the Saudi Prince Talal, who purchased 100,000 feddans at E£99 per feddan (Economist Intelligence Unit, 1997, p. 50).[12]

Many of these cases of land acquisition resulted in conflicts with tenants working the land on customary tenures (such as *Wadi al Yad*) because, as state-owned land, their plots were the product of the Agrarian reforms under Nasser. While the military had ultimate say in the sale of these state lands, it was the Egyptian state – through its various institutions and with the aid of internal security forces – that did the dirty work of dispossessing tenants.

The 2000s

Egypt entered the new millennium with the onset of an economic downturn. While not a full-blown recession, growth halved between 2000 and 2002, raising cause for concern. The regime's response was the appointment of its most neoliberal-oriented government of businessmen under Ahmed Nazif. After a decade of halting reforms, the

---

[12] Toskha was due for completion in 2017 but ended in dismal failure.

mandate of the new government was to accelerate privatization and liberalization. As discussed in Chapter 3, this new government was composed of American educated businessmen close to Gamal Mubarak. Both the composition of the new government, the material interests of its most prominent members and their ideological orientation increased the potential for conflict with the military. Albrecht and Bishara (2011, p. 18) argue that the military remained suspicious of Gamal Mubarak's neoliberal economic agenda, due to its long-standing commitment to Nasserist étatism. The Minister of Defence and Commander in Chief Tantawi was known in U.S. diplomatic circles to have believed that "Egypt's economic reform plan fosters social instability by lessening GOE [Government of Egypt] controls over prices and production" (Ricciardone, 2008). As a result, they disagreed with the Nazif government's liberalization and privatization project. Nonetheless, they *did* take advantage of the liberalization process – rather than obstruct it entirely – to enhance their own economic power, positioning themselves as a competitor to the growing neoliberal fraction within the NDP. Numerous generals joined the NDP's privatization committee, enabling them to take better advantage of the liberalization process. Not only could they strategically protect their own industries from privatization, but they could now also scoop up state-owned enterprises slated for privatization, expanding their influence in the civilian economy. For example, through the AOI, the military acquired the public-sector railway manufacturing company in 2004, enabling the military to produce billions of pounds worth of train and metro carriages for the government. In 2003, the military also created a new corporate entity called the Maritime Industries and Services Organization, which acquired three major state-owned enterprises over the next 5 years: the Egyptian Company for Ship Repairs and Building, Alexandria Shipyard and the Nile Company for River Transport. Most controversially, the military opened a steel factory in 2005 with the blessing of Hosni Mubarak. This move set the military up as a competitor to Ahmed Ezz, close confidant of Gamal Mubarak and wealthy steel monopolist. Despite already owning an automobile manufacturing company, the military also blocked the privatization of the El Nasr Automotive Manufacturing Company in 2010 with the intent on acquiring it for itself.

The military experienced a learning curve during this process, not only establishing new networks with private capital, but also establishing new holding companies. In 2000, the military created the Holding Company for Maritime and Land Transport, which engages in port management, storage, maritime transport services, warehousing, cargo and container handling, freight services, transportation, tourist activities and international and domestic trade.[13]

The military also tightened its grip over its control of state lands from 2000 onward. In 2001, the National Centre for Planning State Lands Uses was created "to act as a supreme organization for the centralization of state land allocations to different ministries and bodies" (Abul-Magd, 2017, p. 138). However, the National Centre for Planning State Lands Uses was directed, by presidential decree, to coordinate with the Ministry of Defence, placing the military in a privileged position above the new authority. In 2002, a new decree enabled the military to "monitor business projects to make sure they abide by the terms and regulations of the military in using their land" (Abul-Magd, 2017, p. 138). Violation of such regulations gave the military the authority to revoke the permission granted for such projects or to demolish the projects without warning.

Over the course of the 2000s then, the military quietly enhanced its economic power by moving back into the civilian sectors of the economy first by expanding its control over land and secondly by participating in the privatization process. While working in concert with private investors, the military remained sceptical of economic liberalization in general, and the clique of rising millionaires tied to Gamal Mubarak in particular. Thus, while its official funding from the state continued to decline, its economic profile quietly expanded, setting it on a collision course with the neoliberals within the regime.

By the middle of the 2000s, the contradictions of the neoliberal growth model became increasingly clear. On the one hand, the new Nazif government hit growth rates of 7 percent by 2006, earning them praise from the World Bank and the IMF after years of disappointing growth at the beginning of the decade (Enders, 2008). Neoliberal reforms, it was argued, were finally paying off under the sound stewardship of the government of businessmen. On the other hand, these growth rates masked the growth of serious socioeconomic disparities and obscured the underlying fragility of the Egyptian economy.

---

[13] For a list of companies that fall under the Holding Company for Maritime and Land Transport, see HCMLT (2018).

Politically, the regime was also under attack from an increasingly popular Muslim Brotherhood, which, as will be discussed in Chapter 5, made extraordinary gains in the 2005 parliamentary elections. This political and economic fragility would be exposed during the global food crisis of 2007–2008 and the growing strike wave that coincided with the intensification of neoliberal restructuring.

The economic crisis of 2008 allowed the military to exercise its authority against an increasingly beleaguered neoliberal government. Between 2007 and 2008, food costs increased dramatically, as numerous countries in the Global South experienced a food crisis. Egypt, as one of the largest countries dependent on food imports, was hit hard. Rising fuel costs, seed and fertilizer costs, demand for staple crops for biofuel production, and speculation on commodities markets all contributed to rising food prices. Over the course of 2007, prices of basic foodstuffs increased 11.5 percent, and between January and March 2008, the cost of bread, grains and other basic foodstuffs shot up 40 percent (Putz, 2008). This occurred in the context of years of reductions to subsidies on basic foodstuffs in accordance with the conditionalities of the various loans Egypt received from international donors like the IMF and the World Bank.

Predictably, discontent with the Nazif government grew. Working-class Egyptians found themselves waiting in long, chaotic – and often violent – bread lines. The regime reintroduced subsidies on sugar, rice and oil. Within the first few months of 2008, eleven people had already died in lines waiting for subsidized bread (Johnston, 2008). Workers in industrial towns like Mahalla organized strikes to pressure the government to increase their wages to meet the rising cost of living. Despite winning plaudits from international financial institutions and the international business press for the impressive growth displayed in the mid-2000s, the government was now on the precipice of what the old guard within the NDP had always feared would result from liberalization: growing social unrest linked to the rising costs of food.

Distrustful of the regime, Egyptians increasingly demanded action by the military (Al Jazeera, 2008; McGreal, 2008). Even the Muslim Brothers seemed unwilling or unable to capitalize on the food crisis. Essam El Erian, a leading Muslim Brother, told the Guardian newspaper that, at that moment, "[t]he only power is the army." He quickly qualified this by stating that although the Muslim Brothers were "against a coup d'état … it is difficult to see who else can change things" (McGreal, 2008). As the crisis escalated, Mubarak called upon the army to increase bread production and distribute it to the poor. He also decreed a 30 percent increase in public sector wages (which was quickly offset by a 35 percent increase in fuel costs). While the army was baking bread for the poor, the regime's internal security services were clamping down on protesters and striking workers.

The public turn to the military in the context of the food crisis reflected the traditionally high levels of popular support enjoyed by the military. A year before the crisis, 70 percent of Egyptians described the influence of the military as "positive," with 30 percent describing the military's influence as "very good" (Kohut, Wike, & Horowitz, 2011, p. 12). This high level of popular support would only grow as the crisis facing the regime intensified over the next few years. While many scholars attribute the generally high approval ratings of the military to its historical legacy of "defeating" Israel in the 1973 war, it may also be due to the military's growing distance from the regime (in terms of its declining role in government and its disassociation – either real or perceived – from regime corruption and repression) and the regime's increasingly neoliberal orientation, as well as its role in providing for the national market and bolstering social protection, regardless of how minimal that social protection was. In effect, the military's intervention into the food crisis consolidated its reputation "as Egypt's least corrupt and most efficient state institution" (Cambanis, 2010).

It is in this context that tensions began to emerge between the military and the increasingly neoliberal NDP regarding the succession of Mubarak on the advent of his retirement. Speculation at the time was that Mubarak was grooming his son, Gamal, to replace him as president. The military's opposition to Gamal had long been an open secret. Most analysts of the military highlighted this tension, and it was well known in diplomatic circles (Scobey, 2008). Surprisingly, military officials themselves would sometimes openly express their reservations of Gamal Mubarak in media interviews. This growing tension was rooted in the competing interests between the military and the NDP as opposing fractions of capital. As mentioned in Chapter 3, Gamal Mubarak was associated with a "younger generation of ruling party cadres who have made fortunes in the business world," while the military is associated with the "old guard" of the NDP, "a substantially less wealthy elite who made their careers as ministers, officers and apparatchiks" (Cambanis, 2010). The privatizing zeal of the neoliberals, and their seeming lack of "national" outlook, was manifest in their continued pursuit of economic growth at the expense of socioeconomic polarization. Major General Mammdouh Badawy, the chairman of a military firm operating under the auspices of the MoMP, "recalled with distaste the days of economic liberalization" during the 1990s and 2000s when "businessmen were eating up the country" (Reuters, 2018). Ultimately, the generals seemed convinced that the neoliberals would eventually target the military's business empire for privatization, thereby completing the marginalization of the military in Egyptian public life.

On the eve of the 2011 uprisings, the military, despite enduring years of budget cuts (Figure 1), remained a significant economic force.[14] Seventy percent of the AOI's production was oriented to the civilian market, while 40 percent of MoMP production was similarly oriented. Estimates of the military's total contribution to the economy vary. Conservative estimates, taking account only of the businesses formally controlled by the military, suggest 5 percent of gross domestic product. Estimates including their control (both formal and informal) over state land and other economic sectors range as high as 40 percent (Blumberg, 2011). The regime, on the other hand, appeared to be suffering some setbacks. The elections of 2005 witnessed the political rise of the Muslim Brothers (to be discussed in Chapter 5) and the regime was forced to slow down the pace of neoliberal reforms after the crisis of 2008. At its 2009 party convention, the NDP committed itself to health care reform, poverty alleviation and the expansion of social policy as a way of responding to the rising social discontent long foreseen by the old guard.

While the military's formal position within the Egyptian state has declined as a result of the economic liberalization pursued by the regime under Sadat and Mubarak, its economic power has expanded significantly. Despite concerns by proponents of liberalization that the increasing role of the military in the economy would stifle the development of a dynamic, indigenous private sector, the military sees itself as facilitating private sector growth – "filling gaps in the market" – rather

---

[14] Determining the military's budget is very difficult due to its lack of transparency. Official figures suggest that the military budget declined from an average of 10 percent of GDP in the 1990s to 4.9 percent on the eve of the uprisings.

than substituting itself for the private sector (Reuters, 2018). At the same time, its participation in the capitalist economy in no way means that the military is unambiguously "neoliberal" as argued by some scholars (Abul-Magd, 2017, p. 113). While neoliberals view the market as the pre-eminent mechanism by which to produce and distribute goods in an economy – often entailing the commodification of "de-commodified" goods and services such as water, healthcare, education and so on – the military has time and again displayed its willingness to intervene *against* the market by reintroducing subsidies, distributing bread, and generally overriding market forces by means of its political power. This latter role is reminiscent of the developmentalist vision the military adhered to in the post-war period. To dismiss the military's developmentalism as self-serving rhetoric not only downplays its interventionist role in the economy but obscures the nature of the conflict between it and the true neoliberals associated with Gamal Mubarak and the Nazif government. The uprisings of 2011 provided the military with an opportunity of assuming control of the state and subordinating the neoliberals to its hegemony. At the same time, the military is not attempting to break completely from neoliberalism. Rather, it is attempting to adhere to its traditional developmentalist role in a context of global neoliberalism without an understanding of how the latter undermines the former.

Conclusion

In the immediate post-colonial period, the Egyptian military became increasingly involved in the economic development of the post-revolutionary economy. Far from representing a form of socialism, the military's role evolved as a pragmatic response to the contingencies of post-colonial development, particularly the lack of capital. Thus, the military gradually developed the organizational capacity to accumulate assets and control strategic sectors of the economy. As Egypt began to liberalize under Sadat, this economic role increased as a form of compensation to the military's formal depoliticization. As Egypt embarked on more dramatic economic restructuring in the 1990s, the military managed to adapt: it expanded its productive assets and benefited from its control over state lands in a context of rising land prices. At the opening of the twenty-first century, the military was emerging as a dominant fraction of capital with interests in all sectors of the Egyptian economy. This economic power was supplemented by a nationalist vision that distinguished it from the neoliberals dominant in the NDP under Gamal Mubarak. While often sitting uneasily alongside its increasingly regional and global economic interests, this nationalist identity would lead the military to promote particular reforms that did not easily fit the mould of neoliberalism. By the time of the Arab uprisings, the military would remain as the one organization with the greatest degree of national legitimacy, enabling it to either expropriate or co-opt the neoliberals, and usurp power from the Muslim Brotherhood. By doing so, it was able to emerge as the dominant fraction of Egyptian capital – the only one that was capable of promoting a vision of national reconstruction.

5 | The Mosque and the Market
The Muslim Brotherhood

The Muslim Brotherhood: Islam, the Market and the Moral Economy

Conceptualizing the Muslim Brotherhood as a fraction of Egyptian capital as opposed to 'an expression of a religious essence abstracted from time, place and social context" (Beinin, 2005, p. 112) results in "de-sacralizing" Islamist politics (Zubaida, 2011, p. 1).[1] It also requires situating the Brothers' ideas and objectives in historical context (Naguib, 2009). As Ismail (2006, pp. 30–31) points out, "Conservative Islamism is ... shaped by the socio-economic context of contemporary Egypt" and "operates in a context of socio-political transformation." In this sense, Islamism is "articulated in relation to power positions, and in turn shapes power relations in society" (Ismail, 2006, p. 30).

It would be a stretch, however, to argue that the leadership of the Muslim Brothers constitute a coherent class fraction in the same way as do the neoliberals and the military. Rather, it is more accurate to conceptualize them as an *aspiring* class fraction who have been building up their capital and their capacities in the context of economic liberalization. At the same time, however, we cannot understand their attempt to constitute themselves as a fraction of capital in the typical ways conceptualized by conventional approaches to class fractions. For example, their capital is not defined largely in sectoral terms (e.g., agricultural, large manufacturing or small manufacturing, commercial, financial); nor does their capital conform to the domestic/transnational and money capital/productive capital divide discussed in Chapter 1. Some Brothers are engaged in the production and distribution of foodstuffs for the domestic market, whereas others are engaged in real estate or finance with regional economic linkages

---

[1] For prominent ideational approaches, Esposito (1983) and Kepel and Richard (1990).

(particularly with the Gulf States). Rather, their fractionalism is rooted in attempts to institutionalize an Islamic economy as an alleged third way between Western capitalism and socialism or communism.

The idea of an Islamic economy signifies an attempt to subordinate capitalism to a traditional body of Islamic ethics (and *shari'a*). Pfeifer (1997) identifies three core principles at the heart of Islamic economics.[2] First is the rejection of the "possessive individualism" that forms the basis of Western capitalism (Macpherson, 1964). *Homo Islamicus* is rooted within a set of communal relationships that forms the moral parameters of his individual utility. In other words, individual utility must correspond with spiritual development. In this sense, the entrepreneur must "pay just wages and charge just prices." The second principle is the prohibition on the payment or taking of interest on loans and proscriptions against speculative economic activity and conspicuous consumption. Interest represents a form of unearned income, speculation diverts capital away from productive investment and conspicuous consumption promotes waste. The implication of this is that "depositors in Islamic banks ... become partners in the banks" investment decisions, sharing in the profits and losses from those decisions in proportion to their deposits" (Pfeifer, 1997, p. 158). Finally, there is *zakat*, a voluntary tax to finance private, religiously administered charitable programs (in opposition to the welfare state), and Islamic inheritance laws that prevent the concentration of property. Between 1949 and 1951, Sayid Qutb – the Muslim Brother most associated with the ideology of the organization – wrote several books (*Social Justice in Islam*, *The Battle of Islam and Capitalism* and *Islam and World Peace*) sketching out an Islamist approach to social justice that required theorizing about the place of the market in Muslim society. Through this work, Qutb "explained how Islam qualified individual gain through charity, the prohibition of usury, and inheritance laws" and argued that Islam demanded that Muslims "govern their economic relationships in an ethical manner, looking to the interests of the

---

[2] Unlike Pfeifer, Asutay distinguishes between Islamic Economics and Islamic Moral Economy. According to Asutay (2013, p. 57), Islamic economics emerged as the "Islamic equivalent of conventional or neo-classical economics in defining but also describing the nature of" Islamic moral economy. In contrast, Islamic moral economy is a "religiously defined response to the economic development failure in the Muslim world, whether capitalist, socialist or nationalist, with an authentic meaning derived from the ontology of Islam" (Asutay, 2013, p. 56).

common person and the community against predatory capitalism" (Calvert, 2009, p. 134).

Islamic moral economy, however, is highly amorphous. Proponents often characterize it as a third way between capitalism and socialism, allowing them to "approve certain aspects of capitalism, including private ownership of the means of production, profit maximization as a motor force in economic behaviour, and free market competition in products, services and labor" (Pfeifer, 1997, p. 157). Indeed, Qutb was less ambiguous in his opposition to socialism than to capitalism, due to the former's mix of materialism and atheism. Calvert (2009, p. 136) argues that in *Social Justice in Islam*, Qutb "attempted to undercut the claims of Western socialism" – not capitalism – by promising to "impose distributive justice upon free enterprise." In fact, more than socialism or capitalism, *communism* received the most severe criticism. As Roy (1994, p. 133) argues, capitalism, "never having been an economic ideology, it is Marxism that is the mirror and foil of the Islamist effort."[3] In *Milestones*, published in 1964, Qutb characterized communism as an ideology that promotes proletarian "hatred and envy of other classes" and creates a "selfish and vengeful society" rooted in "exciting animalistic characteristics"(Qutb, 2006, p. 61). From this point of view, he argues, "the whole of human history is nothing but a struggle for food!" (Qutb, 2006, p. 61). In his analysis of the Brothers' social and economic activism in the 1940s, Kourgiotis (2018, p. 468) argues that the Muslim Brothers "never sought to radically change or substitute the Egyptian capitalism of their time for an economic system *sui generis*." Rather, they sought a *"purification of capitalism from its injustices."* This ambiguity suggests that the meaning of Islamic moral economy is contextual and fluctuates along with changes in the historical context in which it is expressed.

However, the Muslim Brothers also resemble a type of social movement embedded within a growing civil society composed of charitable

---

[3] Western socialism was not yet a significant force in contemporary world politics when the book was published in 1949. Outside of the UK, where the Labour Party had formed government, and Scandinavia where the Social Democrats were in power, conservative parties governed in most Western countries. In *Milestones*, he depicts a socialist economic convergence between the West and the East Bloc (Qutb, 2006, p. 23). Despite this Tripp situates Qutb as a kind of anti-capitalist resister who "hoped that capitalism and the ideas associated with it would be stopped in their tracks" (2006, p. 151).

organizations and nongovernmental organizations. Wickham (2002, p. 6) characterizes the Muslim Brotherhood is a social movement that "marshaled resources and created opportunities for opposition activism outside the formal political channels controlled by the authoritarian state." Using Tarrow's (2011, p. 9) definition of a social movement as "collective challenges, based on common purposes and social solidarities, in sustained interaction with elites, opponents and authorities," Wickham (2002, p. 5) examines the ways the Muslim Brothers use religion to generate "opportunities, resources, and motivations for collective challenges to powerful institutions and elites."

On top of this, the Muslim Brotherhood is an organization composed of a multi-class membership base that has been illegal for much of Egypt's post-war history. The Brothers are committed to a multi-class membership on the presumption that Islam can bind the various social classes together based on morality and proper religious conduct, regardless of their divergent material interests. The socio-economic composition of the core membership of the Muslim Brothers has either undergone a significant transformation in conjunction with the post-war developments in Egyptian capitalism or are not obviously "economic" in any clear sense. For example, the class interests of the large landowners who have consistently occupied the upper echelons of the organization's leadership and comprised the core of the organization's primary donors, have changed as Egypt has become increasingly integrated into the global economy and has experienced a significant degree of industrialization. Second, the heterogeneous urban middle classes that have traditionally comprised the bulk of the organization's active membership are not solely or even obviously economic. Merchants, retailers and small businessmen sit alongside civil servants, doctors and lawyers. With the shift from import substitution industrialization to a more liberal, export-oriented form of capitalist development, the influence of the business classes on the organization increased. By the 1980s and 1990s, the Muslim Brotherhood "appealed to rentier capitalists, the labour aristocracy, petty merchants and professionals" (Tuğal, 2012, p. 36).

The attempts to institutionalize an Islamic economy by using Islamic capital and social welfare services to bind together a pious, cross-class coalition of Muslim Brothers justifies the characterization of the organization as an aspiring class fraction. According to Ayubi (1991a, p. 198), the provision of financial and social services by members of the mainstream Islamist movement (such as the Muslim Brothers) was "capitalism with an Islamic face." Yet, it was a capitalism practiced against the state and one meant to bind Muslims – particularly Muslim entrepreneurs – together. The extent to which these Islamic economic and social institutions formed the basis of an Islamist fraction of Egyptian capital is therefore crucial. Ayubi (1991a, p. 192) suggests that, "the setting up of Islamic economic and financial institutions represents a conscious strategy by the Islamic movements for subsidising and financing their political, social and organization activities, or at least for linking the supporters, the sympathisers and the religiously-inclined to the Islamic movement not only by spiritual ties but also by interest-based institutionalised bonds." In a similar vein, Zubaida (1990, p. 160) argues that the Muslim Brothers are part of a "more general trend in Egyptian society to establish an *Islamic sector*, to parallel and rival the official sector." This Islamic sector is both economic and social, due to the importance of the charitable Islamic organizations of which the Brotherhood is a part. The funding of these services comes, "at least in part, from donations and profits of the Islamic economy." In this sense, the Brothers' ability to mobilize resources, opportunities and motivations becomes particularly important for understanding the way they have attempted to pursue the Islamic economy as the materialization of the *umma* (the global Islamic community) (Vannetzel & Yankaya, 2017).

Islamism against the State: The Brotherhood

The Muslim Brotherhood was founded in 1928 by Hassan al-Banna, the son of a local sheikh, who became active in Muslim organizations from an early age. At the time of its founding, the Brotherhood "was just one of several religious societies seeking to reinforce popular adherence to Islam and combat the threat posed by the spread of Western cultural values and lifestyles in a context of rapid social and political change" (Wickham, 2015). By the late 1940s, the group "expanded into a broad national organization with a large membership base and a network of social and welfare institutions that eclipsed those of any other civic association, religious or otherwise" (Wickham, 2015, p. 22). Estimates of the organization's growth vary wildly: Mitchell (1969, p. 328) estimates that by 1949, the organization had 2,000 local branches and as many as 600,000 members drawn from many sectors of Egyptian society, while Sullivan and Abed-Kotob (1999, p. 42) cite the significantly higher figure of 1–2 million members. Despite the diverse social composition of its members, there was, however, a distinctive urban middle-class dominance within the organization. According to Mitchell (1969, p. 329), the rural and lower class elements within the organization were "only important in a statistical sense," for they played virtually no role in shaping the organization's "political destiny." The working-class component of the Brotherhood also needs to be qualified. While Sullivan and Abed-Kotob (1999, p. 42) refer to the "discontented city proletariat" among the swelling membership of the organization in the 1940s, Ayubi (1991a, p. 159) notes that the "so-called 'workers' who appear on some official lists of Islamic militants are often technical artisans (e.g. mechanics, electricians, metal forgers, etc.) who do not work in large, modern factories." Munson (1988, p. 103) also notes that peasants, as well as the "urban poor and blue-collar workers" have largely been absent from Islamist movements in Egypt and the broader Arab world. The core of the organization remained professionals, university students, civil servants, and from the 1960s onward, small and medium-sized businessmen. At the same time, the Muslim Brothers were beholden to a small number of wealthy rural notables for their financing. According to Kourgiotis (2018, p. 473), the organization was dependent on the donations of just 120 wealthy patrons in the 1940s, most of whom derived their wealth from land.

Under the leadership of al-Banna, the Muslim Brotherhood primarily defined itself as "anti-systemic" in the sense that it was against the prevailing political order. Al-Banna loathed the continued influence of the British in Egyptian life and despised the factionalism and secular orientation of the Egyptian political elite. He was also distressed by the unwillingness of the Egyptian elite – who were primarily landowners and wealthy merchants – to "address the country's highly skewed distribution of wealth and alleviate the suffering of the Egyptian masses" (Wickham, 2015, p. 22). He was also concerned with what he perceived to be the increasing secularization of Egyptian society, such as the adoption of "Western" approaches to "Islamic" issues by Al-Azhar scholars and the abolition of the Caliphate in Turkey by secular modernizers.

The ideological orientation of the Brotherhood was somewhat ambiguous under al-Banna. According to Mitchell (1969, p. 234), the "ultimate goal of the Muslim Brothers was the creation of an "Islamic order (*al-nizam al-islami*)" rather than an Islamic "state." Al-Banna was "less concerned than his followers about the intellectual assumptions of the movement" and gave little thought to the constitutional re-ordering of the Egyptian state (Mitchell, 1969, p. 237). According to Euben (1999, p. 55), al-Banna was "more activist than theorist," whose "theoretical contribution would remain rather limited" (Ayubi, 1991a, p. 134). Ayubi (1991a, p. 131) suggests that this lack of focus on theorizing an alternative Islamic state had to do with contextual factors. In the context of the 1930s and 1940s, al-Banna and the Brothers had "more immediate concerns such as the continued British occupation and the rising nationalist movement."[4]

In the 1940s and early 1950s, the economic platforms of the Muslim Brotherhood and the Free Officers overlapped significantly. The Brothers believed that "economic independence was the foundation of genuine political independence," and that economic and social security were necessary to pre-empt the class struggle and the national disunity such struggle caused (Mitchell, 1969, p. 272). Indeed, they shared with the nationalists the desire to create a national economy and "destroy the control of foreigners over the economy" (Mitchell, 1969, p. 274). In terms of economic policies, they supported the abolition of usury, progressive taxation for *zakat*, profit sharing for workers, the nationalization of natural resources, banks and large-scale industry,[5] land reform, tenure security, and social security.

Immediately after World War II, the Brothers established a program of small industry to address the problems of high unemployment plaguing the country. They set up the Muslim Brothers' Company for Spinning and Weaving in Shubra al-Khayma "as an effort to revive Islamic socialism … liberate the national economy," and "raise the level of the Egyptian worker" (Mitchell, 1969, p. 276). The group also established companies in construction, the production of construction materials, transport and advertising and established a labour section to present itself as a protector of the labourer from exploitation by foreign

---

[4] As a result, he left what Kepel (1985, p. 36) refers to as an "ideological vacuum" upon his assassination in 1949. Sayid Qutb filled that vacuum and became chief propagandist of the Muslim Brotherhood after the 1952 revolution.

[5] However, Kourgiotis (2018, p. 477) argues that the Brothers did not support the nationalization of Egyptian industry; rather, they supported giving the local bourgeoisie a greater controlling share in Egyptian capitalism.

capital and to organize workers into trade unions (mostly transport and textile workers). However, Ayubi (1991a, pp. 172–173) argues that the Brothers were "opposed to the encouragement by the Communists of trade union independence from non-workers patrons" and "never openly supported strikes by workers except, and only in a veiled and implicit manner, against foreign owned enterprises." As the "only available bulwark against the advent of the radical nationalist, anti-imperialist and anti-capitalist forces," the Brotherhood's "views on economy and social justice were indicative of their reluctance to challenge the socio-economic establishment" (Kourgiotis, 2018, pp. 471–474).

After Al-Banna's assassination in 1949, the Brothers entered a period of crisis. Membership numbers declined, and the Free Officer's movement sidelined the organization during the 1952 revolution. While expecting to share power with the Free Officers, the Brothers faced a period of intense state repression instead. Key members of the Muslim Brotherhood were initially part of the revolutionary government and, unlike members of other popular political organizations such as the trade unions, the new regime released many Brothers from prison.[6] Ayubi (1991a, p. 135) argues that some Brotherhood leaders "hoped that through their cooperation with the new regime, leftist, secularist and democratic forces would be liquidated, thus paving the way for a greater influence for, and possibly a total takeover of power by, the Ikhwan."[7] Tensions between the Brotherhood and the Free Officers intensified in 1954 after an assassination attempt on Nasser. The Brothers lost much of the influence they had among the Egyptian working class to the Nasserists. The regime arrested tens of thousands of Brothers – including Qutb – ridiculed them and tortured them. The Brotherhood was dissolved as an official organization in 1954 and many Brothers went into exile in Europe and the Persian Gulf. Any possibility of power sharing came to an end.

Under the repression of the Nasserist regime, Qutb's ideas became a "main feature of the Muslim Brothers' thought" (Ayubi, 1991a, p. 136). However, it was his later ideas, which were increasingly militant, abstract and idealist, that became dominant in the organization, and

---

[6] According to Ayubi (1991a, p. 135), many members of the army belonged to the Brotherhood. At some point, even Nasser is believed to have been a member.

[7] The term *Ikhwan* is often used as a shorthand to refer to one of the Arabic names of the Brotherhood, such as, *al-Ikhwān al-Muslimūn*.

these ideas were moving away from the moral Islamic economy articulated in his earlier work.[8] Part of the reason for this is that – as suggested – the Free Officers movement had integrated the economic ideas of the Islamic moral economy into Nasser's economic reform agenda. As Ayubi (1991a, p. 174) notes, Nasserism represented a similar "secular, State-led version of the same populist/corporatist recipe that the Islamists call *takaful*."

The regime executed Qutb in 1966 and his ideas of a militant armed struggle against the secular state were repudiated by the Brotherhood leadership, paving the way for the eventual split in the Islamist movement going into the 1970s. Throughout the 1970s, the more militant, Qutbian wing of the Islamist movement would break off and eschew political economy altogether, opting instead for a dogmatic, absolutist version of an Islamic state, with very little regard being paid to its socio-economic foundation. The moderate, mainstream Islamist movement within the Muslim Brotherhood would collaborate with the economic liberalism of the Sadat regime and ultimately accommodate Islamic economy to the realities of a Saudi dominated regional capitalism.

Islam against the Left: The Brotherhood under Sadat

The Brothers experienced rising fortunes under Sadat. To consolidate his power, Sadat re-oriented Egypt away from the Soviet Union and towards the West and Saudi Arabia. Over the course of the 1950s and 1960s, Saudi Arabia underwent extensive economic modernization with the help of oil to "stabilize Saudi society and transform its structure so that it could play its role in the world economy" (Halliday, 2013). By 1973, with the first "oil shock," petrodollars "flooded into

---

[8] In his later writings, Qutb's contempt for socialism and communism eclipsed his earlier critiques of capitalism and fused with the bitterness of his sense of betrayal by the Nasserists. From the confines of his prison cell, he characterized the Nasserist regime as an "American regime" in disguise, one that nonetheless originated in "the socialism of Karl Marx," and was characterized by "Communist directives and moral degeneration." Under Nasser, Egyptian society – like its Western and socialist counterparts – existed in a state of *jahiliyya*, meaning "pagan ignorance," and needed to be subverted through struggle (*jihad*). Qutbian discourse "is a position of utter refusal to enter into any dialectical relationship with objective realities or to prepare any societal alternatives to the status quo" (Ayubi, 1991a, p. 141).

the central coffers of oil-producing countries" like Saudi Arabia "in what amounted to one of the most dramatic transfers of wealth in human history" (Jones, 2011, p. 3). A domestic political shift to the right within Egypt accompanied this realignment with the Saudi-American axis as Sadat began the process of de-Nasserization.

De-Nasserization entailed the de-sequestration of Agrarian reform lands back to their original owners among the large landowning class, and the substitution of Nasser's import substitution industrialization economy with the more liberal, export-orientated *infitah* policy. To do this, Sadat needed to shift the balance of forces away from the nationalists and the leftists in favour of the forces of the right and centre-right. Affecting this shift entailed a *rapprochement* with the Muslim Brothers. At a personal level, this was not very difficult, as Sadat was once a member of the Brotherhood and styled himself as *al-rais al-mu'min*, "the Devout President" (Hasan, 2003, p. 105). In 1971, Sadat implemented a general amnesty for the organization and in 1975 he released all imprisoned Brothers and enticed exiled cadres to return home. In fact, Sadat's intention with *infitah* was not just to encourage Arab (the Gulf states in particular) investment in Egypt; it also explicitly targeted Muslim Brothers who had established businesses in the Gulf during their years of exile under Nasser.

In return, the mainstream of the Muslim Brothers generally supported *infitah*. For the most part, *infitah* overlapped with many of the Brothers' economic policies: cut-backs in public sector spending, encouragement of the private sector in the economy, a non-interest bearing banking system, *zakat* as the basis for social welfare, and independence from foreign economic intervention. In this sense, *infitah* paved the way for the organisational and economic rebirth of the Muslim Brothers. Economic liberalization encouraged the import-export trades, particularly in the north, thereby expanding opportunities for small and medium-sized businesses and merchants, a traditional demographic of Muslim Brotherhood support. As *infitah* facilitated the growth of "importers, financiers, middlemen and profiteers," referred to as the "*infitah* class," businesses linked to the Brotherhood proliferated, constituting up to 40 percent of private sector enterprises, with a large concentration in real estate and currency speculation (Beinin, 2005, p. 120).

The 1970s also witnessed the growing dominance of the Muslim Brothers by members of the old landed aristocracy. The third leader of the organization – 'Umar al-Tilmisani – was born into a prominent landowning family that owned up to 300 feddans of land before the 1952 revolution.[9] Tilmisani's deputy, Mustafa Mashhu, was also from a prominent landowning family from Sharqiyya province. Sadat's restitution of landed property clearly benefited these members. Such developments lead Springborg to conclude that, by the late 1970s, the Islamic *infitah* class bought the leadership of the organization with "resources acquired through collaboration with the Sadat regime" (Springborg, 1989, p. 236). At the end of the decade, eight out of the eighteen families that dominated Egypt's private sector were members of the Brotherhood (Beinin, 2005, p. 120). The dominance of the Muslim Brothers by landed wealth would continue into the 1980s and early 1990s.

The Brothers also made significant inroads into finance through the creation of Islamic banking and informal Islamic financial institutions, known as *Sharikat Tawzif al-Amwal al-Islamiyya* (Islamic Money Management Companies [IMMCs]). Islamic banks emerged in the context of the oil boom of the 1970s – itself a sign of the emerging *pax Saudiana* – and represented "an endeavour by the rising Arab commercial bourgeoisie to employ petro-dollars in the highest paying types of mercantile activities" (Ayubi, 1991a, p. 185; Roy, 1991). They also had ties to the more elite members of the Muslim Brother leadership.[10] For example, 'Umar Mar'i – founder of the Egyptian branch of the Faisal Islamic Bank in 1977 – had been jailed as a Muslim Brother by Nasser. He also had family ties with Sadat. 'Umar Mar'i recruited other Muslim Brothers to work in the bank.

According to Ayubi (1991a, p. 184), while "Islamic banks appeared initially to favour financing small artisans and entrepreneurs to emphasise the role of work and diligence, they have ended up financing the already well-to-do." By way of contrast, the IMMCs did more to facilitate the growth of an upwardly mobile segment of the lower middle classes. The IMMCs were informal institutions that emulated the practices of the formal Islamic banks, but were smaller, personalized operations, usually run by an entrepreneur and his family who acquired capital through working in the Gulf States. While the majority remained small, some grew to amass deposits of more than U.S.$10 billion with a

---

[9] Al-Tilmisani's predecessor, Hassan al-Hudaybi, was born to a working-class family. However, Hudaybi's brother-in-law was chief of the royal household.
[10] Osman Ahmad Osman was a big supporter of IMMCs.

client base of up to 500,000 (Zubaida, 1990, pp. 153–154). By December 1986, 190 registered and 90 non-registered IMMCs existed, making Egypt home to the largest number of IMMCs in the Arab world, such as Rayyan, Sharif, al-Sa'd, al-Huda, Badr and al-Hilal. The Sharif group was founded by Latif Sharif, a "staunch member" of the Muslim Brothers (Moore, 1990, p. 251).

At a superficial level, Islamic banks and IMMCs represented attempts to practice the Brother's Islamic economy in the sphere of finance.[11] The IMMCs were particularly popular among small depositors and workers in the Gulf States due to the generous payments. Indeed, the first IMMCs originated from the activities of private currency speculators who offered financial services to migrant workers in the Gulf looking for ways to send their remittances back to Egypt.[12] By the mid-1980s, IMMCs offered between 20 percent and 30 percent dividends, which were considered a form of profit sharing rather than interest to conform to the strictures of Islamic finance (Sadowski, 1991, pp. 229–230; Zubaida, 1990, p. 153). As a result, the IMMCs amassed billions of Egyptian pounds in savings that they invested in various domestic and international markets as the IMMCs transformed themselves into investment companies in the 1980s.

Some of the more doctrinaire Islamists even considered engagement with the IMMCs preferable to "dealing with the institutions of an 'infidel' State" and considered currency speculation to be a lucrative, anti-State form of economic activity that was legitimately Islamic (Ayubi, 1991a, pp. 192–193). Indeed, the IMMCs were the product of the overlapping segments of the more moderate and conservative Islamists and the commercial bourgeoisie. This is not to say, however, that the organizations were the product of the Muslim Brotherhood. As Beinin (2005, p. 122) notes, "the owners and managers of the Islamic investment companies generally did not belong to the Society of Muslim Brothers or other Islamist organizations, although relations were generally supportive." Rather, they served as intermediaries for

---

[11] According to Ayubi, the idea of "Islamic finance" originates in attempts to replicate the types of cooperative societies flourishing in Western Germany after World War II.

[12] Sadowski (1991, p. 223) notes that the while official estimates of remittances stood at U.S.$4 billion, others have argued that remittances reached anywhere between U.S.$12 billion and U.S.$18 billion.

Muslim Brother business activity and contributed to the formation of an "Islamic sector" in the economy.

Another reason the IMMCs remained popular was due to their voluntary support for charity institutions and their provision of social services, such as schools, daycare facilities, hospitals and health clinics and vocational training centres (Ayubi, 1991a; Sullivan, 1990, pp. 329–330). As public investment in social services began to shrink in the 1970s, Islamic charitable associations stepped in to fill the gap. A typical form of service provision was centred on a private mosque that would also contain the abovementioned services. These services required the payment of a modest fee and sometimes required donations for *zakat*. In some of the wealthier neighbourhoods in Cairo and Alexandria, such complexes may be much more elaborate, like the Mustafa Mahmud Mosque in the Cairo suburb of Muhandisin, which contains a large, modern hospital. Private hospitals such as these catered to rich clients and the services were of a higher quality than the deteriorating state hospitals. As the Sadat and Mubarak regimes pursued the dismantling of Egyptian socialism throughout the 1970s and 1980s, the space for Islamic charitable societies grew. Approximately 600 Muslim charitable societies existed in Egypt. By the mid-1980s, that number grew to 2,000.

The Brothers' role in the provision of social services was encouraged by the regime to mitigate the negative impacts of *infitah* on the lower classes. This formed part of the regime's strategy of using the Muslim Brothers against the left during its attempt to shift Egyptian politics to the right and develop a more liberal variant of Egyptian capitalism. Muslim Brothers enticed to return from the Gulf to invest in Egypt were granted tax privileges on the condition that they reserve parts of their buildings for the operation of private mosques that would provide social, health and education services (Ben Nefissa, 1995). In this regard, the Islamic social sector established by the Muslim Brothers was "anything but detached from the state: it lay at the centre of the regime's economic and political policies of welfare relocation" (Vannetzel, 2017, para. 12).

At the same time, however, *infitah* "challenged the coherence of the Muslim Brotherhood" (Ates, 2005, p. 138). Divisions opened up on a number of fronts. While successful, entrepreneurial Muslim Brothers returned from the Gulf to invest in the opportunities available under *infitah*, younger, highly educated Brothers with no capital and no family ties became radicalized by the conspicuous consumption that erupted under *infitah*. These members felt distanced from an organizational leadership increasingly dominated by the wealthy and the propertied. Many of these younger, more radical Islamists came from Upper Egypt, and came from modest families that experienced social mobility from Nasser's educational and social reforms. In this part of Egypt, the *fellahin* benefited from Nasserite agrarian reforms and were now suffering under *infitah*. As Fandy notes, most Islamists from the south "were born after the 1952 revolution and benefited from Nasser's land and educational reforms and graduated from colleges in the 1970s" (Fandy, 1994, p. 613). In fact, this fragmentation of the Islamist movement has contributed to the inability of the Brotherhood to dominate the Islamist "field" like the Islamist Justice and Development Party (AKP) have been able to do in Turkey, a factor that would contribute to their downfall in 2013 (Tuğal, 2012). Splinter groups from the Brothers – namely, *Jihad* and *Gama'a al-Islamiyya* – formed in response to the growing revulsion among certain Islamists of the Brothers' participation in the conspicuous consumption associated with *infitah*. These radical groups would unite to assassinate Sadat in 1981, in response to the regime's sweeping crackdown on Islamists, helping to stall the process of further economic liberalization.[13]

The Brotherhood under Mubarak

President Mubarak attempted to break the cycle of repression and violence that culminated in the assassination of Sadat through the gradual release of political prisoners – including members of the Muslim Brothers – beginning in the late autumn of 1981. The first 7 years of Mubarak's rule thus signified a relative breakthrough by the Brothers into the mainstream of Egyptian politics. Economically, the Brothers were also thriving. A particular political dynamic emerged between the regime and the Muslim Brothers under Mubarak. The organization would remain illegal, yet individual Brothers were able to participate in elections as independent candidates as long as they did not cross a tacit line of seeking to overthrow the regime. Mubarak allowed – and even encouraged – the Brothers to continue their

---

[13] The regime was already backtracking from liberalization due to the violent bread riots of 1977.

charitable work, particularly as the social problems associated with economic liberalization grew more pronounced in the late 1980s. In this sense, Vannetzel (2017) argues that the Brothers ceased being entirely "outside" the state. Economically, however, the regime confined the Brothers to the margins of the economy, forcing them to operate in the informal economy. If the Brothers broke their tacit agreement with the regime, the latter would clamp down and seize the assets of businesses affiliated with the organization.

The growth of Islamic financial institutions and social organizations continued throughout the first half of the decade. More Islamic banks opened in Egypt, some domestic, like the Islamic International Bank of Investment and Development (1980), some operating out of the Gulf, such as the Saudi Egyptian Finance Bank (1988) and some resulting from partnerships between Egyptian and Gulf capital, such as the Al Watany Bank of Egypt (1980). By 1985, Islamic banks comprised 16.8 percent of the market (Moore, 1990, p. 236). The growth of Islamic finance not only demonstrated the growing economic clout of moderately conservative Islamist organizations like the Muslim Brothers, it also signified their integration with what Hanieh (2011) refers to as Gulf-centred "*khaleeji* capital" that formed the basis of the rising *pax Saudiana*. The IMMC also experienced a period of remarkable growth. By December 1986, 190 registered and 90 non-registered IMMCs existed. While the majority remained small, some grew to amass deposits of more than U.S.$10 billion with a client base of up to 500,000 (Zubaida, 1990, pp. 153–154). More and more depositors opted for Islamic investment companies, starving state banks of savings at a time when the Egyptian state subsidized most of its imports through borrowing in a global environment of tight credit. Between 1983 and 1986, it is estimated that the formal banks lost £E8.1 billion in savings, much of which flowed into the IMMCs.

Numerous businesses affiliated with the Brothers flourished throughout the 1980s, including shoe manufacturing in Alexandria, labour contracting for agricultural infrastructure maintenance and repair and Islamic publishing – such as the Dar al-Shuruq publishing house. The most prominent business was the Tali'at al-Iman construction company established by the son of one of the Brothers who attempted to assassinate Nasser in 1954. However, in terms of membership and political support, the relationship between the IMMCs and political Islam is not so straightforward. The illegal status of the

Muslim Brothers means that many businessmen – particularly smaller businessmen – remained wary of publicly declaring their affiliation with the organization. Sharif may have supported his Muslim Brothers, but the head of Rayyan denied any such political involvement. On this basis Moore argues that "the mutual interests of the Islamists and the money dealers could also diverge" (Moore, 1990, p. 252).

As global oil prices declined in 1986, competition to attract the remittances of workers in the Gulf intensified. Islamic banks were in trouble: the Islamic International Bank for Investment and Development was in receivership and the Faisal Islamic Bank of Egypt was paying out lower "profits" to its depositors than the fixed interest rates of the conventional banks. In contrast, the IMMCs were paying out over twice the level of interest rates, enabling their depositors to keep up with inflation. By the end of the year, however, Rayyan reportedly lost $100 million speculating on gold, but was eventually rescued by Saudi banks. Many of the IMMCs "bought up local enterprises and partially restructured themselves to appear more in conformity" with the law (of 1986) (Moore, 1990, p. 251).

In this context, the regime increasingly viewed IMMCs as a threat to the interests of both public *and* Islamic banks. After a series of debates on the role of IMMCs, the Mubarak regime enacted a new investment law in April 1988 seeking to rein in the Islamic investment companies, while transferring their capital into the Central Bank of Egypt.[14] The law clamped down on IMMCs by requiring them to repatriate their assets to Egypt and submit to the supervision of the Capital Markets Authority. All the opposition parties opposed the new law. Islamists decried it as an attack on Islam and a victory for America and Zionism, and the liberal *Wafd* party opposed it because it stifled the development of the free market. After implementing the law, the regime arrested numerous members of the IMMCs, shut down their operations and transferred their deposits – which stood at millions of U.S. dollars – to the official banks (Sadowski, 1991, p. 237). Consequently, many of the IMMCs collapsed by May 1988.

The Brothers also expanded their influence through the provision of social services. The regime was unable to offer employment to university graduates or continue to provide adequate social services as it slashed state budgets. The Brothers took over by offering charity

[14] For details on the debate, see Zubaida (1990).

programmes and social services to rural and impoverished urban areas of the country. According to Vannetzel, the Brothers were "granted space to expand through welfare activities, in the frame of tacit cooperation with the incumbent regime to maintain so-called stability." Thus, despite their formal political opposition, they were unofficially part of the "authoritarian coalition leading the former regime before Mubarak's fall in 2011" (Vannetzel, 2017, p. 220). This relationship between the Brothers and the regime was, however, precarious. Insofar as the Brothers' charitable activities kept the lid on social discontent, the regime tolerated it. If these activities threatened to delegitimize the regime, then the state would crack down on the Brothers. In 1992, when an earthquake struck the slum areas of Cairo, the Muslim Brothers were first to deliver aid and relief for those affected. Slow in its response to the earthquake, the government accused the Brothers of exploiting the disaster for political gains and demanded the group cease all relief work and stop acting like a "parallel state" (Wickham, 2015, pp. 77–78).

In the political sphere, the Brothers entered a political coalition with the *Wafd* party and the Labour party to contest the 1984 and 1987 parliamentary elections, respectively. In 1984, the Brothers won eight of the alliance's 58 seats. The alliance was short-lived as it produced internal divisions within the *Wafd* party regarding its relationship to secularism and its position among the Coptic community. In 1987, the Brothers contested parliamentary elections in an alliance with the Socialist Labour Party, a centre-left party that increasingly moved away from secularism under Mubarak. The Brothers won 35 of the alliance's 56 seats, marking a dramatic increase from the previous election.

The Muslim Brothers and Economic Liberalization

The implementation of the Economic Reform and Structural Adjustment Programme in the early 1990s coincided with what many commentators considered to be a process of political "de-liberalization" (Albrecht & Schlumberger, 2004; Kienle, 1998; Shehata, 2009). The regime adopted an increasingly hard line towards dissent in the context of an upsurge in Islamist violence – particularly by *Jihad* and *Gama'a al-Islamiya* – in the early 1990s. The renewal of the Emergency Law gave the regime the power to stifle legal political opposition as well as prosecute its "war on terror." By the end of the decade, the regime demonstrated an increasing willingness to shut down legal political parties (Stacher, 2004).

Economic liberalization, however, continued. As discussed in Chapter 3, the process of economic liberalization implemented during the 1990s and 2000s resulted in a large degree of monopolization by the so-called "Whales of the Nile" (Sfakianakis, 2004). A relatively small group of capitalists with close links to the neoliberal fraction of the National Democratic Party reaped most of the benefits of privatization and liberalization. These "networks of privilege" (Heydemann, 2004) created an "insider/outsider" dynamic that corresponded to the divide between large firms and small and medium enterprises (SMEs). The lack of institutions of interest representation that would enable small businesses to influence the policy-making process compounded the marginalization of SMEs. Large capital had established a number of business associations to facilitate the representation of their interests in the policy-making process: the Federation of Egyptian Industry, the Egyptian Businessmen's Association, the Junior Businessmen's Association and the American Chamber of Commerce. In contrast, small businesses were significantly under-represented. Despite constituting the vast majority of businesses in Egypt, SMEs were only represented by the Cooperative Society for Small Businesses, a branch of the Cooperative Productive Union, which was a "corporatist entity of industrial cooperatives operating under the supervision of the Ministry of Local Development" (Zovighian, 2013, p. 187). Like many of the interest associations of the old Nasserist state, the Cooperative Productive Union did more to control small businesses than it did to represent their interests to the state.

Attempts were made to change the landscape of SME interest representation in the context of the Economic Reform and Structural Adjustment Programme. In 1997, the Mubarak regime allowed for the establishment of the Federation of Development Associations (FEDA). However, unlike small business associations in other countries, FEDA was a federation of nongovernmental organizations dependent on a handful of Western donors and unrepresentative of the SME community at large. As a result, FEDA's interaction with the regime had little effect on liberalizing the policy-making process. In fact, Zovighian (2013) argues that "networks of privilege" were replicated by FEDA among SMEs due to this dependency and the ability of the regime to control FEDA's access to the levers of state policy. In other words, far from altering the terrain of SME interest representation, FEDA was integrated into the quasi-corporatist structures of the Egyptian state.

In this context, we can understand the Brothers' position on economic liberalization as a mixture of ideological principle and political expediency. First, the ideal of an Islamic economy is not opposed to "free market" capitalism as understood by the Muslim Brothers. As mentioned above, the Brothers formulated their notion of an Islamic economy in opposition to the statism of the Nasser period. The free market remains the driver of economic activity and Islamic charity will provide for social protection. Private property and the family remain core components of a just, Islamic society. In this sense, the Brother's Islamic capitalism is not very different from traditional conservatism within the Anglo-American tradition (Aughey, Jones & Riches, 1992). In more contemporary terms, the Brothers' mix of private property, family, religion, free markets and charitable social provision, resembles post-war Christian Democracy, leading some scholars to characterize the Brothers' as a form of "Muslim Democracy" (Nasr, 2005). From this perspective, the regime's control of the liberalization process – by privileging regime "insiders" against entrepreneurial "outsiders" – is a corruption of the whole process of liberalization. The mechanism of economic liberalization should be free markets, not regime patronage. In this sense, the Muslim Brothers support an idealized version of capitalism as a free market defined by openness to new market entrants. In the same way that segments of the conservative and libertarian right in the United States decry the market dominance of corporations as a product of the politicization of markets that is antithetical to the "free" markets of capitalism, so too do the Muslim Brothers decry the corruption of politically connected business "insiders" operating in close proximity to the regime. In this sense, the Muslim Brothers criticize the failures of liberalization without criticizing liberalization itself. To put it another way, because of the Muslim Brothers' exclusion from the networks of privilege despite its position within Egyptian civil society and its support from small businesses, the organization criticized the process of liberalization, while tacitly supporting economic liberalization as an objective in its own right.

However, the Muslim Brothers' position toward the free market is not just a matter of "outsiders" seeking in "free markets" the power to circumvent the regime. It often appeared to take different positions on liberalization. This can be explained by reference to a number of different factors. First, the Muslim Brothers is a cross-class social movement attempting to bring together lower class Egyptians under the leadership of an ostensibly middle and upper class organization while trying to ignore or downplay the antagonistic class relations that constitute capitalism. This often forces them to straddle the fence on liberalization. On the one hand, economic liberalization – insofar as it opens up opportunities for the Brothers to start up and run successful businesses to finance their activities – is something the leadership supports. On the other hand, economic liberalization has resulted in deteriorating living conditions for the very lower classes the Brothers seek to organize as the basis of its counter-hegemonic project.[15] To openly support privatization or the elimination of food subsidies would alienate lower class Egyptians from the organization. According to Görmüs (2016, p. 63), the Brothers emerged as the prominent opposition group due to its "ability to speak on behalf of the masses who were being impoverished during the process of structural reforms." During the 1990s, the Brothers often opposed the elimination of food subsidies. As Beinin (2005, p. 135) notes, these types of contradictions help to "maintain the primary face of Egyptian political Islam as a social movement opposed to Washington consensus policies."

The political calculus involved in maintaining this cross-class coalition therefore also determined the Brothers' position on liberalization. For example, the early 1990s saw the Muslim Brothers participate – through the "Islamic Trend" or "Islamic Voice" – in the trade union elections for the first time. In doing so, they supported the right to strike – which was new for the Muslim Brothers – criticized privatizations and the abolition of subsidies and promoted inflation-linked wage increases. These positions reflected a more populist side of the Islamic political economy, the dynamics of the Brothers' tactical political alliance with the Labour party forged in 1987 and their desire to carve out an oppositional space vis-à-vis the regime. The Labour Party sought to establish an Islamic political economy to the left of the Muslim Brothers and advocated the protection of national industry – meaning they opposed the privatization of state-owned industries. Although the Labour Party boycotted the 1990 parliamentary

---

[15] More on this in Chapters 6 and 7.

elections, the Brothers maintained its political alliance with the party, which carried over into their trade union work.

However, at the same time, the Brotherhood "was essentially mute" (Springborg, 1991, p. 248) on the issue of agrarian liberalization due to the fact that it was "dominated by wealthy conservative Islamists whose outlooks and class backgrounds predisposed them to support land-owners" (Springborg, 1991, p. 242). While remaining quiet on this issue, they effectively supported the policy. As a result, the "position of the Muslim Brotherhood on the issue of land reform has been almost identical to that of the regime and its supporters" (Mandour, 2016).[16]

The New Guard

By the mid-1990s, the leadership of the Brothers was largely composed of a professional stratum that came out of the universities in the 1970s and were now dominant in the various professional syndicates as well as by a handful of new wealthy donors who made their fortunes from commerce and finance. Unlike previous patrons and members of the old guard, Khairat al-Shater and Hassan Malek were not from landed families. Rather, they had made their fortunes in various business ventures. Al-Shater is the son of a merchant who engaged in socialist politics under Nasser. Under Sadat, he became interested in Islamism and joined the Muslim Brothers in 1981. Before Sadat's assassination, he went into exile in Saudi Arabia, where he made his fortune in textiles, furniture and software.[17] He returned to Egypt in mid-1980s and became the Brothers' chief financier. In 1995, he became the head of the Brothers' Cairo branch. Politically, he is the informal head of the dominant "Persian Gulf" faction within the Brothers, which tends to be politically conservative and supportive of neoliberal economic policies. It is reported that, while head of the Cairo section, al-Shater established "parallel structures" within the organization – effectively creating an "organization within an organization" – that enabled the upward mobility of members who did not meet the criteria of "religiosity, historical legitimacy or knowledge of Islamic jurisprudence" favoured by the "old guard" (Howeidy, 2012). His business interests expanded

[16] In this regard, the position of the Muslim Brothers diverged sharply from that of *Gama'a al-Islamiya* (Fandy, 1994).
[17] Some reports say Shater lived in England for a number of years before returning to Egypt.

into the areas of tractors and car manufacturing, chemicals, pharmaceuticals and management consultancy, and he used his parallel structures to employ Muslim Brothers in his various businesses. It is also
believed that he sits on the executive boards of numerous companies in
Bahrain, Luxembourg and the UK as well as the International Bank for
Development and Investment. As his business empire grew, therefore,
so too did his influence within the Muslim Brothers. This combination
of wealth and power had never existed within the organization.

Al-Shater's business partner, Hassan Malek, is another major patron
of the Brothers. Hassan and al-Shater met in the late 1970s at university and went on to found the software company Salsabil, which
attained lucrative contracts from the military. Malek is also the
founder of Malek trade and runs an extensive import/export business
and the Sarar clothing brand. He is a key investor in the Turkish
furniture company Istikbal and has strong ties to the Islamist business
community in Turkey (MÜSIAD), which would serve as a source of
inspiration for the creation of an Egyptian Islamist business association
after the fall of Mubarak.[18] He established his connections with
MÜSIAD through his role as representative on the Board of Governors
of the International Business Forum (IBF). The IBF was formed in
1994 in Pakistan by the coordinated efforts of the Pakistan Business
forum, the Organization of Islamic Cooperation, the Islamic Bank of
Development and the Islamic Chamber of Commerce.

Another important Brother and member of the IBF Board of Governors is Essam el-Haddad. El-Haddad is a member of the Arabian
Development Group (an organization for introducing foreign investors
to the Egyptian market), the Union of Arab Exhibitions (1995), the
German-Arab Chamber of Industry and Commerce, the British Egyptian Business Association and the Canadian Chamber of Commerce.
He also founded "Inter-Build Egypt," the country's largest exhibition
for the construction sector. El-Haddad would later be appointed as
chief economic advisor to President Mohamed Morsi after the collapse
of the Mubarak Regime.

Other wealthy Brothers, including Youssef Nada in Switzerland and
Kamal El-Helbawy in the UK, were instrumental caretakers of the
overseas finances of the group (Feteha, 2012). Nada was a member
of the old guard who established a cheese factory in Austria in the

---

[18] To be discussed in detail in the post-script.

1950s after fleeing persecution by the Nasser regime. He branched out into construction and cement in Libya in the 1960s as well as steel and agricultural materials. In the 1980s, he co-founded the *al Taqwa* bank with Swiss nationals Francois Genoud, a former financier of the Third Reich, and Ahmed Huber, far right Islamist convert with ties to German neo-Nazi groups.

According to Adly (2014), these Brothers represented a new generation of leaders within the organization. They predominantly earned their wealth through wholesale and retail sales in the commercial, financial and services sectors both in Egypt and abroad. Adly (2014) points out that this

> may be due to the fact that access to assets such as land or divested public-sector companies needed for activities such as industry, construction, or tourism has historically been limited to the network of people close to the state in the Mubarak years. This has left others to focus on less capital-intensive activities and the service sectors—enterprises which also lend themselves to reduce the risk of confiscation or retrieval of these funds in case of a clash with the authorities. While they may remain targets, by not holding wealth in fixed assets like land or concentrated in larger companies, Brotherhood businessmen may more easily relocate or hide their assets to reduce the risk of seizure.

This new generation was more attracted to economic liberalization – particularly in the urban economy – than were the old guard and sought to actively "build an institutional network of like-minded business groups to favour their integration into the world economy and their socio-professional representation in their own countries" (Vannetzel & Yankaya, 2017, p. 2). Important in this endeavour to create Islamist "economic advocacy networks" was the MÜSIAD – the Islamist business association in Turkey. MÜSIAD was established in 1990 and experienced dramatic growth throughout the decade. Between 1990 and 2000, MÜSIAD grew from a membership base of 25 to 3,000. This growth occurred in the context of the export-oriented growth model Turkey implemented from 1980 onwards. Small and medium sized enterprises in Anatolia benefited from this growth model, resulting in the creation of a "devout bourgeoisie" supportive of the new, ruling *Refah* (Welfare) Party (Gumuscu, 2010).[19] MÜSIAD

---

[19] The *Refah* Party came to power in 1996, but the military deposed it in 1997. The Constitutional Court banned the party in 1998, forcing its dissolution.

continued to grow its membership base after the election of the AKP. From its founding, MÜSIAD sought to enhance "cooperation between Muslim countries" against the "domination of Western countries in the world economy" (Vannetzel & Yankaya, 2017, p. 7). To accomplish this goal, MÜSIAD joined the IBF in 1994 and assumed a leading position in the international network by 1995. It is through membership in the IBF that Muslim Brotherhood business-men like Malek participate in the economic advocacy networks forged by MÜSIAD.

The Brothers' path towards an AKP-style *rapprochement* with neo-liberalism was not so straightforward. In 1996, moderate Brothers split off from the Brotherhood to create the *Wasat* Party (Centre Party), under the leadership of Abu'l-'Ila Madi Abu'l-'Ila, to promote liberal-ism and democracy (Stacher, 2002). However, this new party remained marginalized due to the absence of a devout bourgeoisie that could channel its activities through the business activities of SMEs that were independent of the state. The main beneficiaries of liberalization were upper class Egyptians who have opted either for political passivity or for participation through the National Democratic Party. According to Gumuscu (2010), the Muslim Brotherhood remained a less moderate, dominant force of Egyptian political Islam due to the character of Egyptian economic liberalization. Unlike Turkey, the liberalization process did not benefit SMEs, enabling the rise of a devout bourgeoisie. Rather, liberalization benefited large capital and the state elite. How-ever, as Tuğal (2012) points out, the more important factor compli-cating the Brothers' position was its inability to monopolize the "field" of Islamist politics in Egypt. As mentioned, the Brothers have never been able to make inroads into Upper Egypt among the dispossessed *fellahin* where the more radical *Gama'a al-Islamiya* remain dominant (Fandy, 1994).

Either way, the Brothers' ability to constitute itself as a dominant Islamist fraction of capital was frustrated in the 1990s. The new millennium did not introduce any immediate changes. The Brothers contested the election as independents, winning 17 seats. On the eve of the 2000 parliamentary elections, the regime once again clamped down on known Muslim Brotherhood supporters. In a speech delivered in the immediate aftermath of the uprisings that brought down Mubarak, al-Shater claimed the regime cracked down on 9,000 firms and busi-nesses on the eve of the 2000 election (al-Shater, 2011).

Breakthroughs and Crackdowns, 2004–2010

The period from 2004 to 2010 saw the Muslim Brothers expand their political and economic influence. The Mubarak regime had been under pressure from the Bush administration – as part of its democracy promotion program – to open up the political process to opposition forces (Meital, 2006). At the same time, neoliberal restructuring was accelerating under the so-called government of businessmen, intensifying inequality and fomenting social unrest. A wave of strike activity, launched by rank-and-file workers against the official union movement, was beginning to take off, and violence related to land disputes resulting from the liberalization of tenure relations in the countryside intensified. In the urban centres, a new political movement – *Kefaya* – emerged to protest against widely perceived regime corruption. Finally, in the broader context of Islamist politics, the landslide victory of the AKP in Turkey in 2002 inspired the Muslim Brothers to embrace "democracy promotion" by accepting liberal constitutionalism and sidelining any attempt to establish an Islamic state.

As a result, opposition parties focused on amending the constitution, annulling the state of emergency and liberalizing the media during the 2005 election campaign. Commentators noted that the Brothers seemed to be making all the right noises about democracy and constitutional politics (El-Ghobashy, 2005; Leiken & Brooke, 2007; Nasr, 2005). In fact, during the 2005 parliamentary elections, Al-Shater reached out to Western media outlets to demonstrate the Brother's respect for democracy, pluralism and constitutional government (el-Shatir, 2005).

In this vein, the Brothers' 2005 electoral campaign focused on the lack of democracy in Egypt, which – they argued – promotes economic monopolies, concentrates wealth in the hands of the few and breeds corruption (Ikhwan, 2007a). Unemployment, inflation, the budget deficit and the debt and a poor investment environment were the main problems facing the Egyptian economy. During the campaigns of 2005 and 2007, the Brothers strongly criticized the Nazif government's acceleration of the privatization program and the cutbacks to the social safety net. They advocated a "review" of the privatization program and granted the state a greater role in the economy. However, this did not entail a return to "the bitter experience of [the] public sector," but rather, the more efficient management of public assets (Ikhwan, 2007b). In the sphere of social policy, the Brotherhood advocated for the right to healthcare according to people's needs rather than their ability to pay, the right to basic education to link the individual to labour market requirements to fight unemployment, and social insurance in the form of family allowances, maternity benefits, disability insurance and income assistance. The contradiction here resides in the fact that these social policy positions would undermine the Brothers' traditional provision of those services through private, religious-based charities, particularly given their stated commitment to a secular, constitutional state.

However, their election platform also contained an eclectic mix of unspecified economic policy commitments, reflecting the relatively unsophisticated understanding the Brothers have of a modernizing capitalist economy (Ikhwan, 2007a). On the one hand were elements of economic nationalism, such as expanding the local design and industrialization of factories, machines and equipment, and promoting "self-industry and development." On the other hand, the Brothers promoted "Islamic globalization" through increased economic integration with Arab and Islamic countries (including Turkey and Malaysia). The Brothers also needed to appeal to different capitalist constituencies; for example, appealing to large capital by supporting "distinguished" industrial cities, and supporting SMEs by establishing technical, financial and marketing support. There was also some confusion regarding what constitutes "high value-added" industries – which include telecommunications and computer programming with textiles and spinning – and there was a focus on "multidimensional" industries, like chemical fertilizers.

While the platform pulled the Brothers in diametrically opposed directions, privately, many high-ranking Brothers expressed their commitment to the so-called free market, even in the provision of things such as housing.[20] In an interview in late December 2005, Mohammed Mahdi Akef – the Brothers' "Supreme Guide" – expressed his commitment to market liberalization, a position that would be more freely expressed and concretely articulated after the fall of the Mubarak regime in 2011.[21]

---

[20] Although the election platform did say that "achieving economic abundance and living a good life is a religious duty and a human necessity" (Ikhwan, 2007a).

[21] The claim that the "markets should not be touched" was made in the context of a question on Mubarak's neoliberal policies regarding the provision of housing. Interview with author, December 23, 2005, Cairo.

The Brothers were remarkably successful in the 2005 assembly elections. Their candidates – still running as official independents – won 88 seats, or 19 percent of the seats, representing an increase of 71 seats from the previous elections in 2000. This success sparked a crackdown by the regime in 2006 and 2007. During this period, Hamas swept to power in Gaza in January 2006, effectively putting the brakes on America's "democracy promotion" agenda in the Middle East. Fearing that political liberalization was facilitating an Islamist wave in the region, the Mubarak regime launched the most comprehensive crackdown on the Brothers in a generation. In Spring 2006, between 700 and 850 Brothers were arrested (Shehata & Stacher, 2006). The regime shut down approximately seventy businesses with ties to the Muslim Brothers in what Abul-Magd (2012) refers to as "competition between two groups that controlled capital in Egypt, namely between Gamal's group and the Brotherhood." These companies "were rentier-based and primarily produced consumer products that targeted upper and middle classes" (Abul-Magd, 2012). Among these businessmen was al-Shater, who was imprisoned by a military tribunal until the collapse of the Mubarak regime in 2011. Hundreds more Brothers were arrested before the 2007 Shura Council elections, a move that ensured the organization failed to win a single seat.[22] In the lead up to the 2008 municipal elections, the regime arrested another 800 Muslim Brothers. The regime accepted only 10 of the 5,754 candidates registered for the elections by the Brothers, leading the Brothers to withdraw from the elections.

The crackdown resulted in the reformers losing the initiative inside the organization. Many of them were in prison between 2005 and 2010, enabling the conservative faction to consolidate its power over the Guidance Council, resulting in what Hamzawy (2007) refers to as a regressive shift in the organization's political orientation. The leadership produced a draft platform containing a proposal for the creation of an independent religious council mandated to ensure legislation conformed to Shari'a, raising questions about the organization's commitment to the Egyptian constitution. According to Wickham (2015, p. 127), the power of the conservative faction was "reinforced by the outcome of Guidance Bureau elections in 2008 and 2009, as well as by the election of a new Supreme Guide in January 2010."

---

[22] The Shura Council is the Upper chamber in Parliament.

The conservatives were spread across two different tendencies: a more ideologically dogmatic "old guard" that experienced the repression of the Nasser era, and a group of pragmatic conservatives grouped around al-Shater and Muhammed Morsi. The latter served as a "bridge" between the reformers and the old guard and came to represent the new mainstream of the organization. By contrast, the reformist tendency was clearly on the wane by 2010.

Conclusion

Since the beginnings of liberalization under Sadat, the Muslim Brotherhood has been growing as an aspiring fraction of capital rooted predominantly in commercial capital, with an emphasis on the growing import-export sector tied initially to the growth of the economies of the Gulf states. The attempt to establish an Islamic economy, however, required the Brothers to attempt to branch out into other sectors. In the late 1970s and early 1980s, this resulted in the growth of Islamic finance, in the form of both Islamic banking as well as IMMCs. The growth of Islamic finance, and the attempts to branch out into manufacturing, however, were met with resistance from the National Democratic Party and the dominant fraction of capital that had close ties to the regime. By the late 1990s, a new guard of conservative, business-oriented Brothers ascended through the ranks of the movement and attempted to replicate the successes of the AKP in Turkey. The deposition of Mubarak in the context of the Arab uprisings opened up space for the Brothers to attempt to expand their economic power beyond their commercial base. The attempt to do so, however, would bring the Brothers into conflict with an emboldened and extremely powerful military that managed to establish itself as the hegemonic fraction of capital in Egypt.

6 | "Strike like an Egyptian"

Workers and the Collapse
of the Authoritarian Bargain

The Corporatist Compromise and the Authoritarian State

Since 1952, industrial workers have enjoyed numerous economic rights and benefits that were enshrined in the Constitution of 1956, which also stipulates that the state will guarantee citizens' access to social and health insurance, including pensions and unemployment benefits.[1] These rights form the basis of the current social insurance system, which was first introduced in the 1950s with the introduction social assistance (1950), social insurance (1955) and employment injury, sickness, and disability benefits (1959). In 1962, employers' contributions to social insurance schemes were increased from 7 percent to 17 percent (King, 2009, p. 57). These programs were reformed and consolidated in the Social Insurance law of 1975 and subsequently expanded in the Universal Social Security Scheme of 1980. Despite the liberalizing tendencies of Sadat, Nasserist social policy remained largely intact due to the increasing prospects of food insecurity and its negative impact on working class Egyptians (Bayat, 2006).

In terms of the rights of workers, the constitution guarantees public sector workers 50 percent of the seats on the boards of directors of state-owned enterprises and 25 percent of their profits. Small farmers and small craftsmen are guaranteed 80 percent of the membership on the boards of directors of the agricultural and industrial cooperatives. The constitution also commits the state to the principle of full employment, a fair distribution of income and the reduction of economic inequality. Upon assuming office after the 1952 coup, the Free Officers' regime doubled the minimum wage, increased the rate of disability pay and introduced paid sick leave. Workers also benefited from the implementation of employment protection legislation. Attempts to lay-off

---

[1] Article 17: "The State shall guarantee social and health insurance services. All citizens shall have the right to pensions in cases of incapacity, unemployment, and old age in accordance with the law."

workers required employers to take into account the seniority, age, and family responsibilities of the workers facing dismissal. Permission to implement collective dismissals required approval by relevant administrative authorities, and workers facing dismissal were entitled to severance pay – up to 27 months for workers with 20 or more years of employment – and judicial redress in the event of unfair dismissals.

However, Egyptian workers paid a heavy price for these goods and protections in the end. As Bianchi points out, approaches to labour legislation and trade union representation indicate "a steady shift by successive governments from pluralism to corporatism as the preferred strategy for molding and coopting the emerging associations of the working class" (Bianchi, 1986, p. 430). This shift towards corporatism would not have been a problem were not for the growing authoritarian tendencies of the post-revolutionary state. The Free Officers' regime sought to simultaneously strengthen trade union organizations and expand trade union membership while developing mechanisms of state control over that same trade union movement. While the processes of unionization were easier than under the previous *Wafd* government, and while unionization extended to agricultural workers, the new regime also required the creation of only one national peak trade union association that would possess a monopoly of trade union representation over the entire labour movement. In 1957, Egyptian unions were organized into the Egyptian Trade Union Federation (ETUF), which transformed into a highly centralized, hierarchical structure of corporatist interest representation by 1964.[2] While the prohibitions on union activity in force under the *Wafd* were abolished under Nasser, new prohibitions were introduced, such as bans on strikes and work stoppages, and on inciting class antagonisms. In this sense, the ETUF simultaneously became the official representative of the labour movement and the main vehicle by which to control it. According to Beinin (2009a, p. 449), the ETUF has approved of only two strikes since 1957. Ayubi refers to this as a form of populist corporatism, which represents "a way of mobilising the lower classes and bringing them into politics [and the modernization process] more or less for the first time," as opposed to fascist forms of corporatism, which represent "attempts by middle classes, who feel threatened by working class

---

[2] For the complex history of the formation of the ETUF, see Beinin and Lockman (1987), chapter 13.

movements, to push their social inferiors back out of the political arena" (Ayubi, 1992, p. 98). Such conservatism regarding working-class challenges to employers and the propertied classes would increasingly come into conflict with the growth of working-class militancy in the context of the neoliberal transformation of the Egyptian economy beginning in the 1990s.

As the official trade unions were integrated into the one-party state system, they became organizational vehicles "to ensure that workers fulfilled their responsibilities" (Posusney, 1997, p. 73).[3] As Nasser once famously said in response to the ETUF president's criticism of the absence of any reference to the trade unions in the 1957 constitution, "The workers don't demand. We give" (Beinin, 2016a, p. 18). For its part, the state bestowed upon the trade union leadership "highly attractive and unprecedented legal guarantees concerning job security, promotions, and retirement benefits," resulting in "the selective cooptation of a collaborative, powerful, and handsomely rewarded segment of the non-communist union leadership" (Bianchi, 1986, p. 432).[4]

Under Sadat, the ETUF became even more centralized and undemocratic. In 1976, Sadat introduced the Trade Union Law, which "sanctified the hierarchical structure of the union movement, specifying explicitly that it have a pyramid form where the lower bodies were subordinate to the higher ones" (Posusney, 1997, p. 105).[5] Indirect elections were introduced to ensure the self-reproduction of the collaborationist leadership. Throughout the 1970s and 1980s, ETUF leaders were increasingly represented in the leadership structures of the National Democratic Party and ETUF presidents began to be appointed to various ministries – including the Ministry of Labour and the Ministry of Manpower and Professional Training (Paczynska, 2006, p. 53). They were also appointed to numerous economic planning councils, public sector management boards, parliamentary committees and ministerial consultative bodies.

While the evolution of the ETUF clearly stifled the ability of Egyptian workers to form independent unions that could more effectively challenge the regime, the "corporatization of the Egyptian labor

[3] By 2007, Egypt had a trade union density rate of 27.5% (ILO, 2018d). The bulk of this centres on the public sector.
[4] This includes appointing the ETUF president as the Minister of Labour.
[5] For different interpretations of what the 1976 law meant for the relationship between the unions and the state, see Posusney (1997) and (1986).

movement has not been a simple matter of subordinating the working class to the authoritarian order" (Bianchi, 1986, p. 434). Rather, Bianchi argues that this corporatist arrangement "provided union leaders with new means for defending workers' interests and, ironically, for limiting the decisional autonomy of the authoritarian regime in certain critical issues" (Bianchi, 1986). Over the course of the 1970s and 1980s, the ETUF obtained an increasing number of concessions from the state in return for support for the ruling party's policies. One of the outcomes of these concessions was the increasing financial autonomy of the ETUF from the state, such that the "corporatist institutions established by President Nasser in the 1960s were no longer effective in ensuring that the regime's policy preferences would not be challenged by labor" (Paczynska, 2006, p. 54). Indeed, Beinin (2001, p. 159) argues that Mubarak's half-hearted implementation of neoliberal reforms in the latter half of the 1980s was a result of resistance from the rank-and-file within the trade unions. This particular relationship between the authoritarian state and the trade unions – and the types of social and employment protection regimes implemented over the course of the post-war period – formed the basis of the corporatist compromise that legitimized the authoritarian state in the eyes of Egyptian workers (King, 2009).

Labour Market Dualism and Informality in the Egyptian Labour Market

Liberal critics of Egypt's corporatist system of industrial relations attribute to it the peculiar problems of the Egyptian labour market. Egypt's labour market is characterized by a high degree of dualism between the public and private sectors. This dualism assumes the form of a highly protected, unionized public sector and a highly precarious, private sector increasingly characterized by informal labour untouched by labour market regulations. On the one hand, unionized public sector workers enjoyed employment protection, pensions, and higher wages and received health coverage.[6] On the other hand, private sector workers were non-unionized, subject to a greater degree of employer discretion in the labour process and had less social protection.

---

[6] Public sector wages average 48 percent higher than private sector wages (Beinin, 2016a, p. 38).

For example, Assaad (2014, p. 2) argues that this dualism is a legacy of the 1960s "authoritarian bargain" between "authoritarian regimes and politically significant groups to provide them with well-compensated jobs in the bureaucracy and the security forces, ... privileges such as access to subsidized commodities, housing and services, in exchange for political quiescence, if not loyalty." On the one hand, this creates a large class of labour market insiders with privileged jobs and de-commodified benefits who are difficult to dismiss. This creates disincentives for hiring by managers and employers: in times of increasing labour demand, managers rely on exploiting their existing labour supply due to the inability to shed their excess labour when the demand for labour declines. As a result, informal labour markets expand to absorb the surplus labour. Because public sector employment provides higher wages and more secure jobs, labour market entrants come to prefer public sector jobs over work in the formal private sector, which remains "anemic and small." This further weakens the private sector and, in the context of a ruling class fearful of social unrest, results in the further expansion of public sector employment.

On top of this dualism between the public and private sector labour markets, the private sector is further segmented between a formal sector and an informal sector. Portes and Böröcz define the informal sector to include "all productive and distributive income earning activities which take place outside the scope of public regulation on the macrosocietal level" (Portes & Böröcz, 1988, p. 17). This growth of *informality* is a corollary of the undynamic nature of formal private sector activity, which is – so the argument goes – a result of the public sector driven growth at the heart of the authoritarian bargain. In contrast with the formal sector, the informal sector is characterized by "a general instability of employment, an avoidance of most labour laws, and a tendency to remain outside normal capitalist rules of contract, licensing and taxation" (Munck, 2002, p. 113). It is also characterized by the dominance of low-waged, labour-intensive forms of production.

Informality "contributes to the long-term survival of a particular regime of accumulation" by reducing the average cost of social labour by circumventing labour protection legislation (Portes & Böröcz, 1988, p. 25). Portes and Böröcz also point out that informal labour does not benefit from the existence of systems of social protection, including healthcare, pensions and unemployment benefits; rather, "the informal working class ... subsidizes business by partially absorbing the costs of the reproduction of labor" (1988, p. 22). To put it another way, informality "does not provide the same occupational safety and medical care 'umbrella' [i.e., social protection] for its participants as does its formal counterpart" (Portes & Böröcz, 1988). This is the case in Egypt. Working in "contracted," or formal employment determines whether a worker receives social protection benefits or not. According to Wahba and Assaad (2015, p. 6), "[a]lmost 92% of contracted workers have social security coverage, compared to less than 9% among non-contracted workers." However, these rights to social and employment protection – whether constitutional or statutory – are highly contingent upon trade union membership, which itself is predominantly located in the public sector. Non-unionized private sector workers have never enjoyed access to these protections. In the private sector, employment protection was often circumvented by informal practices that reflect the power of employers over their employees. For example, workers in newly privatized industries are often forced by their employers to sign an undated resignation letter at the time of employment, granting the employer the ability to arbitrarily dismiss the worker at will, even though a formal contract has been signed. This also allows them to avoid paying the dismissed workers severance pay, which may often be costly in a labour market characterized by high levels of employment protection. Other practices included transferring the worker to another plant, often hundreds of kilometres away. In the context of an increasing dearth of affordable housing in Egypt, this often represents an unfeasible alternative to dismissal by the worker. In many of these cases, workers simply resigned (Paczynska, 2006, p. 59).

The authoritarian bargain of privileged public sector employment puts excessive financial demands on the state. To pre-empt the outbreak of industrial unrest, the regime dispenses numerous public sector wage increases, annual bonuses and cost of living increases – often to reproduce its paternalistic control over workers – that tend to inflate the state's public-sector wage bill. As a result, fiscal crises pose specific problems for the states in the Arab world. As the rents required to sustain this arrangement between the state and public sector workers begin to decline, authoritarian regimes face pressure from labour market insiders (i.e., public sector workers) to preserve their privileges and maintain their employment protection and subsidized goods at the expense of labour market outsiders. The concessions made by regimes to protect these labour market insiders is said to further exacerbate the growth of informality. In the context of neoliberal restructuring, the regime is under greater pressure to reduce deficits which preclude its ability to dispense with these "giveaways."

Proponents of economic liberalization associated Egypt's employment and growth problems with the protections imposed on the labour market and argued that liberal reforms would resolve these interrelated crises. Employment protection, it was argued, provides disincentives for employers to hire more workers due to the costs of dismissals, resulting in the intensification of work among the existing labour force and the forcing of new entrants to the labour market into the unregulated informal sector. By doing this, employment protection stunts job growth in the formal labour market and encourages the growth of precarious, informal labour. Labour market flexibilization would provide incentives for entrepreneurs to allocate labour in a more efficient manner, thereby creating job growth, reducing unemployment and formalizing informal employment.

Policy proposals from liberal think tanks like the Egyptian Centre for Economic Studies therefore blamed unemployment on labour market rigidities – such as minimum wage legislation, employment protection, working time regulations, overtime pay, trade unions and social security contributions – and the general dominance of the economy by the public sector (Abdelgouad, 2014; Hassan & Kandil, 2011). Not surprisingly, liberal reformers have made numerous proposals for labour market reform that result in the diminution of workers' rights and workers' benefits. The reduction or elimination of social security contributions would give employers an incentive to hire more workers by reducing their non-wage labour costs, thereby reducing unemployment levels and increasing employment.[7] Employers have also proposed restrictions on workers' rights to strike and have proposed reforms to make strikes illegal (Ehab, 2012). The favoured means of attaining these goals – weakening workers' rights and reducing social protection to make it cheaper and easier for employers to hire and fire

---

[7] It is notable that of the 75 firms surveyed in Ehab's study (2012), only 27 percent identified labour market rigidities as a problem, hampering their ability to perform well in the economy.

workers – entailed the privatization of state-owned enterprises, which would also achieve the goal of reducing public spending.

Privatization, Liberalization and the Decline of the Corporatist Compromise

Egypt's implementation of the Economic Reform and Structural Adjustment Programme program of 1991 altered the terrain upon which the post-war corporatist bargain between labour and the state was constructed. The Mubarak regime committed itself to a program of privatization and labour market liberalization. One of the foreseeable consequences of privatization was the elimination of social and employment protection for the workers employed in newly privatized industries due to the fact that social insurance is tied to public sector employment. While the reforms to social security introduced in 1975 extended coverage to all workers in the public and formal private sectors, the "expansion of social protection under the current system was heavily based on growth in government employment and the extension of social protection benefits to public sector employees" (Sieverding & Selwaness, 2012, p. 4). Given the greater incidence of social protection in the public sector, privatization posed a potential threat to the benefits that workers had won during the 1950s, 1960s and 1970s.

Due to the history of the ETUF's opposition to privatization throughout the 1970s and 1980s, the regime had to bargain with the labour movement to gain the latter's acceptance of the reform project. The ETUF initially refused to endorse the government's privatization plan in 1991, fearing that it would threaten the interests of workers. Yet, a change in leadership moved the federation closer to the regime's position. For example, future ETUF president and member of the People's Assembly, Sayyid Rashid, voted in support of the government's privatization law, foreshadowing the union's official endorsement of the bill after its passage. Yet, lower down in the union hierarchy, there was stronger opposition to the privatization drive led by Niyazi 'Abd al-'Asiz, the president of the Electrical, Engineering, and Metal Workers Federation (and one time member of the left-wing Tagammu' party).

Despite having endorsed Law 203, the ETUF was at odds with the regime over its application of the law by the end of 1992 (Posusney,

1997, p. 228). Indeed, although having supported the privatization law, Rashid, now president of the federation, criticized the regime for facilitating mass layoffs, exacerbating social instability and mishandling the Social Development Fund. In 1992, the ETUF leadership condemned privatization and called for the legalization of strikes in the event of public sector layoffs. They also condemned the elimination of subsidies on basic goods and refused – for the first time –its traditional declaration of support for the government. At the same time, however, the leadership did nothing to mobilize the rank-and-file against privatization and liberalization. Rank-and-file workers would indeed push back against the attempts by employers to roll back wages and benefits, or to weaken job security, but they did so without support from the Federation leadership.

In response, the government made numerous concessions, including protection from mass layoffs and the rollback of health and pension cuts, retention of the profit-sharing scheme for workers, and – crucially – guarantees that only a wholesale reform of the Labour Code could undo these protections (Weiss & Wurzel, 1998). In effect, the ETUF was able to ensure that the social and employment protections that public-sector workers had won over the course of the 1960s, 1970s and 1980s would be carried over into the private sector. Having done this, the ETUF finally gave its blessing to the privatization drive in 1994.

The maintenance of the status quo – at least in terms of labour market policies – posed problems for the government's privatization agenda, as such labour market rigidities proved unattractive to foreign capital – and without foreign capital, the privatization agenda would be stillborn. Given that the government could not roll back the social and employment protections the ETUF had managed to safeguard without reforming the Unified Labour Code, the issue of labour reform now had to be put on the agenda, virtually ensuring another confrontation with the trade unions. In 1995, the government attempted to reform the Unified Labour Code to weaken employment protection and impose more stringent conditions on the ability to strike. To get the ETUF on board, the government proposed to extend the terms of office of ETUF officials, enabling them to retain their positions after retirement, and making it more difficult for opposition trade unionists from rising up through the ranks of the confederation. Passage of the legislation, however, became bogged down as the demands of the

ETUF and the Federation of Egyptian Industry were extremely far apart on the issues of the right to strike and employment protection. Repeated attempts by the regime to alter the draft legislation in ways that were more acceptable to the unions failed partly due to the pressure felt by the ETUF leadership from an increasingly militant rank-and-file that was hostile to privatization. At the same time, however, pressure on the government from international lenders and multinationals for labour market reforms was increasing. As this pressure mounted, the regime "offered fewer concessions to rank-and-file protest, and its response to them became more repressive and violent" (Posusney, 1997, p. 230).

The 1990s, then, were characterized by a dualistic dynamic of state-labour relations. At the elite level, the ETUF engaged in negotiations with the regime over the pace and scope of liberalization through the corporatist institutions of interest representation and policy-making that had been established over the course of the 1970s and 1980s. Public statements and backroom negotiations were the favoured strategies of the ETUF. At the grassroots level, rank-and-file workers engaged in direct industrial action to protest the state's reform agenda. While these forms of industrial dispute were not sanctioned by the ETUF leadership, they "nonetheless bolstered the Confederation's negotiating position since its leadership could play on the regime's fear of widespread social unrest" (Paczynska, 2006, p. 57).

However, as unemployment increased and growth declined between 2001 and 2003, the government sought to push its neoliberal agenda more aggressively. The manufacturing sector experienced a significant slump as the growth experienced during the mid-1990s came crashing down in the context of the East Asian crisis of 1997 and the slump in oil prices in 1998 (Figure 2). Exports began their long decline in 1999 as a result. After 4 years of declining manufacturing capacity and stalled reforms, the government sought to increase privatization efforts, albeit with little success (as discussed in Chapter 3).

To accelerate the privatization process, the Labour Code needed to be reformed to create more flexible labour markets, which were believed to be key to attracting foreign investors and reducing unemployment. The reforms would introduce the types of labour market flexibility that were already standard practice in the Special Economic Zones introduced in 2002. For instance, according to the Special Economic Zones Law, investment companies in the zones were

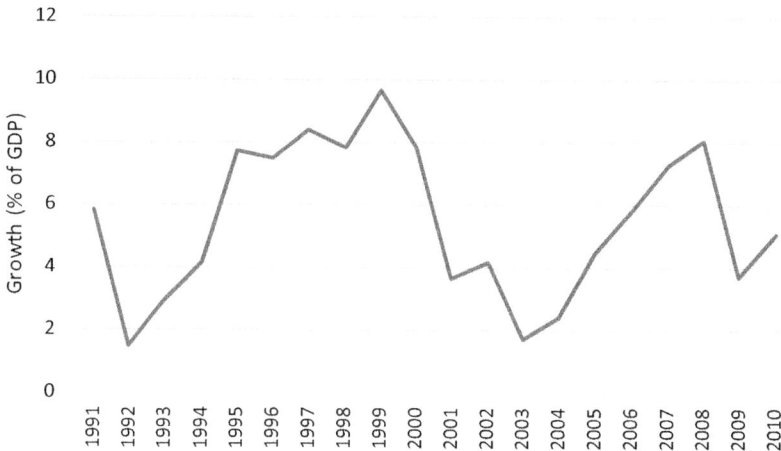

Figure 2 *Manufacturing growth rate, 1991–2010*
Source: World Bank Development Indicators: Manufacturing, Value Added (annual percent growth) (2018)

exempted from "complying with legal clauses relating to labour organizing, depriving workers of the rights set up in local union committees" (Wahba, 2009, p. 20). With this in mind, the Nazif government tabled the Unified Labour Code in 2003 (Law 12/2003).

While the new labour code granted workers the legal right to strike (albeit with specific limitations), it also significantly increased the power of employers. First, it weakened the employment protection that protects workers from arbitrary dismissals. The significant aspect in this regard are the provisions regarding collective dismissals. Employers are now free to lay off workers under certain economic conditions, such as a decline in firm profitability, a recession and so on. No statutory requirement exists compelling employers to consider alternatives to dismissal, such as job transfers or retraining. This new flexibility was justified as a necessary means of enabling firms to adjust their labour force to changing market conditions. Under the new code, employers can also fire workers based on "some custodial sentences, which are listed under Article 129, such as "breach of honor, honesty or public morals" (International Business Publications, 2013, p. 50).

Second, the new code has eliminated any statutory limitations on the successive renewal of fixed-term contracts and on the maximum duration of fixed-term contracts. Employers were particularly keen to normalize fixed-term contracts because workers on such contracts would be excluded from standard benefits and would be paid lower wages. Such reforms would effectively weaken the insider/outsider dualism that came to define Egypt's labour market.

Despite its name, however, the new Unified Labour Code does not apply to the entire Egyptian labour market. The main concession that the ETUF won from the government was the exclusion of "[p]ublic servants of the state agencies, including the local government units and the public authorities" (2003, para. 4) from the new legislation. This includes bureaucrats, state administrators and members of the police services. Contrary to the claims by Wahba and Assaad (2015, p. 5), however, the law does not exempt the entire public sector. Thus, it applies to workers in public sector enterprises, just as it applies to workers in the formal private sector. As a result of this, it reinforced the gap between blue collar public sector workers working in state owned enterprises and white collar workers employed in administration, while closing the gap between blue collar workers in the public and the formal private sector.

In the wake of these labour market reforms, Egyptian manufacturing experienced a period of significant growth starting in 2004, after a 5-year period of decline (Figure 3). Growth in this sector peaked at 8 percent in 2008 before declining in the wake of the global financial crisis of 2007. Much of this growth occurred in small firms of 15 workers or less (OECD, 2007a, p. 240), and included fabricated

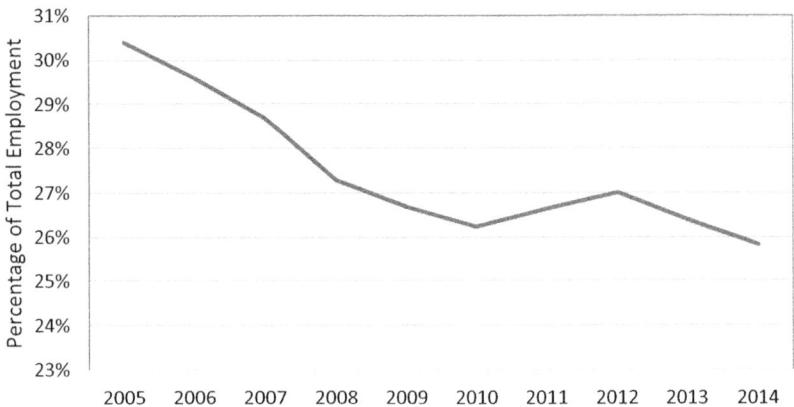

Figure 3 *Public sector employment, 2005–2014*
Source: ILO LFS Public employment by sectors and sub-sectors of national accounts

metal products, printing, transport equipment, paper products, non-metallic industries, chemicals, ready-made garments and food products. Total investment in manufacturing increased 862 percent between 2003 and 2007, with private sector investment registering a remarkable 1,006 percent over the same period (Central Bank of Egypt, 2018). Neoliberals attributed this to the reinvigoration of the liberalization project, including the 2003 passage of the reforms to the Labour Code. However, growth in the manufacturing sector failed to surpass the levels attained in the late 1990s and began to decline as Egypt became caught up in the global financial crisis; and as we will see, this growth was accompanied by rising levels of labour market insecurity, poverty and income inequality.

Increased Employer Power, Unemployment and Informality in the Labour Market

Despite the growth of industry and manufacturing after 2004, the impact of neoliberal reforms on workers and the labour market was not so positive. In contrast with the belief, held by neoliberal reformers, that privatization and labour market flexibility would result in the formalization of the informal sector, thereby bringing down unemployment, it seems the opposite has occurred. While Wahba and Assaad (2016, p. 6) argue that "the evidence suggests that there has been an increase in contracted jobs" in the non-agricultural private sector since the introduction of the 2003 labour market reforms, privatization and labour market reform did nothing to transform Egypt's informal labour market. In fact, layoffs from privatization resulted in the *growth* of the informal sector, making it the fastest growing sector in the 1990s. After a decade of privatization, "half of employees worked with no contract or social security coverage" by the mid-2000s (Paczynska, 2006, p. 56). Radchenko (2014, p. 172) notes that in the period 1998–2006, the share of informal employment increased by 9 percent while public sector employment declined by 8 percent. In a recent assessment of the Egyptian labour market, Assaad and Krafft (2015, p. 47) noted "increases in the share of informality in all firm sizes in 2012 as compared to 2006." Wahba and Assaad (2015) have also noted that under-employment – referring to the generalization of precarious labour – has increased substantially. According to the International Labor Organization (ILO) labour force survey data, the percentage of informal employment in Egypt has increased from 55.8 percent in 2008 to 58.7 percent in 2011, with the percentage increasing to 62 percent in 2016 (ILO, 2018b).[8] In the non-agricultural sector, the number of informal workers has risen from 38.3 percent in 2008 to 50.6 percent in 2016 (ILO, 2018a).

In fact, privatization and labour market flexibility has imported aspects of informality – such as increased precarity – into the formal labour market that renders the concept of informality increasingly problematic. While neoliberals like De Soto (2001) assumed that widespread informality in the Global South would be formalized in ways resembling the labour markets of the West, the obverse seems to be occurring. As Breman and van der Linden (2014, p. 920) argue, "the 'Rest' [meaning the Global South] is not now becoming like the 'West', but the other way round." What they mean by this is that the formalized labour contract of the advanced capitalist West was not the natural outgrowth of capitalist development, but rather the product of contingent historical developments like the rise of free trade unions, and perhaps even linked to the development of wage-led growth models like Fordism. The growth of precarious employment in these countries is bringing the labour markets of the West closer to the labour markets of the South, rather than the other way around.

The result is that debates on informality in the Global South are limited regarding the extent to which they adequately depict insecurity in the labour market. While informality refers to insecure forms of employment that exist outside of the formal labour market, atypical or precarious forms of employment – characterized by a greater degree of flexibility in favour of the employer – exist within the formal labour market (Standing, 2011). Thus, the growth of a formal labour market at the expense of the informal labour market may downplay the extent to which the growth of precarious employment coincides with growth of the formal labour market. Workers in the formal labour market are increasingly experiencing the "destabilization of the stable," in the sense that "precariousness now reaches into previously stable zones of employment" (Castel, 2003, p. 387). The example of "zero-hour contracts" in the UK serves as a case in point. Under zero-hour contracts, workers *contractually* consent to a level of precarity reminiscent

---

[8] The Central Agency for Public Mobilization and Statistics estimates the total percentage of informal workers at 40 percent in 2010.

of the informal sector. Workers on zero-hour contracts must be available for work despite having no guarantee of a minimum number of hours of employment. In this sense, Wahba's and Assaad's claims that formal employment increased after the implementation of the labour reforms of 2003 may be perfectly compatible with the findings that such formal employment was also increasingly precarious.

Privatization and labour market liberalization, therefore, has resulted in a rise in labour market insecurity and precariousness, regardless of the level of formal employment in the labour market. First, privatization and labour market liberalization weakened the types of employment protection and social protection that workers had gained throughout the post-war period. As mentioned, reforms to the Egyptian labour market increased flexibility by making it easier for employers to hire and fire workers and by increasing the growth of temporary employment. As a result, current levels of social insurance coverage have declined in conjunction with the decline in public sector employment. Health insurance coverage has also declined. Data remains incomplete, but by 2008, only 51 percent of the population had health coverage.[9] In rural areas, the coverage rate dropped to just under 30 percent (ILOSTAT, 2018b). More important, levels of social insurance coverage have also declined among public sector workers as a result of the growth of temporary employment contracts. Between 1998 and 2012, social insurance coverage for public sector workers declined from 97 percent to 93 percent, while the coverage for private sector workers remained unchanged at 24 percent. This contradicts Wahba's and Assaad's (2015, p. 6) claim that social insurance coverage has increased as a result of the increase in contracted employment since 2003, since the "acquisition of a job contract not only implies job security but also other important benefits." Not only has coverage among public sector workers declined, the huge gap between those working in the public sector and those working in the private sector has not been reduced as a result of privatization despite the claims that increased labour market flexibility has resulted in an increase in formal employment. In fact, the biggest decline in social insurance coverage occurred for the non-waged workforce – those who are self-employed – with a drop from 29.6 percent in 1998 to 14 percent in 2012 (Roushdy &

---

[9] There are data only for 2008, making it difficult to assess the trajectory of health coverage.

Selwaness, 2014, p. 2). Such claims understate the extent to which precarity has become formalized in neoliberal labour markets. New entrants to the labour market have an even more difficult time as they struggle to find work that has any coverage whatsoever.

Second, average real wages have deteriorated in the context of liberalization. By the end of the 1990s, the average real wage declined to 68 percent of its 1985–1986 value (Radwan, 2002, p. 12). While real wages did register some growth – 1.7% per year – between 2000 and 2005 (and a 6 percent increase in 2006), they began to decline again in 2007 (ILO, 2010). While nominal wages increased significantly from 2008 to 2010, they barely kept up with inflation: while average nominal wages grew by an annual average of 14 percent, inflation rose by an annual average of 13.8 percent during this period (CAPMAS, 2018b; World Bank, 2018k). Partly as a result, real average monthly incomes declined by an annual average of 9.6 percent between 2006 and 2009 (ILO, 2010). At the lower end of the wage scale, the statutory minimum wage remained unchanged at £E35 from the early 1980s until 2010, failing to keep up with the significant spikes in inflation over this period. Indeed, inflationary trends have resulted in a generalized decline in real wages and has been identified as one of the primary drivers of poverty in Egypt (Bargawi & McKinley, 2010).

Third, the impact of liberalization on employment has also been unimpressive. While unemployment dropped in the late 1990s, it rose steadily during the first half of the 2000s, reaching 11.2 percent in 2005 (Figure 4). Langot and Yassine (2015) argue that the 2003 reforms have contributed to an "increase in the levels of the Egyptian unemployment rate." The reform's impact on Egypt's *employment* rate has also been unimpressive. While the employment rate rose to 47 percent in 2007, it dropped back down to 45.1 percent in 2010 (CAPMAS, 2018a). The subsequent drop in unemployment to 9 percent in 2010 was quickly offset by the outbreak of the uprisings of 2011, when unemployment shot back up to 12 percent. The particularly troubling feature of the Egyptian labour market is the persistently high levels of unemployment among the youth. As successive neoliberal governments scaled back on public sector employment (Figure 5) and ended the programs of guaranteed employment for university graduates, youth unemployment began to increase significantly over the first half of the 2000s, demonstrating an upward trend over the period in question (Figure 5 and Figure 6). By 2005 it had reached 32.5

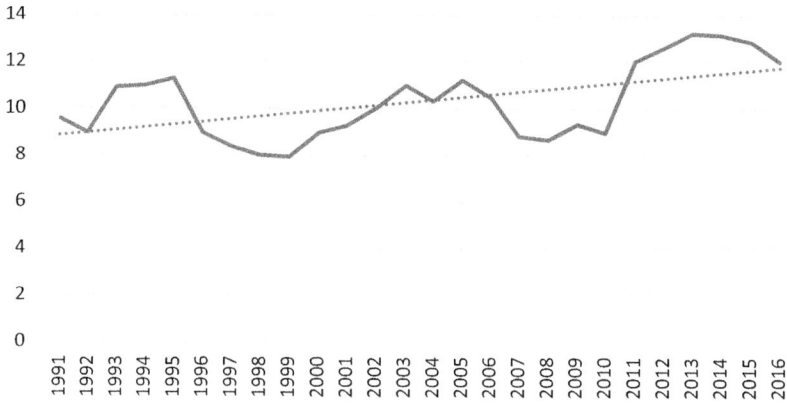

Figure 4 *Unemployment, total (percent of total labour force) (modelled ILO estimate)*
Source: ILOSTAT (2018e)

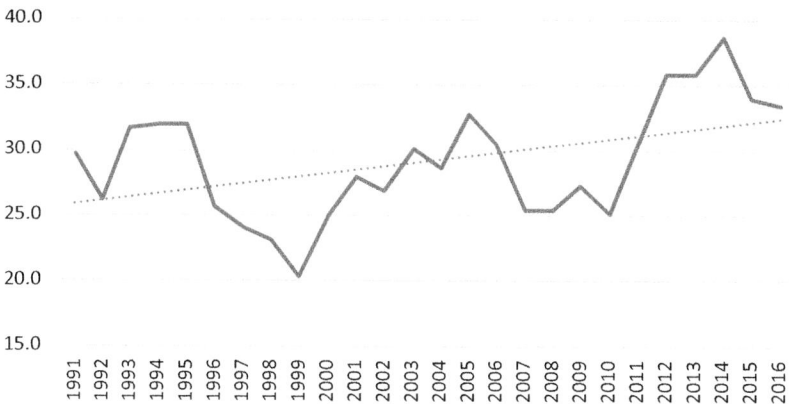

Figure 5 *Unemployment, youth total (percent of total labour force ages 15–24)*
Source: ILOSTAT (ILOSTAT, 2018e)

percent (World Bank, 2018u).[10] Perhaps more significant is the fact that the number of young Egyptians (ages 15–24) not in employment, education or training rose from 29.7 percent in 2008 to 33.1 percent in 2010 (ILOSTAT, 2018d).

[10] Some estimates suggest that unemployment among 15- to 29-year-olds is as high as 60 percent (Barsoum, 2015).

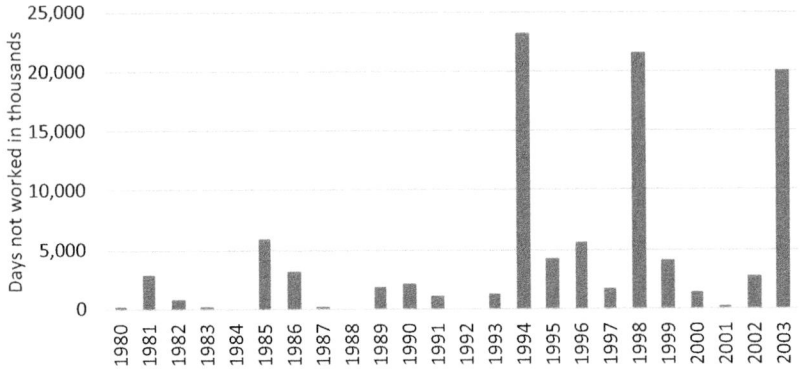

Figure 6 *Days not worked due to strikes and lockouts by economic activity*
Source: ILOSTAT (2018a)

These negative labour market outcomes have had an impact on poverty and inequality in Egypt. However, the question of income inequality remains rather contentious. World Bank data suggests that income inequality remained relatively static between 1991 and 2010. Measured in terms of the Gini coefficient, Egypt entered the 1990s with an inequality of 0.320 and ended the decade at 0.328. By 2010, inequality had declined to 0.315 (World Bank, 2018g). Kheir-El-Din and Heba El-Laithy (2006) argue that income inequality actually declined from 0.446 in 1991 to 0.320 in 2005, suggesting a much greater degree of declining inequality than that indicated by the World Bank. Indeed, the data collected by the World Income Inequality Database indicates just how conflicting the data on income inequality in Egypt is (UNU-WIDER, 2017). However, recent studies have emphasized the difficulties faced in gathering the income data needed to record levels of income inequality and have suggested that World Bank estimates have consistently downplayed income inequality in Egypt and, once corrected, stands closer to 0.47 for 2008 (Van der Weide, 2016).

Data on income shares is also rather ambiguous for the same reasons. According to the World Bank, the income-share of the top 10 percent of income earners increased from 26.7 percent in 1990 to 28.3 percent in 1999. By 2010, however, the top 10 percent of income earners dropped down to 27.3 percent. At the other end of the income spectrum, the shares of the bottom 10 percent of income earners remained unchanged right up to 2010 (indeed, it has remained unchanged right up to 2015) (World Bank, 2018j). However, these income shares may not reflect the true extent of growing income inequality in Egypt for some of the reasons discussed above. On top of this, the top ten percentile often masks a growing disparity among the top income earners. In Egypt, the growth of multi-millionaires has occurred within the top 0.04 percent of income earners (Ahram Online, 2013).

While the trajectory of income inequality may be debatable, the data on wealth inequality paints a much starker picture of the impacts of neoliberalism. Wealth inequality incorporates the distribution of property in any measurement of inequality. By these measures, the levels of wealth inequality have grown significantly, as an increasing amount of landed property, urban property, and capital that has been accumulated by the wealthy. Measured in terms of the Gini coefficient, Egypt's wealth inequality stood at 67.8 percent in 2010. By 2017, it had risen to an astonishing 91.7 percent (Credit Suisse, 2010, p. 86, 2017, p. 113). Thus, even if we take the most generous estimates of Egypt's income inequality, when wealth inequality is taken into account, Egypt becomes one of the most unequal societies in the world (Diab, 2016a).

There is also clear evidence that poverty rates have increased in the context of liberalization. Between 1999 and 2010, Egypt's poverty headcount ratio increased from 16.7 percent of the population to 25.2 percent (World Bank, 2018q).[11] However, this measurement is based on the lower, or absolute, poverty line; measurements based on the upper poverty line takes the percentage of Egyptians living in poverty up to 42 percent in 1999 (El-Laithy, Lokshin, & Banerji, 2003). Based on these latter measurements, Paczynska argues that by the early 2000s, "half of the population was living below the poverty line and income disparities grew" (Paczynska, 2006, p. 56).

Far from resulting in an upsurge of employment, the Egyptian labour market has remained plagued by high levels of unemployment and growing precarity as the informal sector has grown to absorb the surplus labour created by privatization. In this sense, the process of privatization – and its corollary of labour market flexibilization – resembles a form of capital accumulation by dispossession discussed in Chapter 3. The privatization of state-owned enterprises – as a means

---

[11] The urban poverty headcount increased from 9.3 in 2000 to 15.3 in 2010 (World Bank, 2018v).

of transferring public assets to the private sector – only makes sense if the rights and benefits granted to workers in previous periods are eliminated. In this sense, the dispossession refers to the act of being dispossessed not of one's property, but rather of one's socioeconomic rights – the rights that form the basis of the post-war social contract in Egyptian society. In light of the negative impact liberalization has had on Egyptian workers – in both the unionized public sector and the informal private sector – it is not surprising that the intensification of privatization and labour market reforms have eroded this social contract and coincided with the explosion of labour unrest.

The Rise of Worker Protest

Given the integration of the labour movement into the authoritarian corporatist structures of the Egyptian state discussed above, strike activity has been relatively rare in Egyptian industrial relations. Periodic strikes would break out here and there, usually without the support of the ETUF. For example, in the early to mid-1970s, in the context of Sadat's *infitah* program, a wave of strikes rocked Egypt. Between 1972 and 1976, just under 300,000 days were lost in 573 strikes involving 70,000 workers (ILOSTAT, 2018c). In the aftermath of the strikes of the mid-70s and the bread riots of 1977, a "chilly and repressive climate descended upon Egypt" (Beinin, 2001, p. 157). The Sadat regime implemented Law 3 of 1977 penalizing striking workers with imprisonment and hard labour.

In the early years of Mubarak's rule, labour unrest subsided once again. As mentioned in Chapter 3, the first few years of Mubarak's regime resulted in the easing up of state repression. In the sphere of labour relations, worker protest remained at a low. Between 1980 and 1993, just over 19,000 days were lost to strikes and lockouts, and between 1980 and 1997, records indicate that only 27,000 workers had engaged in strike activity (Figure 6). However, industrial unrest began to erupt in the mid-80s, particularly in response to legislation doubling workers' contributions to health and pension programs. Beinin (2016a, p. 44) estimates that an average of 33 strikes occurred per year between 1986 and 1993. Strikes broke out in mid-decade at the Misr Spinning and Weaving Company in opposition to these reforms. In late 1985, worker action in Kafr al-Dawwar turned violent, including damage to property and infrastructure, culminating in a massive security crackdown resulting in the deaths of three protesting workers at the hands of security forces. In early 1986, close to 40,000 textile workers in Shubra al-Khayma and Ghazl al-Mahalla went on strike, with the support of the Workers' Defence Committee, an organization that had broken away from the Tagammu'. In 1989, workers at the Iron and Steel Company went on strike for higher wages, occupying the factory on the second day of the strike. The occupation met with violent repression by security forces, resulting in the death of one worker, the wounding of dozens and the arrest of hundreds. As Alexander and Bassiouny note, the "ferocity of the state's response to the Iron and Steel Company strike can be seen as reflecting a desire to forcibly contain dynamics of collective action which had begun to spawn processes of reciprocal action between economic and political struggles perceived as deeply threatening to the existing political order" (2014, p. 110).

Confrontations between workers and the regime intensified after the implementation of Economic Reform and Structural Adjustment Programme reforms beginning in 1991. Indeed, after 1994, strike activity began to escalate. Between 1994 and 2003 – the last year for which the ILO has data – more than 84,000 days were lost to strikes and lockouts (Figure 6). The main confrontation during this period occurred at the Misr Spinning and Weaving Company at Kafr al-Dawwar in October 1994. The strike was broken after security forces stormed the plant, killing four members of the strikers' families. In 1998 alone, approximately 12,000 workers went on strike and engaged in 80 protests (ILOSTAT, 2018f).

This upsurge in worker militancy coincided with the attempts by the regime to privatize state-owned enterprises in line with its agreement with the International Monetary Fund under successive governments throughout the 1990s. In response, veteran labour activists formed the Centre for Trade Union and Workers Services in 1999. The Centre for Trade Union and Workers Services was an independent organization that Beinin (2016a, pp. 47–48) refers to as "Egypt's leading labor-oriented NGO [nongovernmental organization] for the next twenty years." The growth of labour organizations like the Centre for Trade Union and Workers Services was a response to the ETUF's close relationship to the regime and the propensity of the leftist political opposition to align with the regime in the face of the growing strength of the Islamist opposition.

Over the course of the 2000s, as the effects of liberalization and privatization began to be felt, workers increasingly engaged in sit-ins, strikes and protests against their employers, demanding better representation in their workplaces and demanding unpaid back wages. A new wave of strikes and protests broke out in 2004, the same year that the Egyptian state stopped publishing official data on strike activity and the same year that Egypt's most neoliberal government (under Nazif) took power.[12] Workers protested the breaking of pre-existing contracts and agreements by new, private owners; the failure of public sector enterprises to pay workers their share of the profits, as required by law; low wages; and non-payment of overdue bonuses and wage supplements, and the prospect of layoffs resulting from privatization.

From 2004 to 2006, there were well over 700 labour actions, and between 550 and 614 reported strikes and labour protests in 2007 alone (Abdalla, 2012, p. 2; Farah, 2009, p. 46; Rutherford, 2008, p. 227). The peak year before the uprisings in Tahrir square was 2009, with 700 strikes and labour protests (Abdalla, 2012, p. 2). Between 2004 and 2008, approximately 1,900 strikes took place and an estimated 1.7 million workers were involved (Beinin, 2016a, p. 66; Lee & Weinthal, 2011). Beinin (2009a, p. 449) claims that between 1998 and 2008, approximately 2 million workers participated in 2,623 factory occupations, demonstrations and protests. This growth of a militant workers movement "constitutes the largest and most sustained social movement in Egypt since the campaign to oust the British occupiers following the end of World War II" (Beinin, 2009a, p. 449).

There are a number of discernible trends to the rise of worker protest during this period. First, the strikes began to incorporate political demands into the traditional economic grievances expressed by workers. As Abdalla (2016, p. 203) points out, workers were aware of the "unwritten rules" of the Mubarak regime: that is, that economic grievances, detached from broader political demands, will be met (often in a one-off, ad hoc fashion), while political grievances will be met with repression. By integrating political and economic demands, workers crossed the "red line" of regime tolerance, inviting sporadic

---

[12] More than a quarter of the public and private sector strikes that broke out between 1998 and 2004 occurred in 2004, the year when the Nazif government accelerated the pace of the privatization of public sector enterprises (Beinin, 2009b, p. 77). In 2004 the number of protests had reached 267 (Paczynska, 2006, p. 63).

instances of state repression. At the same time, however, the regime appeared more reluctant to respond with brute force, considering such moves may panic foreign investors. Second, the strikes increasingly involved private sector workers as well as public sector workers. Some of this was the result of the increasing number of privatized factories, but it also included original private sector firms, including those established in the numerous Free Economic Zones created in the 1990s. This blurring of the traditional lines between public and private sector workers was the result of labour market liberalization, through which public and private sector workers began experiencing similar forms of workplace exploitation. Third, the strikes included a growing number of women workers, often in leadership roles. Finally, the strikes also laid the foundation for the nascent growth of an independent trade union movement outside of the organizational structures of the ETUF.

In 2006, workers at the Misr Spinning and Weaving factory in Mahalla al-Kubra went on strike when the management of the company refused to pay workers a profit-sharing bonus decreed by the government. The strike was initiated when 3,000 female garment workers left their stations and challenged the men to join them. The General Union of Textile Workers and the ETUF both opposed the strike. Unlike strikes in the 1990s, the state security forces refrained from employing violent repression against the workers – many of whom were women. As Abdalla (2012, p. 2) notes, "since 2005 the regime had mostly reacted to workers' protests with a mixture of indifference, toleration, and concessions." Also, unlike the strikes of the 1990s, this strike lasted more than the usual 24 hours and involved a cessation of production, foreshadowing the prolonged and more disruptive industrial actions that were to come over the next few years. The strike was successful in that workers were offered bonuses equal to 45 days of their work, assurances from management that the factory would not be privatized and promises that 10 percent of the profits would be distributed to the workers in the event that the firm earned at least E£60 million in profit.

The strikes in Mahalla had a demonstration effect among the other textile factories along the Delta over the next 2 years. Up to 30,000 workers in ten different textile mills engaged in strikes, protests and other forms of collective action over the course of 2006 and 2007. The number of strikes and protests nearly tripled, from 222 in 2006 to 614 in 2007 (Abdalla, 2012, p. 2). In January 2007, the textile workers at Indorama walked off the job. This action was followed the next month by strikes at the Misr Fine Spinning and Industrial Silk companies in Kafr al-Dawwar and the Delta Spinning factories in Zifta and Tanta. This represented a rapid geographic expansion of strike activity outside of traditional sites of industrial unrest (Alexander & Bassiouny, 2014, p. 111)

However, Mahalla al-Kubra remained ground zero of the workers' struggle. In late 2007, the workers at Ghazl-Mahalla went on strike again in response to government's failure to fulfil the promises made at the conclusion of the pervious strike. The 2007 strike would become the turning point in the workers' struggles. Up to 12,000 workers participated in the strike. For the most part, the workers' demands were confined to economic grievances. However, some of the leaders "explicitly framed their struggle as a political contest with national implications" (Beinin, 2016a, p. 78). They called for regime change, expressed their grievances against the ETUF and called for an end to the "colonialism" of the International Monetary Fund and World Bank. Conceptualizing the linkages between economics and politics in this way would ultimately test the regime's patience.

The local strike committee at Ghazl al Mahalla called for a national strike in April 2008 to address the crisis of rising food prices during the food crisis that was sweeping across numerous countries of the Global South. Despite lacking the capacity to organize such a nationwide general strike, security forces occupied the factory and the ETUF executive sanctioned the local union leadership and pressured them to call off the strike. While management made concessions to the workers, prompting the strike committee to abort the strike, tensions in the city persisted, culminating in protests against the rising cost of food. Security forces responded with violence as protesters burned electoral posters of prominent National Democratic Party candidates – including Mubarak. The security forces arrested 331 people – including journalists – killed one and wounded hundreds. The state authorities cancelled council elections in Mahalla al-Kobra and in other parts of the Nile Delta fearing an electoral victory for pro-labour and Muslim Brotherhood sympathizers. However, as Benin (2016a, p. 80) points out, the level of repression employed by the regime in Mahalla al Kubra was "exceptional" and most likely due to "the government's sensitivity about the high profile of Ghazl al-Mahalla and fear that workers there might successfully organize a national protest." Ultimately, this incident of violent state repression "did not affect the overall dynamic of the strike wave" (Alexander & Bassiouny, 2014, p. 112).

The regime's general reluctance to employ systematic violent repression to crush the strikes facilitated their spread to other sectors of the economy. Between 2007 and 2009, strikes spread from the textile and clothing sector to the building, transport, food processing, and oil sectors. According to the Egyptian Workers and Trade Union Watch, strikes and other forms of protest spread to telephone and electrical goods manufacturing, light and heavy engineering, energy, food production, construction and hotels. Miners at the Sinai Manganese mines, dockworkers at the Port Said shipyards, transport workers in Imbada and Mahalla, oil refinery workers in Suez, and poultry workers in Cairo all joined the strike wave in 2007. Cairo Transport workers – drivers, ticket collectors and mechanics – also went on strike, first in 2007 and then in August 2009. The transport workers demanded an end to the Emergency Law, the removal of the National Democratic Party from state institutions, the introduction of a new constitution and a minimum wage. They also withdrew their support from their union committee on grounds that it failed to convey the demands of the workers to the government.

During 2009 alone, there were estimates of close to 700 workers' actions (Abdalla, 2012, p. 2). In May 2009, 400 workers at the recently privatized Tanta Linen, Flax and Oil Company staged a 5-month-long sit-down strike in front of the parliament to protest worsening conditions, late payments and the firing of workers engaged in strikes at the plant over the previous 3 years. The striking workers also called for the renationalization of the firm, which had been sold to a Saudi company in 2005. This represented a significant prolongation of strike action in Egypt.[13] The strike was also important in another sense. As Duboc (2015, p. 232) points out, the staging of the sit-down strike in front of the parliament established "spaces of visibility," which "helped to undermine the foundations of the regime's corporatist ruling bargain."

What is also significant about this new strike-wave is that it incorporated workers in both private and public sectors. As indicated above, public sector workers in state owned enterprises were not exempt from the concessions exacted from the regime that protected public servants

---

[13] It was also the only strike supported by the ETUF.

from the increased flexibility introduced by the 2003 reforms. Increasingly, public sector workers were sharing the same fate as their counterparts in the formal private sector. In October 2004, workers at the Ghazl Qaliub textile company went on strike. In January 2005, workers at the Asmant Tora cement factory engaged in a work stoppage after the firm's privatization. Over the course of 2007, workers at numerous private sector companies in spinning and textiles engaged in strike activity. At Marakem Group factories in Sadat City, 2,700 workers went on strike; at Arab Polvara, 6,000 workers went on strike in the same year. In October 2007, workers at the Needlecraft Egypt garment factory in the Shibin al-Kawm Free zone "illustrates the reach of the protest wave even into parts of the economy which the Egyptian government has attempted to detach most completely from the old model of Nasserist state capitalism through the provision of incentives to foreign investors" (Alexander, 2010, p. 249). Workers at the privately owned Mansura-España garment factory in Talkha staged a 2-month-long strike to protest the rumoured liquidation of the firm. What made this strike particularly exceptional was not just its private sector status, but the prominence of women workers in the strike. By 2009, 37 percent of all collective actions organized by workers occurred in the private sector; by 2010, it had risen to 46 percent (Beinin, 2016a, p. 68).

During this period of intensified class conflict, tensions between rank-and-file workers and the ETUF leadership also increased. Grassroots activists struggled against the leadership of the ETUF in a bid for greater independence. While the extent to which the ETUF was always a "bureaucratic faction in the state apparatus that was detached from and unresponsive to" (Beinin, 2016a, p. 73) its membership is a matter of debate, the fact remains that a growing number of workers increasingly viewed it as such after 2004, thereby eroding its legitimacy.[14] What is less disputable is the fact that it made no concerted effort to

---

[14] Beinin (2009a, 2016a), Alexander and Bassiouny (2014), Duboc (2015), Abdalla (2012) and Weiss and Wurzel (1998) argue that the ETUF is a tool of the authoritarian state, while Bianchi (1986) and Paczynska (2006) argue that the ETUF successfully defended the interests of labour market "insiders," which often brought it into moderate conflict with the regime. The point made here is that the distinction between insiders and outsiders began to break down with the passage of Law 12 of 2003, thereby increasing the distance between the ETUF leadership and the rank-and-file.

organize any of the private sector workers employed in the factories in the Special Enterprise Zones around Cairo.

Labour activists formed the Coordinating Committee for Trade Union and Workers' Rights and Liberties to observe the ETUF elections in 2001. Reforms introduced in 1995 had strengthened the power of the ETUF executive over the local committees by further institutionalizing its executive power. In this case, the 2003 reforms that appeared, on paper, to extend the right to strike were effectively countered by reinforcing the power of the ETUF elites. Lower level committees elected by workers were weakened to insulate pro-regime elites. In this sense, Alexander and Bassiouny (2014, p. 132) argue that, "despite gaining the *theoretical* capacity to act as a trade union through the Labour Law of 2003, the ETUF bureaucracy did not, in fact, utilise any of its power to call strikes or even win gains for its members through negotiations or campaigns over the issues that were mobilising tens of thousands of workers."

The gap between the ETUF leadership and the mobilized rank-and-file increased during the new round of union elections held in 2006. Even by Egyptian standards, the level of fraud was considered extremely high. The purpose was to purge popular, militant trade unionists and prevent the Muslim Brotherhood from making inroads into the unions. In Mahalla, the ETUF leadership intervened in the union elections at the Misr Spinning Factory to remove popular leaders and install "regime sycophants" close to the ETUF leadership (Beinin, 2016a, p. 75). This intervention prompted a campaign by the original elected committee to impeach the ETUF local leadership. Similar cases occurred elsewhere, prompting similar responses by rank-and-file activists. In August 2007, Aisha Abd al-Aziz Abu-Sammada – member of the local ETUF committee – organized a strike at the Hinnawi Tobacco Company in Damanhur and struggled against the ETUF leadership for failing to support the striking workers. As a result of her defiance, she was fired and suspended from the union. While the firm ultimately rehired her in the wake of a legal battle, her suspension from the union remained in force.

The strikes that broke out during the 2000s also formed the basis of an emerging, independent trade union movement. In 2007, local tax collectors formed the Independent General Union of Real Estate Tax Authority Workers – the first independent trade union in Egypt since World War II. Up to 8,000 tax collectors went on strike to protest against wage inequality. In a remarkable turn of events, the Independent General Union of Real Estate Tax Authority Workers won a 325 percent wage increase. By December 2008, the new union had close to 30,000 members. This opened up space for the formation of other independent trade unions, including the formation of an independent union of healthcare technicians in 2009. The collapse of the regime in 2011 would provide workers the opportunity to establish an independent umbrella trade union, the Egyptian Federation of Independent Trade Unions, to compete against the ETUF in the ensuing power vacuum that accompanied the deposition of Mubarak.[15]

Conclusion

Liberalization had a profound effect on the livelihoods of Egyptian workers. After a slow start, the pace of liberalization began to accelerate in the mid-1990s, sparking the beginning of the largest strike-wave since the early 1970s. In response, the regime sought to placate the workers by increasing wages and public sector employment. Beginning in 2004, the government of businessmen reinvigorated the neoliberal project. Between 2004 and 2008, privatizations accelerated significantly and labour market reforms stripped workers of what rights they retained. By 2008, class conflict intensified in industrial towns like Mahalla and Helwan. The number of strikes increased dramatically, and the official trade union movement was unable to contain the discontent against the regime. A new generation of workers, many of whom were radicalized women, would begin to question the legitimacy of the regime and struggle to create an independent union movement. These struggles, while not as visible as the student protests of Tahrir Square in 2010–2011, would ultimately signal the beginning of the end of the Mubarak regime.

---

[15] The EFITU had a membership of 1.4 million belonging to 72 individual unions (Alexander, 2012).

7 | "You Let the Dogs Eat the Peasants"
Peasants, Small Farmers and Accumulation by Dispossession

Agricultural Liberalization

In 1974, Sadat passed Law 69, abolishing the state's custodianship of land, restoring more than 147,000 feddans to previous owners among the large landowners and disempowering pro-tenant agrarian relations dispute committees. That same year, Egypt became the third largest importer of grain, signifying the beginning of a crisis of Egyptian agriculture and a growing state of food insecurity. In 1970, Egypt was producing a $300 million surplus in agricultural goods. By 1977 – the same year as the bread riots – that surplus had turned into an $800 million deficit. By the mid-1980s, Egypt's agricultural trade deficit stood at U.S.$2.5 billion (Bush, 2009, p. 56).

Proponents of agrarian reform argued that the liberalization of the rural economy would increase the productivity of agricultural labour and promote the export competitiveness of the Egyptian economy. The debate regarding the reform of tenancy laws began in 1985. Liberals argued that, by the late 1980s, Egyptian agriculture absorbed 34.5 percent of Egyptian manpower, while contributing only 19.3 percent to Egypt's gross domestic product, which was seen by the Egyptian authorities as a sign of "unproductivity" (National Bank of Egypt, 1990, 1992). Increasingly, state control of pricing and marketing, ownership of cooperatives and agricultural industries, and support of small holdings and traditional communal lands were seen as the main determinants of agricultural stagnation. Initial attempts at agricultural liberalization began with the help of USAID in the early 1980s. The goal was to replicate the U.S. factory farm system of export-oriented agriculture by facilitating capital-intensive investment and liberalizing pricing and marketing. On their own terms, the reforms were somewhat successful. For example, between 1980 and 1990, wheat production increased from 1.7 million tonnes to 4.2 million tonnes, while the yields in wheat production – measured in terms of hectograms per hectare – increased by 67 percent over the same period, signifying a substantial increase in agricultural productivity (FAOSTAT, 2018).

However, the zeal for agricultural reform did not stop there. Reformers sought to extend the reform process to the tenure system. Critics of the tenure system had long claimed that the agrarian reforms of the Nasser period lay at the root of Egypt's agricultural crisis. As discussed in Chapter 2, the Nasserist reforms of the 1950s and 1960s had reduced the concentration of land through its redistribution to peasants and farmers and by securing their rights through rent controls.

After 1991, the voices in favour of liberalization grew louder (Saad, 1999, 2000, 2002). They argued that fixed rents made the tenant-farmer lazy, for "he does not exert any effort to increase his production, since the very least of produce will suffice to pay the rent." Market rents, which were more "reasonable," would force him to "exert an effort to increase his production," which would be "beneficial for society as a whole" (Saad, 2002, p. 109). Nasser, it was argued, had tilted the balance between the tenant and the landlord, to the effect that "the tenant became the owner." Pro-government journalists, notably *Al-Akhbar*'s Jalal al Hammamsi, argued that tenants were raking in exorbitant profits from rising agricultural prices while landlords had become poor peasants. Similarly, the ex-Vice President of the State Council argued that the land reforms of 1952 produced a "feudalism of the tenant," whereby tenants oppressed the landlords (Saad, 2002, p. 108).

Aspiring reformers called on Mubarak "to get rid of those laws," implying that they were imported from Communist countries and contradicted Shari'a law (Saad, 2002, p. 109). To this end, reformers proposed a new law – Law 96 of 1992 – to liberalize the system of tenure that governed the Egyptian countryside since 1952. The reforms contained in the new law removed rent controls, thereby enabling landlords to charge market rents and issue short-term leases. The law also reduced or eliminated input subsidies for small farmers and peasants. These changes were deemed a necessary means of increasing agricultural productivity, employment and value-added (Abdel Khalek, 2001; De Soto, 2000; Nassar & Mansour, 2003).[1]

The government also framed the reforms within the need for greater food security in an increasingly integrated world economy. However,

---

[1] The law did not apply to either state lands or *awqaf* lands.

no tenant or peasant organizations were consulted in the drafting and passage of the agrarian reforms, and no tenants or peasants had representation in the People's Assembly during the debate on the law. The Tagammu' was the only party to support tenant interests in opposition to the reforms, and even it ultimately conceded a lot of ground – including the right of eviction by the landlords – to the ruling National Democratic Party (NDP) in the final draft. While the government declared that new lands would be made available – through land reclamation – for tenants to inhabit after the implementation of the law, this stipulation was "vague and not binding," the process of relocating evicted tenants on reclaimed land was unplanned, and the reclaimed land remained unavailable (Saad, 2002, p. 117).

When the law was finally passed, there was a general sense among tenants and peasants that the government would eventually retreat from the reforms, or that the president would repeal it or, at the very least, extend the deadline of evictions. Evicted tenants expressed shock that the "constitution of the revolution" could be so easily undone. In a statement that foreshadowed the type of land-based conflict that would soon emerge in the Egyptian countryside, the head of the Peasant Union Committee likened the situation to that of "Land for Peace" in Palestine: "If the government wants peace, we have to keep the land" (Saad, 2002, p. 116).

Accumulation by Dispossession and Agrarian Change

The agrarian reforms of the early 1990s had dramatic effects on rural Egypt. They signified the culmination of a decades-long process of reconstituting the power of the old landed class. By engaging in this process of reform, the Mubarak regime engaged in a "long-term policy of repression, preventing rural resistance to economic reform and, under the new law, pursuing what amounts to a national land grab" (Bush, 2011, p. 52). Simply put, the agrarian reforms of the 1990s initiated a process of accumulation by dispossession in the Egyptian countryside, facilitated by increasing levels of state repression, by which a growing number of small tenant farmers and peasants were, to paraphrase Marx, divorced from their means of production and subsistence.

The reforms enabled landlords to terminate the leases of its tenants with the prospect of renewal at higher, market-based rents. Rents per feddan rose on average from E£500 in 1997 to more than E£2,000 (and more than E£3,000 in the Delta) in 2000, and rents of E£4,000 to E£4,500 were not uncommon. In Beni Suef and Monoufiya, Qalyoubiya, Kafr Elwan and Qena, rents had increased from E£300–400 to E£3,000–4,000 per feddan between 1997 and 2008. A real estate boom soon followed, seeing land prices rise at a rate of 148 percent per year between 2007 and January 2011 (Shawkat, 2015). By 2011, annual rental rates per feddan topped E£4,000–6,000 (Ayeb, 2012, p. 82). For instance, Ahmed Abdel Bey from the village of Abu Swailem south of Beni Suef rented 14 qirats of land from an absentee landlord who was also a government employee. Prior to Law 96, Abdel Bey paid a fixed rent. After the implementation of Law 96, landlords gave no viable option to tenants and small holders except to pay higher rents or face evictions. Faced with unaffordable rents, Abdel Bey was evicted and began renting again only in 2002, subjected to higher, market-based rents.[2] In the village of Mattiaa in Qena governorate, "Fatima" – a mother of four – described rising levels of conflict in her village between peasants and landlords. Fatima's husband was a teacher, but they also had a half feddan of land they used to cultivate food for their own consumption. Fatima said that many landlords complained to the police about the large number of land occupations by evicted peasants resisting eviction. Eventually, the police used force to evict the peasants off the land. New, market-based rents rose to E£4,000 per feddan, preventing any of the peasants from renewing their leases. As a result, many of them became day labourers.[3] In 2005 in Qena, the governor conducted a property assessment according to which the value of houses was inflated subsequent to which the governor not only increased the rents, but also demanded back rents (Land Centre for Human Rights [LCHR], 2005a).

In the aftermath of the reforms, there has been a noticeable conversion of arable land away from the cultivation of staple crops such as wheat, rice and lentils and towards the production of cash crops like vegetables for export to European markets. While the acreage devoted to the cultivation of wheat increased by 26 percent between 1997 and 2010, acreage devoted to rice and lentil production has declined by

---

[2] Interview with Abdel Bey, 2007.
[3] The village witnessed an increasing number of feuds over the inheritance of land because land values dramatically increased after 1992 (Joya, 2008).

29 and 64 percent respectively. Conversely, vegetable production has increased by 447 percent over the same period (FAOSTAT, 2018). At the time that rice production has been declining, imports of rice increased by 2,429 percent between 1997 and 2010.[4] At the same time, vegetable exports increased by 418 percent between 1997 and 2010.

While peasants and smallholders had the option of purchasing their plots of Agrarian Reform land, the dramatic increase in the price of land effectively priced most peasants and smallholders out of the market. For example, the Abdel Hadi family of Kafr-elwan owned two feddans of land upon which they grew wheat, corn and clover for the local market. Over the course of a decade, starting in 1997, their rent increased from E£500 per feddan to E£3,000 per feddan per year (Joya, 2008). Those who could afford to purchase their land often had to resort to private forms of financing – at liberalized rates of interest – that resulted in unsustainable degrees of indebtedness that eventually resulted in dispossession.

Those tenants who did have their leases renewed (albeit at higher rents) were often compelled to cultivate cash crops, leaving them increasingly vulnerable to fluctuations in global commodities markets. The most prominent example is the case of cotton growers. On top of being subjected to rising rents, cotton prices bottomed out, declining by approximately 50 percent between 1997 and 2002, continuing the sector's decline (Baffes, 2004, p. v). Between 1997 and 2010, the area of land devoted to cotton production subsequently declined by 57 percent (FAOSTAT, 2018). Having accumulated massive debts as a result, cotton growers in the governorates of Beheira, Qalyoubiya, Fayoum, Minya and Beni Suef were unable to pay their increased rents, resulting in the loss of their land (LCHR, 2005f, 2007h).

The elimination of food subsidies and cheap credit intensified this precarious market dependence. As a condition of the liberalization process, the Principal Bank for Development and Agricultural Credit transformed into a profit-oriented financial institution through the divestment of its developmental role over the course of the 1980s and 1990s.[5] Under Sadat, the credit services of the agricultural cooperatives

---

[4] It increased by 13,463 percent between 1997 and 2011 (FAOSTAT, 2018).
[5] In 1976, Sadat destroyed agricultural cooperatives. He transferred the resources and capital of the cooperatives into the PBDAC. Once he had created this centralized credit agency for agriculture, he encouraged agribusiness to develop and reclaim land across Egypt.

were transferred to the Principal Bank for Development and Agricultural Credit through a new system of village banks, in what is largely considered to be a political move intended to counter the attempts to increase the autonomy of the co-operatives from the state (Sadowski, 1991).[6] The Principal Bank for Development and Agricultural Credit provided loans to individual tenants (bypassing the cooperatives) at subsidized rates and was granted a monopoly over the sale of fertilizers and pesticides. Throughout the 1990s, however, the bank was gradually stripped of its non-banking functions and transformed into a liberalized financial institution. It raised interest rates for agricultural credit by 16 percent, reduced fertilizer supplies and eliminated agricultural subsidies at the same time that rents and land prices were increasing.[7] From 1980 to 1992, the percentage of agricultural loans distributed by the Principal Bank for Development and Agricultural Credit averaged 75 percent of total agricultural loans. By 1995, it had dropped to 23 percent, with commercial banks rounding out the total (LCHR, 2003, p. 13). The Principal Bank for Development and Agricultural Credit also reduced its purchases of crops limiting it to wheat and maize while its storehouses were privatized and their staff either reduced or laid off (Nassar & Mansour, 2003, p. 149). As a result of this liberalization, Egypt's 4,222 agricultural cooperatives were "left unaided to face the liberalized market forces, and compete directly with the private sector both in the supply of farm inputs and in the marketing of crops" (Nassar & Mansour, 2003, p. 149).[8]

As a result, tenants struggled with the general upkeep and improvement of their tenures. Outlays for irrigation, sewage maintenance and other farm equipment became the sole responsibility of the tenant just as the costs of water, fertilizer, seeds and other basic inputs were rising. Government spending on agriculture declined by 17 percent between 2004 and 2010 (FAOSTAT, 2018).[9] The elimination of state credit programs and the decline in public investment in agriculture significantly increased the costs of farming. The cost of fertilizers doubled three times between 1992 and 1994 and the cost of power rose 40 percent in 1999 (LCHR, 2003, p. 13). The privatization of farming

---

[6] Leaders of the cooperatives were not represented on the boards of the village banks.
[7] They were subsequently lowered to 7.5 percent in 1999.
[8] Egypt had 5,999 agricultural cooperatives in 2004 (Mohamed, 2004, p. 57).
[9] FAO data do not go back further than 2004.

infrastructure exacerbated the problem. In 2005, the privatization of water delivery systems in Fayoum and Beheira governorates resulted in reduced access to water by smaller farmers as most of the water was directed towards agribusiness projects.

Rent increases, exacerbated by the proliferation of short-term (12-month), often unwritten and revocable, contracts meant that an increasing number of tenants could not pay their rent (Ibrahim & Ibrahim, 2003, p. 120). The inaccessibility of new loans and the burden of high interest rates on their past loans effectively forced peasants and tenants to abandon their lands. In 2007, in various governorates across the country (Sohag, Minoufiyya, Minya, Qena, Kafr el Sheikh, Alexandria, Qalyoubiya, Giza and Damietta), thousands of farmers were threatened with imprisonment because they were unable to repay their debts to the Principal Bank for Development and Agricultural Credit. By 2010, an estimated 225,000 farmers had been imprisoned due to unpaid debts (Golia, 2011; LCHR, 2007b). Other indebted farmers went in hiding, some in the mountains of Qena.

The Expropriating State

The significance of the agrarian reform, however, goes beyond merely empowering landlords to impose market rents on their tenants, however important this may be. Despite the fact that the law did not sanction the privatization and redistribution of public lands, landlords and corrupt public officials took advantage of the new political climate to "enclose" the various forms of public lands comprising the Egyptian tenurial system, evicting longstanding tenants in the process. Egypt's system of state property was comprised of a variety of different forms of property.[10] Communal forms of property, such as *Wad el Yad* is a form of public land that, if occupied and worked continuously for 15 years (and with no counter-claimant), can become the property of the occupant without the need for a deed to demonstrate ownership. *Waqf* lands were religious lands brought under state ownership during Nasser's time. Finally, Agrarian Reform lands were state land comprised of appropriated private lands as part of Nasser's agrarian

---

[10] The land tenure system in Egypt is the culmination of various laws and decrees rooted in Roman law, Islamic Sharia, Ottoman laws and French laws as well as secular Civil Codes.

reforms in the 1950s and 1960s. As mentioned in Chapter 2, private lands that exceeded the land ceilings established under the Free Officers, along with the lands of the royal family, were nationalized and redistributed to peasants and small farmers. All three forms of property have been the subject of sustained legal attacks by the proponents of capitalist property relations.

Together, these de-commodified forms of tenure formed the basis of a peasant based "moral economy" in rural Egypt. Thompson (1971, p. 79) described the "moral economy of the poor" as being comprised of a "consistent traditional view of social norms and obligations, of the proper economic functions of several parties within the community" that are common in a subsistence based economy that has not yet been subsumed to the "cash-nexus" of capitalism. The subjection of the production and distribution of staple goods like corn and bread to the impersonal forces of the market promoted behaviour that violated the social norms and obligations of this moral economy, sparking direct action – such as bread riots – on the part of the poor. In his work on South East Asian peasants, Scott (1977) demonstrates that the notion of a moral economy of the poor translates into the peasant societies beyond Thompson's European focus, forming the basis of a moral economy of the peasant. In a similar way, the Nasserite agrarian reforms – particularly the security of tenure – formed a cornerstone of the peasant moral economy in Egypt, a moral economy that was increasingly under siege by the liberalizing reforms of the 1990s.

The moral economy exists at odds with the development of capitalism and tends to be "embedded" within pre-capitalist social relations that resist the commodification of land, labour and money. The types of social relations comprising the moral economy resemble the primary organizing principles of pre-capitalist economies identified by Polanyi (1944): reciprocity, redistribution, and perhaps most important, self-sufficiency. Given the embeddedness of this type of agrarian moral economy, it often falls upon the state – acting in conjunction with the dominant propertied class – to "disembed" property from these pre-capitalist social relations through acts of dispossession designed to further commodify the land.

Although nationalized, the titles to these Agrarian Reform lands remained in the hands of their previous owners. Thus, recipients of such redistributed lands lacked the official documentation that served as proof of ownership. Under Sadat, the original owners expropriated under Nasser began reclaiming their rights of ownership to such lands, and this process continued under Mubarak, particularly during the 1990s and 2000s. A similar problem faced tenants working on other forms of state land as well. For example, holders of *Wad el Yad* lands lacked documentation proving their ownership, relying instead on custom and oral history. In the context of neoliberal reforms, the state no longer recognized customary claims to property, making it easier to evict tenants. This process of expropriation and the elimination of customary rights accelerated in the context of neoliberal reform. In some cases, tenants were expropriated and evicted through a process of titling that was set up to formalize customary tenures. In these cases, tenants were encouraged by neoliberal reformers to register their land-holdings with the relevant authorities. Such a process was promoted by the World Bank and Hernando De Soto – who argued that such formalization would "breathe life" into the "dead capital" of the poor (Economist, 2004).

In many other cases, smallholders working on Agrarian Reform lands and other state lands were forcibly evicted by the state in the face of rival claimants bearing pre-1952 property deeds. After 1997, successful claimants did not have to pay compensation to the dispossessed and the pace of dispossession accelerated, particularly after the appointment of Nazif and the renewed surge of neoliberal reform, which aimed to attract large-scale agribusiness to the countryside.[11]

The reassertion of landlord power, and the prioritization of capitalist forms of property rights over customary forms of property became part of a widespread process of peasant dispossession through the institutions of the state. As mentioned in Chapter 3, a crucial part of the process of neoliberalization was the transformation of the Egyptian state from that of a redistributive state to a disciplinary, market-oriented state the primary goal of which is to produce and reproduce the social relations of capitalism through the protection of capitalist forms of private property. The Egyptian state, in this sense, became a primary agent of dispossession. Various state authorities such as the Ministry of *Awqaf* (also known as the Ministry of Endowments

---

[11] Article 33e of Law 96 states: "If the landlord chooses to sell the land before 1996/97, the tenant can choose to buy the land or leave it in return for a compensation by the landlord (equal to forty times the value of land tax, for every agricultural year from 1992 to 1997). Or the tenant can keep the land until 1997."

[MoE]), the Ministry of Housing, the Ministry of Agriculture, the agricultural cooperatives, such as the Agricultural Cooperative Association (ACA) and various governors took advantage of the precarious nature of Agrarian Reform lands by forcing tenants off their land and from their homes.

Dispossession therefore accelerated after 1997 with the aid of state institutions and organizations. At the beginning of 2000, the Ministry of Agriculture stated that it would evict approximately 15,000 farmers from 18,450 feddans of state land because they "had failed to keep up with rental payments" (LCHR, 2002, p. 135). As a result, approximately 100,000 people were now exposed to homelessness. By the time of their dissolution under Sadat in 1976, the boards of the cooperatives were increasingly dominated by rich farmers and landlords. As mentioned above, the credit functions of the co-operatives were transferred to the Principal Bank for Development and Agricultural Credit to grant the state more leverage over the cooperatives. Sadat's new cooperative law, introduced in 1981, brought cooperatives more firmly under the control of the Ministry of Agriculture and provincial governors through the creation of a new cooperative confederation. The new law enabled the regime to appoint the leaders of co-operatives, veto the decisions of the cooperatives' elected councils, supervise their accounts and meetings, and shut down co-operatives by simple administrative order.

This process of centralization would facilitate the cooperatives' transformation into instruments of dispossession in the context of neoliberal reform. Under Nasser, possession cards were issued to small farmers and peasants by the ACA to provide them legal backing for the Agrarian Reform lands and entitle peasants and small farmers to subsidized agricultural inputs provided by the co-ops.[12] In this sense, the corporation played a crucial role in validating and legitimizing peasant clams to Agrarian Reform Lands. Throughout the 1990s and 2000s, however, farmers registered numerous complaints against the cooperatives for not representing their interests.

Between 2004 and 2011, the ACA facilitated the dispossession of small holders by issuing new possession cards to landlords and terminating their traditional support services to tenants (LCHR, 2004b,

---

[12] In Yusef El Seddeq and Ibshwai villages, tenants filed complaints stating that the ACA owes them the value of their capital stock invested in the co-op. Having been evicted from their lands in 1997 and 1998, their possession cards have been cancelled (LCHR, 2004a).

2004d). By issuing new possession cards to landlords, the ACA denied receiving decades of rent from peasants and farmers (LCHR, 2006b). In 2006, the ACA in Edko, Beheira governorate, took over the lands of local smallholders and transferred them to influential individuals with the help of local police and armed thugs, known as *baltagya*. In other words, the ACA directly participated in the expropriation and upward redistribution of land through its authority to issue possession cards. In the same year in Minya, farmers claimed that the elections for the Minya Association for Agrarian Reform were fraudulent. In response, farmers organized a boycott of the association and filed a lawsuit before the administrative judiciary court in Alexandria (LCHR, 2007d).

The MoE also played an important role in evicting tenants. Under Nasser, the MoE served as a trustee for public domain endowment lands. Operating under a centuries old system of public property, the MoE is responsible for looking after public domain lands that cannot be mortgaged or sold. Any revenue received from such lands serves the beneficiaries of the estate. The main goal was to prevent the subdivision of property that would sew conflict among the beneficiaries of the land. After Law 96, the MoE actively engaged in expropriating tenants with the goal of exploiting rising land prices that resulted from the passage of the land reforms.

For example, as early as 1995, the MoE seized and claimed ownership of the homes of the farmers in Izbet Rashwan, Beni Suef. The farmers were arrested and imprisoned on charges of trespassing on the property of the MoE. Although released, the tenants were again arrested on the same charges in 2009 (LCHR, 2009b). In 1997, the MoE brought charges of trespassing against the villagers of Rashwan estate, in Beni Suef governorate, south of Cairo. The Principal Bank for Development and Agricultural Credit claimed that the same villagers were in arrears to the bank and sought their imprisonment. Despite numerous court rulings in their favour, the inhabitants of Rashwan estate were arrested and evicted by police in July 2009 (LCHR, 2009d).

In 1996, in Serso, just outside of Mansoura in Daqahliya governorate, 23 veterans of the Yemen war were evicted from the 44-feddan plot of land that had been given to them as part of the land reforms of the 1960s. Despite having his initial ownership claim denied by the Supreme Administrative Court in 1986, the rival claimant – Abdel Aziz al-Masry, a local businessman and member of the ruling NDP – obtained, under dubious circumstances, a court order validating his claim of ownership from the newly formed local reconciliation committee. Coercive police force was used to evict the tenants. One of the veterans, Ali Mohamed Abdullah, recalled the "humiliation and beatings" doled out to the tenants by security forces. When attempting to submit their documents demonstrating their ownership claims, local officials told them to "bring Abdel Nasser back from the dead" to give them their rights. In 2007, a lower administrative court ruled in favour of the tenants' claims, but the state neglected to enforce the court order. The conflict would intensify in the context of the 2011 uprisings (Esterman, 2015).

The farmers in Ezbet El Hakim, in Beni Suef governorate, were given 2 feddans each back in the 1950s as part of Nasser's agrarian reforms. In 1985, the Agrarian Reform Corporation transferred 51 feddans of these lands to the MoE, for which it received E£30 of rent per feddan from the farmers. In 2006, the MoE raised the rents to E£1,200 and converted to yearly leases to increase the rents on an annual basis (LCHR, 2006a). At the same time, a "judicial agent" made competing claims on these lands and threatened to ruin the farmers' crops if they did not start paying rents to him. Upon receiving the farmers' grievances, the MoE instructed them to ignore the intimidation. In the meantime, the Agrarian Reform Corporation issued an ownership certificate to the judicial agent, who sold the land to new owners who demanded payment of market rents.

In December 2007 in Ezbet Ahmed Rashed, Monofeya, the MoE threatened to evict and imprison 3,000 tenants from their land and homes if they did not pay the high rents demanded of them. Villagers claimed that the MoE provided no documentation confirming its ownership of the land and the houses on the land, and they further claimed that they had ownership that predated the existence of the ministry itself. Similarly, the Agrarian Reform Corporation also demanded payments from the villagers and prohibited housing renovations on pain of imprisonment (LCHR, 2007c). In another case in 2007, local villagers were denied alternative housing because the mayor of Ezbet Mohammed Aweys, Beni Suef confiscated land that was designated for building a new village, leaving the former residents homeless (LCHR, 2007a). During the same year, the governor of Sohag decided to build an airport on land that small farmers had reclaimed and improved back in 1981. While there were vast tracts of desert land for building the airport, the farmers could not comprehend the governor's decision to build the airport on their reclaimed agricultural land and, because the farmers' property rights were not recognized by the state, they were threatened with eviction and dispossession without any compensation (LCHR, 2007g, 2009g).

In West Tahta in 2008, thousands of farmers on 5,000 feddans of land were threatened by *pashas* (large landowners) seeking to "seize their lands making use of the fact that they lack documents that indicate their ownership of the land." The land was given to the farmers by the General Authority for Reconstruction Projects and Agricultural Development, which subsequently refused to validate their claims of ownership. The farmers were also denied ownership over another 7,000 feddans of "reformed" land and feared that the General Authority for Reconstruction Projects and Agricultural Development would "take over their lands to sell it to big investors, or landlords in the governorate" (LCHR, 2008a).

Similarly, in villages in the North of Giza, local authorities and the Ministry of Irrigation served eviction notices to tenants occupying land for generations. The land in question stretched from Almnashi to the village of Wardan, adjacent to "Hathor Land," a property owned by a very wealthy landlord. The tenants were issued removal notices by the Ministry of Irrigation, and the local *pasha* hired a team to try and forcibly remove the farming equipment of the tenants but were met with resistance. Upon petitioning the Ministry of Irrigation, the tenants were assured that the removal order would be reconsidered. At the same time, the landlord used his influence to manipulate the possession records at the Property Taxes Department, validating tenant claims that the landlord colluded with local authorities and the Ministry of Irrigation to evict tenants from their homes (LCHR, 2008b).

In October 2009, in a village in Dakahleya governorate near the town of Mansoura, tenants testified to the corruption within the MoE, and its collusion with numerous housing officials and construction companies. The MoE sold numerous feddans of agrarian lands to private investors, after turning down an offer – of 10 percent over the sale price – by the tenants themselves. According to Egyptian law, the tenants should have been given the opportunity to buy the land, but it is clear that the state wanted to redistribute it to private developers (LCHR, 2009a).

In 2010, in the northern governorate of Kafr el Sheikh, the Governor along with the Ministry of Endowment and representatives of the Arab

Company for Land Reclamation expropriated the lands of farmers in the villages of Mostorod, Abyaneh and Al-Aaly despite the fact that the farmers had paid the rent for three years in advance and improved the lands. The agents of the state invaded the land and arrested the farmers for three days without cause. The expropriated lands were transferred to the Arab Company for Land Reclamation (LCHR, 2010a).

These cases demonstrate the crucial role of the state in the creation of markets, particularly in the commodification of land. As Polanyi (1944) argued long ago, state intervention is necessary in the construction of the "self-regulating market." "The road to the free market," argued Polanyi, "was opened and kept open by an enormous increase in continuous, centrally organized and controlled interventionism" (1944, p. 140). In the case of liberalizing Egypt, however, the expropriating state coincided with a degree of decentralization that enabled governorates and local authorities to become proactive agents – in collusion with local notables – in the forcible expropriation of the *fellahin*.

The Violence of Dispossession

The processes of accumulation by dispossession often involve acts of violence, most often (but not always) initiated by the appropriators. As Marx noted of the dispossession of the English peasantry during the transition to capitalism in the early modern period, the history of their expropriation "is written in the annals of mankind in letters of blood and fire" (Marx, 1976, p. 875). The violent expropriation of the peasantry – encapsulated in a history of "conquest, enslavement, robbery, murder, in short, force" – is an experience shared by peasantries across time and geography, and links together the peasant experience from early modern England to contemporary Egypt (Marx, 1976, p. 874).

While class-based violence is not something new to rural Egypt, instances of such violence did increase with the implementation of Law 96. Indeed, the advent of liberalization has given rise to what Abdelrahman (2017) refers to as the "securitocratic" state, characterized by the growth of the Ministry of Interior, "extensive secret police networks and collusion between landowners and local police" (Bush, 2009, p. 61). The growth of the securitocratic state includes the "outsourcing" of informal practices of coercion to groups of armed criminal thugs called *baltagya*, who "carry out duties of 'disciplining' members of the public in return for the police turning a blind eye to their criminal activities." Such duties include "breaking up demonstrations" and forcibly removing farmers from their land (Abdelrahman, 2017, pp. 189–190).

Between 1990 and 1997, the Egyptian state was engaged in a fierce conflict with several *takfiri* (extremist) groups, providing the necessary pretext to "strengthen the control the police apparatus had over the regions and its security grip over villages, preventing or curbing any political activity" (El Nour, 2015, p. 202). The continued renewal of the 1981 Emergency Law – undertaken to combat rising Islamic extremism – also gave the Egyptian state the capacity to increase its level of surveillance and repression in the countryside as the effects of law 96 became apparent.

The summer of 1997 – mere months before the passing of law 96 – witnessed an upsurge in rural violence and unrest. In Bani Suef, Minya, Fayyum, Asyut and Suhag provinces in upper Egypt and the Delta village of al-'Attaf, peasants protested the impending reforms with the support of Nasserist, Islamist and leftist parties. As the protests turned violent, the offices of Agricultural cooperatives were burned down, and one landlord was killed. In Minya, thousands of protesting peasants torched the houses of local landowners, blocked the main roads into the village and set fire to rail and bus infrastructure. Three protestors were killed in the police crackdown. In the Delta village of al-'Attaf, protesting tenant farmers set fire to the local office of the agriculture ministry to destroy official property records. Immediately following its implementation in October 1997, the new law sparked a violent reaction from enraged tenants. Clashes between tenants and landlords broke out in more than 100 villages, resulting in 32 recorded deaths, 751 injuries and 2,410 arrests (Beinin, 2001; Bush, 2009; El-Gawhary, 1997; El Nour, 2015).

Documenting instances of rural violence related to property disputes is not an easy task. Some civil society organizations, like the Land Centre for Human Rights and the Sons of the Soil Land Centre, have attempted to compile data of such incidences over the past two decades. Figure 7 reveals an interesting trajectory of property-based violence in rural Egypt. The implementation of law 96 in October 1997 witnessed a dramatic surge in land-based violence – the above-mentioned "uprising" – followed by a period of manageable violence as security forces gained control of the countryside. While no data

	1997	1998	1999	2000	2001	2002	2003	2004	2005	2006	2007	2008	2009	2010
■ Deaths	100	20	81	34	58	34	30	49		92			192	297
■ Injuries	1,000	289	445	195	302	100	215	328		257			1,066	1,451
▨ Arrests	1,400	267	401	318	666	225	322	429		465			1,333	1,687

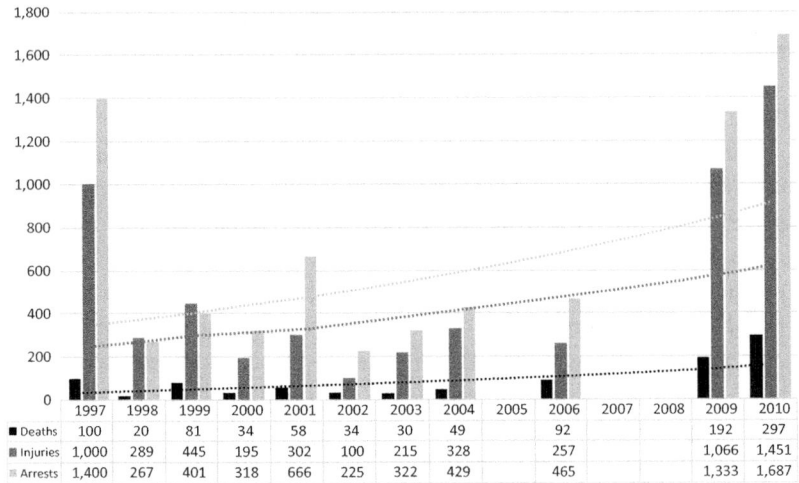

Figure 7 *Land-based violence in Egypt, 1997–2010*
Source: Land Centre for Human Rights, Sons of the Soil Land Centre (Bush, 2011)

seem to be available for 2005, 2007 and 2008, land-based violence
and state repression is clearly on an upward trajectory heading
into 2011.

Some notable examples serve to convey the character of the conflicts.
In March 2005, Salah Nawar, a powerful landlord, arrived in the
village of Sarando demanding the eviction of tenants from Agrarian
Reform lands. Nawar had filed a police report accusing the tenants of
trespassing, stealing his crops and preventing him from going to his
land. On the morning of March 4, Salah arrived in the village accompanied by an armed entourage, including numerous armoured cars and
five tractors to help with the eviction. Nawar's men shot at farmers
who were busy ploughing their lands. The police arrested the wives
and children of the farmers to pressure them to submit themselves to
the authorities (LCHR, 2005b, 2005c, 2005e). Peasants and tenant
farmers claimed that they were coerced by police to sign documents
confirming Nawar's ownership of the land. Nawar claimed that activists from the cities brainwashed the peasants into believing that the
land was theirs, not understanding that his land was "put under
government protection by Nasser the leftist in 1965" and released
again by Sadat in 1972 (Murphy, 2005). Such insolence needed to be
met with repression, for, according to Nawar, "[i]f the peasants get

away with this, such things will spread all over" and they "will revolt and attack all the owners" (Bush, 2009, pp. 51–52).

Farmers claimed the land as their own, insisting that they "always had contracts with the Land Reform Institute."[13] After the implementation of Law 96, however, Nawar began acting like "a little dictator," sending his men around "demanding rents" and evicting entire families (Murphy, 2005). Contrary to Nawar's claims of brainwashing by external agitators, one villager, going by the name "Mohammed," said that he and some others actively sought legal help due to Nawar's attempts to evict them. For the villagers, said "Mohammed," "[l]and is everything ... it's our food, our livelihood, and it prevents us from being thrown out into the world with nothing" (Murphy, 2005).

Another incident in March 2005 ended in a massacre. The Hammam brothers sought to enforce a court order to reclaim 23 feddans of land in the town of Surad in Al-Garbiya governorate. Arriving in the village at dawn with an entourage of farmers from the southern town of Manfalout in Assuit, they immediately met resistance from the town's residents. As the town mayor said of the incident, "coming in [to the village] with strangers is a sign of threat" in village culture, and the residents rightly suspected that the strangers were there for the land (Fathi, 2005). Police reports and eye witness accounts differ, but conflict intensified when one of the tenant farmers – Nadia El-Babli – was shot by one of the Hammam brothers. In the end, the Hammam brothers and their lead hand were killed. Whether they were killed by a mob of tenants enraged at the death of one of their own, or whether – as eye witnesses claim – they were killed by the farmers in their own entourage who ultimately turned on them is unclear. What *is* clear is that the incident serves to highlight the chaotic and violent nature of the land disputes opened up by the agrarian reforms.

In El Mounira village, Qalyoubiya governorate, a former ambassador claimed ownership of a piece of agricultural land owned by the state. Peasants had farmed the land for more than fifty years. The powerful ex-official used the security forces and hired *baltagya* to threaten the farmers to leave their lands and homes by firing their guns indiscriminately in the air. They destroyed water wheels, destroyed

---

[13] The Land Reform Institute, also known as the Land Reform Authority, is the government agency that administered land reform efforts.

irrigation canals, burned crops and storage facilities and even allegedly stole from the farmers (LCHR, 2005g).

In February 2006, the farmers of Yousif El Seddiq area, El Fayoum governorate, claimed that a rival claimant to their lands blocked the roads leading into the village, "seized their lands and damaged their plantations with tractors and drilling machines . . . assaulted them and threatened to kill them" by burying them alive on the land (LCHR, 2006c). Local police arrested and detained the farmers defending their lands.

In 2008, the residents of Ezbet Khairi, Dakahlia governorate were besieged and threatened with eviction from their homes by a powerful figure in their village, Dr. Ahmad El-Hefny, who claimed ownership over all the lands in the village. His hired *baltagya* surrounded the village with barbed wire, cut the electricity, shut off the water supply and demolished some of the residents' homes (LCHR, 2008d). In the same year, Sabera El Masreya had her 4 qirats[14] of land violated by a "person of influence" and his hired *baltagya* near Helwan. They burnt crops and filled in her irrigation canals. She and her five children were evicted from the land, her home was demolished and she became landless and homeless (LCHR, 2009e). In the same year, police used excessive force against protesters in the Delta village of Borolus. Farmers protesting the elimination of food subsidies in the context of the food crisis that affected countries in the Global South blocked the main highway around their village with burning tires. Police responded with tear gas, birdshot and mass arrests. The unrestrained police violence resulted in numerous injuries of women and children (Abdel-rahman, 2017, p. 190).

In 2009, farmers of Tatwan village in Fayyoum filed a report to the office of public prosecutor and the minister of interior alleging they were harassed by the El-Kheir brothers – Mamdouh, Antar and Azzam – to reclaim lands that were distributed to the farmers back in 1960. The El-Kheir brothers hired an entourage of *baltagya* armed with knives and firearms, to assault the farmers and expel them from their homes and agricultural lands. The farmers also claimed that the local authorities in Southern Fayyoum colluded with the interlopers to evict them (LCHR, 2009c). In Al-Ad'adeyya village in the town of Damanhour, security forces assaulted fifty farmers with tear gas and

---

[14] Twenty-four qirats equal 1 feddan.

subsequently beat them in an attempt to evict them from 104 feddans of land. When the farmers refused to comply with the eviction order, local authorities – including the village council and the security forces – arrested, detained and forced the tenants to sign concession papers. While receiving compensation for the concessions, the tenants were also forced to consent to having all their private assets seized in the event they fail to comply with the concession (LCHR, 2009f).

The violence of dispossession shares several common features. It occurs due to collusion between landlords, criminal gangs of *baltagya* and various state authorities – both within the security apparatus and within the broader administration. All incidents involve damage to peasant property in the form of burning crops and damaging or destroying agricultural infrastructure, like storage facilities, irrigation canals and water pumps. They all involve the exercise of physical violence, both by state authorities as well as criminal elements, often resulting in deaths, injuries and mass arrests. Finally, all incidents involve the corruption of legal and administrative institutions that wilfully neglect to uphold the rights of peasants. This violence is also not incidental. Rather, it is a fundamental characteristic of accumulation by dispossession. The incidents of state violence are indicative of the transformation of the state from one that redistributes property and wealth to the lower orders in the interest of maintaining an authoritarian populist social contract into one that facilitates the accumulation of capital by the dominant class in the interests of enhancing economic competitiveness.

Dispossession for Industrial Development

The dispossession of peasants and tenant farmers from state lands often entailed the appropriation of land for the purposes of creating industrial zones to develop Egypt's export-oriented manufacturing. This was a result of changes in Egypt's public land management system. Since the 1970s, Egypt has been attempting to attract foreign investment for industrial development by establishing special industrial zones earmarked for development. In the 1970s, Sadat established "Public Free Zones" as part of his *infitah* policy. Over the course of the 1990s and 2000s, numerous reforms were implemented as a means of advancing the industrialization of the Egyptian economy. Investment Law 8/1997 offered unlimited land based on freehold to foreign investors mainly along the coastline (Suez, Alexandria and the Red Sea). The government also sought to develop numerous other industrial zones. The first of these were located in various "New Cities" and encompassed a planned area of 16,648 ha and 6,840 industrial projects. In 2001, a presidential decree offered free land to investors in numerous cities in Upper Egypt to develop "Planned" Industrial Zones. By 2006, 22,847 ha were assigned for Planned Industrial Zones for 2,304 industrial projects. The Ebeid government introduced legislation in 2002 (Law 83) to introduce Special Economic Zones as a means of attracting foreign direct investment.[15] Firms setting up shop in such zones enjoyed significant tax holidays, exemption from tariffs and import duties, and other privileges as a means of enticing them to invest. Special Economic Zones were regulated and managed by the Special Economic Zone authority, which was independent of the larger Egyptian bureaucracy. Finally, the Nazif government negotiated the first Qualifying Industrial Zones with Israel and the United States in December 2004.[16]

However, investors complained that the public land management system was based on a supply-side model in which the Egyptian government selected specific areas for industrialization in accordance with its regional development policies and priorities. This entailed developing sites in peripheral, underdeveloped regions as well as areas intended to "de-concentrate" the population in the Greater Cairo area. Examples of these types of development projects included the New Cities and the controversial Toshka project.[17]

In its assessment of Egypt's public land management system, the World Bank complained that the current system "constrains existing industrial establishments that are seeking to expand by acquiring adjacent lands" (World Bank, 2006, p. 7). Instead, the bank proposed

[15] Law 83.

[16] Qualifying Industrial Zones enable duty and tariff free access to American markets for good produced in a Qualifying Industrial Zone and containing 11.7 percent of Israeli inputs.

[17] Once fully operational, Toshka was expected to resolve the problems of food scarcity and urban overcrowding by creating an alternate delta parallel to the Nile Valley with the capacity to settle 6 million people while providing 800,000 to 2.2 million feddans of land for cultivation. The infrastructure for the project was provided by the government while the main investment came from a Saudi Prince Talal, who purchased 100,000 feddans at £E99 per feddan (Economist Intelligence Unit, 1997, p. 50).

"selecting locations based on demand and market analysis," which required a reform of the "current incentive system whose bias towards remote underdeveloped areas comes at the expense of competitiveness" (World Bank, 2006, p. 32). Anticipating the World Bank's proposals, the Nazif government transformed the role of the General Authority for Investment and Free Zones away from a "regulatory focus" to a focus on "proactive investment promotion" (OECD, 2007c, p. 36).[18] This entailed "streamlining" the General Authority for Investment and Free Zones by turning it into a "one-stop-shop" for investors.

The General Authority for Industrial Development was created by a Presidential Decree in 2005. Acting as an economic authority with judicial powers, the General Authority for Industrial Development was "to consolidate control over all existing industrial estates in Egypt, in both new communities and Governorates, and oversee the development, management and operation of these zones and any new planned zone" (World Bank, 2006, p. 2). Having established an industrial land bank, the General Authority for Industrial Development aimed to reduce the long and complex bureaucratic procedures that investors faced while attempting to buy state land.

What this all means is that international investors and the World Bank pressured the Egyptian government to set aside its regional development policies and grant investors land based on their perceived market needs, such as being close to existing markets and established infrastructure. In concrete terms, given the highly concentrated nature of arable land in Egypt, this set investors on a collision course with tenant farmers and intensified the struggles over land. While investors were getting their new investment regime that eliminates "red tape," trumpets transparency and the rule of law, and provides protections against expropriation, Egyptian tenant farmers were increasingly subject to arbitrary power, expropriation and state repression.

This has established a destructive dynamic in the Egyptian countryside. Peasants and tenant farmers in possession of Agrarian Reform lands or *waqf* lands, upon which they have farmed for decades or even generations, are displaced from their arable land to make way for industrial development. In turn, they are promised new, uncultivated

---

[18] The General Authority for Investment and Free Zones was changed by Law 13 of 2004.

lands in the desert that they are expected to improve without access to the types of subsidies and preferential agricultural loans characteristic of the previous, statist development model. In many cases, displaced farmers are promised alternative lands that never materialize. This has led activists from the Land Centre for Human Rights to question the rationality of a developmental model that destroys arable land for industrial development in a country characterized by extremely high levels of food insecurity. Indeed, such a development strategy seems to envision agriculture without farmers (Bush, 2000).

For example, in 2009 in Kafr El Mahrouk village, Gharbia Governorate, farmers were forcibly evicted without any compensation or alternative housing to develop an industrial zone on 262 feddans of fertile *waqf* land they had occupied since 1952 (LCHR, 2009a, 2009c). Fertile lands in other parts of Gharbeya – 255 feddans of arable land outside Tanta, 388 feddans in Shandalat village and 300 acres near Mahalla – were similarly appropriated by the authorities for the purposes of industrial development, resulting in a total of 1,205 feddans in the governorate (LCHR, 2010c).

In 2007, the governor of Sohag earmarked a 7,000-acre area of land upon which to build a new airport, including significant sanitation infrastructure. Within this area was agrarian land that numerous farmers had reclaimed decades earlier. Rather than build the airport on desert land, the local authorities chose arable land and evicted the farmers without compensation (LCHR, 2007e).

In 2010, a Prime Ministerial decree sanctioned the appropriation of 115 acres of farm land for the installation of a gas pipeline to the Fayoum Sugar Factory near Kasr El Basel (LCHR, 2010b). During the same year, farmers on the outskirts of 6th of October City had land confiscated to build a massive transit maintenance workshop and an extra underground metro line (LCHR, 2010d).

In all these cases, industrial development was driven by the interests of investors rather than the developmental and demographic priorities of the Egyptian state. As a result, industrial development resulted in the expropriation of land under cultivation due to its proximity to existing markets and infrastructure. As outlined by the World Bank (2006), this demand driven process of industrialization was considered key to enhancing the competitiveness of Egypt. The corollary of this, of course, is that it resulted in the dispossession of farmers in a context of rising food insecurity and rural poverty.

Dispossession and Tourism and Luxury Development

State lands were also appropriated to develop the tourism and luxury housing sectors (in the "New Urban Communities"). In the early 2000s, the tourism industry grew more rapidly than any other sector of the economy and became Egypt's top foreign currency generator. As such, it was "considered by the Government as the most promising industry in terms of job creation potential in the near future" (World Bank, 2006, p. 34). As discussed in Chapter 3, numerous ministers in the Nazif government of 2004 had interests in the real estate sector.

While real estate development began to take off in Egypt in the 1970s, much of it was still largely in the form of public-private partnerships. By the late 1990s and 2000s, the real estate sector underwent a "radical change ... away from heavily-subsidized housing schemes for the urban poor and into private sector-led real estate projects aimed at the middle and upper middle income demand markets" (World Bank, 2006, p. 53). This change corresponds with the development of new strategies of capital accumulation among Egypt's propertied class.

The investors in the tourism sector gained greater access to state lands through the creation of the Tourism Development Authority (TDA) in 1991, a new institution authorized to manage and dispose of public land for tourism development. In 1992, a Presidential Decree transferred most undeveloped public desert land along the Mediterranean Sea, Red Sea and Aqaba Gulf (578 million square metres) to the TDA. To carry out its mission, TDA set up 13 branches across the country to dispose of all land under its jurisdiction at the fixed price of U.S.$1 per square metre. The change in Egypt's public land management system, which gave private investors greater freedom in determining the location of their investment, and the 2004 annulment of the military decree proscribing the use of agricultural land for non-agricultural purposes facilitated the TDA's role in the disposal of state lands.[19]

Predictably, such developments sparked the real estate boom of the 2000s, resulting in land speculation and rampant tourist development. It also led to an increase in land disputes regarding tourism development.[20] Many of these conflicts occurred further up the Nile valley in Qena,

[19] Military Decree 1/1996. The Decree introduced a fine in the amount of E £10,000 and jail term of 2–5 years (El-Hefnaway, 2004, pp. 13–15).

[20] The most infamous incident was the attack on the Pharaonic temple complex in Luxor in 1997 (Jehl, 1997).

Luxor and Aswan governorates. Communities in and around Luxor experienced dispossession since the implementation of Law 96 back in 1997, under the pretence of restoring the area to its "Pharaonic heritage" (Mitchell, 2002, p. 186). In 1999, Abt Associates Inc. developed a comprehensive twenty-year development plan for the Luxor area, called the Comprehensive Development Plan for the City of Luxor. Referred to as a "masterful work of tourism governmentality," development around Luxor and Karnak resulted in the construction of "an enormous separate tourism enclave south of the city called El-Toad, centred on a golf course and ringed by high-end hotels and villas" (Schmid, 2015, pp. 121–122).

The Comprehensive Development Plan for the City of Luxor received renewed impetus through a 2007 Prime Ministerial decree[21] confiscating 1,000 feddans of agricultural land in El Maris, near Luxor, resulting in the dispossession of 8,000 families and 2,400 homes (12,000 people) (LCHR, 2007f). The farmers' legal challenge to the evictions was thrown out of the local courts, precipitating an appeal with the Supreme Court in Cairo (Mohsen, 2010). In 2008, residents in Karnak, Luxor, faced the demolition of their houses to expand the pavilion around the Luxor Temple as part of a larger plan to create an open air museum for the purposes of increasing tourism in the area (Abraham & Bakr, 2000; Kamil, 2008). The construction of the museum was carried about by Talaat Mustafa Group, which also won a contract to build a five-star hotel and develop 19,589 square metres of land on the Luxor Corniche. The residents had mixed titles to the land on which their houses were built: it was either *Wad el Yad* or Agrarian Reform land. They reported that the state property appraisers underestimated the value of their property to reduce the potential compensation the state would owe the residents (Joya, 2008).

The residents of Karnak view the government's promotion of tourism and tourism-related projects as the source of their problems. A young man expressed his frustration with state policies in the following terms: "if tourism means the loss of our houses, do you think we would like tourists and welcome them here?" Other Karnak residents said that tourism had not created any meaningful jobs for the local people. The stonecutters in the small alabaster factories said they

---

[21] Prime Ministerial Decree 264/2007.

rarely sold enough of their carved statues to tourists to make a decent income. Others said the hotel industry brought workers in from Cairo rather than hire locals. At best, they got menial service jobs as dish-washers in the local hotels, as opposed to better paying jobs in the larger resorts. They also complained about the big malls and hotel conglomerates that directly competed with local tourist guides and small shopkeepers, reducing their already marginal income even fur-ther. One resident expressed the view that "the master plan for Luxor is driven by foreign shopping-centre designers," and that the author-ities intended to "make Luxor look like a Disney version of an Egyp-tian town" (Kamil, 2008).

Another case where real estate development expropriated *Wad el Yad* agricultural land occurred on Isis Island in Aswan. Developers appropriated land for the development of a massive luxury hotel – the Pyramisa Isis Island Hotel – that opened in 1993. The people of Isis Island were forced to give up their land without any compensation and moved to Mount Tajoj (Joya, 2008). In nearby Nubian village, women described the state's coercive role in facilitating tourism devel-opment. In the early 2000s, the government forced residents to register their houses to get electricity and water. Unregistered houses were demolished. Police normally began by destroying homes incremen-tally, to intimidate and coerce residents to register their houses. Resi-dents resisted registering houses because the government would then demand either back rent or payment totalling the value of the house (Joya, 2008). Houses that were registered were forced to be painted indigo to present the façade of an "authentic" Egyptian Nubian village to attract tourists.

In 2008, more than 50 families were evicted from their agricultural lands – constituting more than 350 acres – on El Dom Island in Qena. Ownership of the land had been transferred to the Ministry of Irriga-tion to build a promenade for the Ministry to make way for the Qanater development project (LCHR, 2008c).

The Northern Coast and the Sinai Peninsula were also regions opening up to new tourism developments. In 1995, 150 farmers from Northern Ter'at El Nasr area in Borg El Arab City, Alexandria were threatened with eviction from their lands to develop an amusement park. Having cultivated and improved the land for more than 70 years, and possessing title to these lands in accordance with various reform laws implemented over the course of the 1950s, 1960s and 1970s, the farmers were surprised to learn that the "public body for the civilizational societies" refused to complete the ownership procedures for the farmers (LCHR, 2005d). Legal proceedings carried on for a decade.

In 2004 in Dahab, a coastal town on the Southern Sinai Peninsula, local authorities appropriated land belonging to members of the Muzayna Bedouin tribe. Authorities were able to do this because the registration of the land in question – *Wad al Yad* land – had not been recognized by the state. Local authorities bulldozed palm trees and filled in the well on the Bedouin land to build a go-cart racing track. The Bedouin claimed this was to erase any sign of their continued occupation of the land, which, according to a 1980 Presidential Decree, is all that is needed to demonstrate legal claim to the land. Contrary to standard practice, the Bedouins received no compensation for their losses. Rising land prices have merely served to increase the tensions between the Bedouin, the local authorities and various investor groups (Loza, 2005).

Poverty, Agrarian Change and Rural Discontent

The result of this process of dispossession has been a rapid concen tration of land in the hands of a few. With the removal of the limits on landholding, Law 96 resulted in the creation of large landholdings on the one hand and a mass of landless day labourers on the other (Bush, 2002; Ibrahim & Ibrahim, 2003). Land was already highly concentrated in 1990, where almost 70 percent of the landowners had less than one feddan of land totalling 18 percent of all cultivated land. At the other end of the spectrum, 0.25 percent of landowners (9,000) possessed 15 percent of the total cultivated area (Ikram, 2006, p. 263). Between 1997 and 2004, approximately 904,000 rental contracts were terminated. During this same period, peasants incurred close to E£2 billion in losses, and up to 400,000 peasants were turned into day labourers or were simply left without any means of subsistence (LCHR, 2004c, p. 42). Wages for agricultural labourers varied between E£15 and E£30 per day depending on the governorate, and many labourers were paid "in kind." As we saw in Chapter 3, wealth inequality – that is, inequality regarding the ownership of property – has increased dramatically in Egypt over the course of the 2000s. From this, and from the case studies available, it is reasonable infer that peasant dispossession continued, if not accelerated after 2005.

In cases of peasant dispossession, the official government line is to compensate smallholders for the loss of their lands. This may or may not include relocation to newly allocated plots (often in the desert). In practice, however, the state does not always fulfil its promises. Between 1997 and 2005, only 12,664 out of 904,000 smallholders – around 1.5 percent – received compensatory properties (LCHR, 2004c, p. 58). As a result, rural poverty has been on the rise. Between 2000 and 2010, the rural poverty headcount rose from 22.1 percent to 32.3 percent (World Bank, 2018r).[22] However, according to the 2009 UN Arab Human Development Report, the rural poverty headcount reached 52 percent by 2005, based on upper national poverty lines (UNDP, 2009, p. 114).

These socioeconomic developments have a negative impact on the legitimacy of the regime among the rural population. As is the case with the Egyptian working class, the relationship between the regime and the *fellahin* can be characterized as an authoritarian bargain, in which the *fellahin* receive land and/or secure tenure in exchange for deference to the authority of the state. Insofar as the state manages to secure what Sedgwick (2010) calls its "output legitimacy" – such as subsidized inputs, tenure security, preferential credit, debt relief and so on – tenant farmers and peasants may overlook the undemocratic character of decision making in rural Egypt. While the agrarian organizations of this populist corporatism – such as the cooperatives – were always spaces of contestation and class struggle between landlords and *fellahin* – the increasing capture of these organizations by landed interests has not only increased the distance between them and the tenant farmers, it has turned these organizations against them by acting as an expropriating force. In the context of liberalization and the dismantling of the agrarian basis of the authoritarian bargain, the regime has had to "build new constituencies among those benefiting from neo-liberalism to substitute for the old populist coalition" (Hinnebusch, 2014, p. 46). This "post-populist" authoritarian coalition incorporates the rural notables, affluent farmers and real estate investors interested in buying and selling land for tourism development.

The instances of property-based violence and conflict, and the endemic corruption of political institutions rooted on the Egyptian

---

[22] The World Bank defines the rural poverty headcount ratio as "the percentage of the rural population living below the national poverty lines."

countryside associated with the processes of accumulation by dispossession have increased rural discontent and undermined the legitimacy of the Egyptian state among a majority of the *fellahin*. State sanctioned appropriation and rural disinvestment, coupled with establishment of Islamist forms of alternative socioeconomic provision (e.g., of social services or financing) have weakened the regime's base in the countryside. The expropriation of agricultural land for industrial zones at a time of rising food insecurity – culminating in the food crisis of 2008 – suggests that the state has forsaken the small tenant farmer. The mass evictions and house demolitions under the guise of tourism promotion is seen by many as an act of subordinating the interests of Egyptian citizens to those of foreign tourists.

Commentators have noted the rise of rural discontent, and interviews with peasants and tenant farmers demonstrate the extent to which the government is increasingly viewed as an external appropriator acting in the interests of large landowners and investors (Murphy, 2005). Residents in Karnak affected by the Comprehensive Development Plan for the City of Luxor likened their situation to that of Palestinians whose land is taken by force by Israel.[23] Under Mubarak, the Egyptian state is equated with a militarized, occupying force engaged in the dispossession of its own citizens. They also expressed a willingness to resist the state – to kill or be killed, and to never surrender their houses and life savings without a struggle – despite lacking arms. It is a common occurrence that children in Karnak make petrol bombs out of soda bottles in case of an attack by the police on their community. Further up the Nile in Nubian village in Aswan governorate, several women complained that the police destroyed local shops if they did not receive kickbacks from proprietors. They also complained that the government no longer provided services – such as health care – in the village.

As a result, many smallholders believe that living conditions were better under Nasser. Magdi al-Azab, the head of a Nubian family from Isis Island in Aswan, expressed this belief, claiming that, back then, the government compensated residents with money and accommodation when they were relocated for development projects, unlike the current practice under Mubarak. While these expressions of popular discontent are anecdotal, given the absence of public opinion surveys in rural

---

[23] Interviews in Karnak, 2007–2008.

Egypt and the impossibility of conducting wide ranging surveys in the countryside, it is reasonable to infer that this sentiment is relatively popular, given the way local officials and members of the landed elite refer to Nasser in pejorative terms. As noted earlier in this chapter, a family fighting to retain possession of their Agrarian reform lands was told by a state official that, to retrieve their land rights, they should "bring Abdel Nasser back from the dead." Expressions of contempt for Nasser by local notables and local authorities suggests that Nasser's reforms are still a reference point for many *fellahin* in rural Egypt.

This growing discontent has altered the political relations of the countryside, particularly in terms of the declining electoral support for the regime among the *fellahin*. As an authoritarian system, Egypt is peculiar in the sense that, while elections are designed to ensure the dominance of Mubarak and the NDP, the regime often does little to inflate voter turnout numbers to enhance the perceived legitimacy of the regime. For example, during the 2005 election official figures placed voter turnout at just 23 percent, while unofficial sources put it as low as 15 percent (Sharp, 2006, p. 5). In some polling stations in Cairo, it was reportedly as low as 4 percent (Wright, 2005). According to Lust, turnout in the 2005 legislative elections was 7 percent (Lust, 2009, p. 128). This represents a historical decline in voter turnout for the regime.[24]

Historically, voter turnout is higher in the more underdeveloped, rural areas than in the cities (Lust, 2009). Through the co-operatives system, the NDP were able to establish clientelistic relationships between the party and rural constituents. In the late 1970s and 1980s, parliamentarians paved roads, built schools and helped constituents to find jobs in return for votes. There is reason to believe these established forms of clientelism began to break down in the late 1990s and 2000s. Blaydes (2006) argues that the clientelistic relationships binding voters to parliamentarians has been breaking down in the context of liberalization. Austerity has strained budgets, preventing party notables from being able to use state resources to distribute the material goods necessary to maintain these clientelistic relationships. At the same time, from 2004 onward, parliament – and the NDP – became increasing dominated by neoliberal minded businessmen who

---

[24] In 1987, official sources state that turnout for the presidential election was 54 percent (although unofficial sources say it was more like 25 percent) (Post, 1987).

changed the dynamic of the party. As this chapter has demonstrated, party and state officials openly colluded with landlords and business interests to dispossess peasants of their property. In the context of this type of party-sanctioned landlord offensive, traditional relations of clientelism cannot be expected to survive. For all these reasons, the regime has been losing its grip on the *fellahin*, destroying its traditional social base and laying the groundwork for the outbreak of the contentious politics of the 2011 uprisings.

Contentious Politics, Collective Action and Class Struggle

From the enclosure movement in early modern England to the rise of the Zapatistas in contemporary Mexico, peasants have resisted dispossession (Kennedy, 2008; Vergara-Camus, 2014). Egypt is no different in this regard. This fact makes the absence of research on peasant resistance in the current literature on contentious politics in the Middle East so perplexing. Unlike the earlier studies of contentious politics from which it is derived, the current literature on contentious politics in the Middle East is conspicuously silent on the growing conflicts between accumulating landlords and dispossessed peasants.[25] Neither Gerges' (2015) nor Lynch's (2014) collections of essays on contentious politics in the contemporary Middle East address the issue of rural conflict and struggles around land. Even Bayat's (2013, 2017) notion of the "non-movement" of the dispossessed is focused solely on urban subjects, such as those living and working in the informal sectors of Middle Eastern cities.

A generous interpretation of this silence may attribute it to the difficulty of studying rural conflict in countries like Egypt. Travel to rural areas is often fraught with difficulties, not least of which are the numerous restrictions imposed on researchers by domestic security forces.[26]

---

[25] Tarrow (2011) discusses peasant occupations of land as examples of contentious politics, and highlights their often leaderless character.

[26] Conducting fieldwork on land-based issues in rural Egypt is extremely difficult. In Mattiaa village in Qena governorate, the local police inspector questioned me about my interest in issues related to land and property. He also asked if I was married or engaged and inquired into the whereabouts of my husband. In Abyouha, an interview I was conducting was cut short because the policeman accompanying me sat right outside the door and continuously peeked into the room. My translator said we could not stay there any longer, so we left.

However, it may also be a product of the implicit urban biases shared by researchers of contentious politics. The dispersed, and sometimes isolated, nature of rural life often leads scholars to downplay the agency of the peasantry. Marx himself wrote pejoratively of the "idiocy of rural life" and dismissed the peasantry as "sacks of potatoes" (Marx, 1973; Marx & Engels, 1967).[27]

This is not so say, however, that peasants do not resist. Under such conditions, resistance often assumes an unorganized form, what Scott (1985, p. xvi) refers to as the "everyday forms of peasant resistance – the prosaic but constant struggles between the peasantry and those who seek to extract labour, food, taxes, rents, and interest from them" that "stop well short of outright collective defiance." These "weapons of the weak" include acts such as "foot dragging, dissimulation, desertion, false compliance, pilfering, feigned ignorance, slander, arson, sabotage, and so on." Such resistance is not meant to overthrow the existing social structure, but rather to work within the existing system to minimize the damage.

Scott's formulation of peasant resistance to class power intends to shift focus away from the rare conflagrations of peasant rebellions and urban uprisings to the everyday instances of quiet, individualized resistance. In this way, it shifts the focus away from collective (even if unorganized) expressions of resistance. However, Scott's formulation of the "weapons of the weak" implies a context of normalized class exploitation. To put it another way, the "everyday" refers to the constant, routine forms of exploitation that are intrinsic to the system of exploitation as it operates on a daily basis. The "foot dragging" peasant bears a remarkable resemblance to Frederick Taylor's (1913) "soldiering" industrial worker. Dispossession, however, while intrinsic to capitalist exploitation, is not the "everyday" of its *modus operandi*. Rural Egypt of the 1990s witnessed an onslaught against peasant tenure; in this regard, it represented a *disruption* of the "everyday" of rural life, a profound transformation of the type of exploitation experienced by peasants. In this sense, tenants experienced not an

---

[27] Marx may have been using the traditional Greek meaning of "idiocy," signifying the highly privatized and autarchic – as opposed to public and interdependent – nature of rural life. In the Eighteenth Brumaire, he goes on to say: "Each individual peasant family is almost self-sufficient, directly produces most of its consumer needs, and thus acquires its means of life more through an exchange with nature than in intercourse with society."

intensification of exploitation per se, but rather, the marginalization from their everyday forms of subsistence.

All of this is to say that the stakes of class conflict were much higher in the 1990s due to the implementation of Law 96. As discussed, much of the resistance was spontaneous and ad hoc, entailing collective protests against attempts by landlords and *baltagya* to seize the land. Many of the challenges to landlords "took the form of proxy conflicts relating to land access, border and irrigation disputes, and other skirmishes" (Bush, 2016, p. 158). Instances of sporadic violence against landlords and other institutions of authority – such as the burning of local offices of the Ministry of Agriculture, as discussed – bear the hallmarks of peasant protests in Europe in the early modern period. Tenant farmers also hung black banners from buildings, signifying a state of mourning regarding the reforms. Part of this had to with the authoritarian political context. As in the urban labour movement, the formation of independent unions was banned under Mubarak (King, 2009, p. 100). Like the official trade unions, the agricultural cooperatives had evolved into organizations designed to control, rather than represent, the peasantry.

However, the period also witnessed the development of networks of resistance – however embryonic – initiated by smallholders themselves. At the beginning of the agrarian deregulation process, numerous farmers and opposition parties formed Farmers' Committees for Resistance to Law 96. The National Committee for the Defence of Farmers was formed in 1997, comprised of urban and rural activists, but lasted only a few months before its members were arrested by the regime. These committees held 219 meetings to address the issue of dispossession before they were shut down. However, none put forward a strategy to stop the evictions. In the same year, urban intellectuals and radical activists interested in the plight of peasants and tenant farmers formed the Peasant Solidarity Committee. The Peasant Solidarity Committee established networks of small farmers, largely residing in the Nile Delta, urban intellectuals and human rights activists.

Also in the late 1990s, a number of legal organizations emerged to support peasants and tenant farmers in their pursuit of legal remedies to the problems of dispossession. The LCHR was formed in 1996 and became one of the most effective proponents of the legal rights of Egyptian tenant farmers. Aside from litigation and legal support, the

LCHR holds workshops to raise awareness of the *fellahin* of the issues pertaining to their livelihoods and the rights they possess, as well as providing a space for creating a network of activists and volunteers devoted to strengthening the cause of human and labour rights in Egypt.

The Hisham Mubarak Law Centre (HMLC) was founded in 1999 to provide legal support for Human Rights cases. The HMLC helped farmers in Sarando pursue legal action against crop burning by an alleged police informer, and against duplicity by the police in 2008. While the HMLC predominantly focuses on human rights violations – as opposed to economic and social rights – it emerged as "one of the most outspoken and stubborn human rights groups among Egyptian NGOs" (Albrecht, 2013, p. 65). Together, the LCHR and the HMLC "defied, more often than not, the unwritten rules and guidelines established by the security apparatus" (Albrecht, 2013, p. 65).

On the whole, however, farmer organizations have been "sporadic, defensive and ineffective in driving alternative policy scenarios" (Bush, 2016, p. 156). The Middle East lags behind when it comes to forging transnational networks of peasant resistance to dispossession and alternatives to neoliberal globalization. With the exception of Palestine, Tunisia and Morocco, no Arab country has developed organizations affiliated with Via Campesina, the transnational organization of farmers and peasants that fights for food sovereignty and agroecological alternatives to financialized cash crop agriculture. However, regardless of how ephemeral they may have been, these organizations laid a foundation for peasant organizing that would take off in aftermath of the collapse of the Mubarak regime.

Conclusion

One of the most significant changes to Egypt's political economy occurred in the countryside during the period of liberalization. Touted as a solution to Egypt's agricultural productivity problems, the liberalization of agriculture resulted in an extended process of dispossession in the countryside. The abolition of tenure security for peasants and small farmers, forced evictions and skyrocketing rents brought immiseration to the small producers of rural Egypt and further increased Egypt's deep dependence on food imports. What is more, dispossession resulted in the intensification of land related violence, particularly after the introduction of the agrarian reforms of 1997. While the intensification of class conflict in the countryside did not have the same dramatic effect on Egyptian politics as did the growing strike waves in the industrial cities, it did contribute to the breakdown of traditional relations of authority and the erosion of rural support for the Mubarak regime.

Conclusion

The preceding chapters demonstrated the negative effects of liberalization and neoliberal restructuring on the social, economic and political
order of Egypt over the past three and a half decades. The post-war
order institutionalized a populist authoritarian bargain, in which
workers and peasants accepted the authoritarianism of Nasser's one-
party state in return for job guarantees, employment protection, health
care, pensions and tenure security. The Egyptian state assumed a
leading role in the economy, first through import substitution
industrialization and later through wide-ranging nationalizations and
economic planning under the rubric of "Arab socialism." In this context, the public sector grew dramatically because of an expanding
(albeit patchy) welfare state and the need to fill the gaps left by
Egyptian capital's unwillingness to invest in the economy. Political
Islam, in the form of the Muslim Brotherhood, was repressed and
reduced to insignificance as key aspects of its Islamic "moral economy"
were pre-empted – and surpassed – by the Nasserist regime.

Egypt's defeat by Israel in the 1967 war initiated a legitimation
crisis for Nasser's brand of Arab socialism. His untimely death in
1971 coincided with the beginnings of a dramatic shift in the global
economy as the United States unilaterally dismantled the post-war
arrangements established at Bretton Woods and a reactionary Saudi
Arabia exhibited pretensions to regional hegemony. In this context,
Sadat re-oriented Egypt away from the Soviet Union, abandoned
Nasser's commitment to the non-aligned movement, and allied Egypt
closely with the United States and the oil monarchies in the Persian
Gulf. Sadat's political conservatism and his economic liberalism led
him to promote the de-Nasserization of the Egyptian state and economy, implement a program of liberal restructuring (*infitah*) and support Islamism against the left. In this context, Egypt witnessed a
resurgence of the old landed class as well as a rehabilitation of the
Muslim Brotherhood.

The liberalization of the 1970s facilitated the growth of private capital. This capital, however, remained fragmented along politically constituted lines. First, *infitah* resulted in the growth of private sector capitalists close to Sadat's new political organization, the National Democratic Party (NDP), formed out of the conservative wing of the Arab Socialist Union. Second, Sadat's tolerance of the Muslim Brothers resulted in the growth of Islamic capital, particularly with the aid of Islamic banking and Islamic Money Management Companies. More peculiar was the rise of the military as an increasingly autonomous economic force. As Sadat sought to make peace with Israel and de-militarize the Egyptian state, he provided the military with the space to develop its own productive capacity and cultivate its own economic interests as a means of "coup-proofing" his rule.

Sadat's *infitah* also signified the beginning of the end of the populist authoritarian bargain that underpinned the legitimacy of the regime. The distribution of land back to the old landed classes resulted in a dramatic shift of power away from the peasants and towards the landlords. Attempts to privatize state-owned enterprises and intensify the exploitation of Egyptian workers by further integrating the Egyptian Trade Foreign Union into the regime resulted in the rise of worker discontent, expressed in the strike waves of the first half of the decade.

The 1970s ended on a note of crisis. Egypt's increased dependence on food imports coupled with the attempts to abolish bread subsidies sparked the most intense domestic unrest since the revolution. The so-called bread riots of 1977 would serve as a landmark event in contemporary Egyptian history, one against which attempts to further liberalize the economy were assessed. The hollowing out of the authoritarian bargain, coupled with Sadat's toleration of political Islam, resulted in the increasing radicalization of a new generation of Islamists repulsed by the perceived corruption of the *infitahi* classes. This radicalization was particularly salient amongst the increasingly dispossessed communities of Upper Egypt who had gained from Nasser's reforms and were losing out under *infitah*. Heavy handed repression by the state against the Islamists once cultivated by the regime eventually led to Sadat's assassination in the early 1980s.

Egypt under Mubarak

Mubarak's reign began with a brief period of increasing pluralism. As a pragmatist, Mubarak was wary of the disruptive social effects of liberalization and slowed down the process of reform. A political amnesty resulted in a period of greater toleration – within limits – of the Muslim Brotherhood. Attempts to placate the military resulted in policies that would facilitate the expansion of its business interests in the hopes of "coup-proofing" the regime.

Nonetheless, the Third World debt crisis of the mid-1980s increased the pressure on Egypt to dismantle the statist development model it had inherited from the Nasser era. By the end of the decade, Mubarak was cashing in his geostrategic rents to reduce some of its external debt as it entered negotiations with the World Bank and the International Monetary Fund. The result was Economic Reform and Structural Adjustment Programme, a comprehensive structural adjustment program conforming to the broad agenda of the so-called Washington Consensus.

However, the Economic Reform and Structural Adjustment Programme of 1991 represented a more comprehensive process of liberalizing reform than that of Sadat's *infitah*. Here we must distinguish between liberalization and neoliberalism. The former often refers to the elimination of constraints on economic activity and can be understood as a process of negative reforms, in the sense of removing legislation and regulation. The neoliberal project sweeping the globe in the 1980s and 1990s entailed far more substantive reforms that targeted the nature of the state. In this sense, neoliberalism is far more ambitious and radical than mere liberalization. Reforms entailed not merely removing constraints on market activity, but also transforming the Egyptian state in the interest of creating new markets and enhancing market discipline. The World Bank outlined this new role in detail in its 1997 *World Development Report* called *The State in a Changing World*, in which it advocates a shift from the planned economies of the era of "Third Worldism" to the free markets of the post-Cold War period (World Bank, 1997). This requires states to strengthen judicial institutions with the goal of enforcing the rights of private property, to promote business-friendly environments for the growth of private firms, to allow the unrestricted repatriation of profits and to substantially open the economy to the private sector.

In this sense, the state becomes a crucial actor in the implementation of the neoliberal project. In terms of strategies of capital accumulation, this requires active state involvement in the process of making markets and disciplining market behaviour through the rigorous enforcement of private property rights. In Egypt, as in most countries experiencing a neoliberal transition, this entails processes of accumulation by dispossession. In rural Egypt, this resulted in attempts by landlords – with the active support of key state actors – to reclaim land previously redistributed to small tenants during the Nasser period. In such cases, coercive force was used to evict tenants who had worked the land for generations. Yet, dispossession could occur through "market" means as well. The elimination of tenure security exposed smallholders to the imperatives of competitive rents. Being unable to meet the costs of rising rents, numerous tenants were subsequently evicted. To anyone familiar with the history of primitive accumulation in the making of capitalism – notably the enclosure movement of early modern England – the ensuing tensions and violence that erupted in the Egyptian countryside in the late 1990s was predictable.

In the urban economy, accumulation by dispossession assumed different forms, but had similarly disruptive effects. One of the key reforms in the neoliberal toolkit was the privatization of state-owned enterprises – of which there were many in Egypt. The dispossessive aspect of privatization is linked to the assault on workers' rights entailed in the process of privatization. Often characterized as "bloated" and "inefficient," state-owned enterprises often exist within a web of workers' rights and forms of social protection that inhibit the ability of employers to maximize profits and enable workers to resist the intensification of exploitation and maintain a relatively decent standard of living. Such was the case in Egypt. Workers in state-owned enterprises were public sector workers whose access to health care and housing, and the provision of pensions were "decommodified" through their public sector employment. In this sense, they were perceived as social and economic "rights" that constituted the social contract between rulers and ruled in Egyptian society. Similarly, workers in state-owned enterprises often benefited from protection against arbitrary dismissals. The process of privatization effectively eliminates these forms of social and economic rights as ownership is passed from the state to the hands of private capital, granting power to the latter to commodify those goods and services hitherto enjoyed as rights. As with rural Egypt, a result of the neoliberal transformation of the urban economy was rising inequality and intensifying industrial unrest, particularly in the context of the acceleration of neoliberal reforms under the Nazif government of 2004.

The period of Egypt's neoliberal transformation – roughly from 1991 to 2011 – exposed numerous significant fault lines amongst the Egyptian elite. The politics of the period can thus be viewed as a struggle – within the NDP – of neoliberal modernizers pushing forward with their structural reforms, and pragmatic conservatives – many, but not all linked to the military – cautioning restraint. Particularly in the 1990s, the pendulum swung back and forth between accelerated neo-liberalism and redistributive populism. By the early 2000s, however, the neoliberal modernizers were clearly ascendant – at least politically – within the NDP. The period can also be viewed as the continuing fractionalization of Egyptian capital. The dismantling of the statist economy revealed the divisions amongst Egyptian capital that – in many ways – resulted in the creation of the statist economy in the first place. No unified class of capitalists stepped into the breach opened by two decades of neoliberal reforms. Instead, what we see in Egypt are the growing tensions between the three politically constituted fractions of Egyptian capital that began to emerge during Sadat's *infitah* project: the neoliberals, the Islamic capitalists and the military. Contrary to the fantasies of liberal reformers, neoliberalism aggravated the political divisions constituting these different fractions of capital.

Accumulation by Dispossession and the Fragmentation of Egyptian Capital

Egypt's integration into the global capitalist economy has resulted in a significant transformation of the social relations of class. Liberalization and structural reforms – understood here as a process of neoliberal transformation – are not neutral phenomena resulting in the "modern-ization" of the Egyptian economy. Rather, they accompany substan-tive shifts in the balance of class forces within Egyptian society – away from workers and peasants and towards landlords and the owners of capital – that are expressed as forms of dispossession by the popular classes. In contrast with the technical language of structural reform used by neoliberal "modernizers" and the international financial insti-tutions seeking to impose the Washington Consensus on debtor states, capital accumulation by dispossession is a fundamentally political development that alters the power relations within society.

Harvey's (2003) characterization of accumulation by dispossession helps us to understand the qualitative transformations underway in an

Egyptian economy that is increasingly integrated into the neoliberal global economy. Beyond the quantitative metrics of growth favoured by mainstream economists, the neoliberal transformation of the Egyptian economy has resulted in peasants being dispossessed of their land and workers being dispossessed of the socioeconomic rights that formed the basis of the authoritarian bargain of Egypt's post-war socioeconomic order. The erosion of the social basis of Egyptian authoritarianism subsequently helps us understand the increasing fragility of the Mubarak regime.

While the shift towards neoliberalism has unequivocally resulted in a weakening of the class capacities of the working class and the peasantry vis-à-vis Egyptian capital, it is not the case that neoliberalism has resulted in the creation of a unified capitalist class out of the ashes of the statist development model of the Nasser period. Rather, Egyptian capital is fractured along numerous lines, resulting in growing competition between "fractions" of capital. These fractions of Egyptian capital, however, are significantly different from those commonly found in the countries of so-called advanced capitalism. Whereas the latter tend to be differentiated on the basis of sectoral composition – for example, industrial capital versus financial capital, domestic capital versus transnational capital – the fractions of Egyptian capital are politically constituted. The neoliberal period has seen growing competition between the neoliberals associated with Gamal Mubarak and the "modernized" NDP, an increasingly business oriented military, and the Islamic sector, organized around the Muslim Brotherhood.

The politically constituted character of Egypt's fractions of capital means that the politics of neoliberal transformation become all the more salient to the analysis. What this means for the long-term trajectory of these fractions is an open question. Whether the political divisions will give way to the coalescence of common capitalist interests rooted strictly in private property remains to be seen. The immediate aftermath of the uprisings of 2011 witnessed an intensification of this fractional conflict as the military first went after numerous prominent neoliberals associated with Gamal Mubarak before clamping down on the Muslim Brotherhood. Recent developments suggest a certain qualified rapprochement between the military and the neoliberals, albeit under the hegemony of the former, which retains a certain nationalist political orientation.

Neoliberal Authoritarianism and Contentious Politics

The period of neoliberal restructuring in Egypt did little to dismantle the authoritarian infrastructure of the Egyptian state. While liberalizers and democratization theorists were misguided in their general belief that implanting neoliberal capitalism in Egypt would facilitate the growth of democracy, theorists of authoritarianism are perhaps too quick to proclaim that nothing significant has changed in Egypt. The burgeoning literature on authoritarianism has viewed the events that unfolded after the uprisings of 2011 as evidence for their characterization of Egypt – if not the Arab world in general – as being composed of a persistent or resilient authoritarianism. A central claim of this book is that while neoliberal capitalism did not result in democratization (indeed, that capitalism does not in general result in democratization), Egyptian society and Egyptian authoritarianism has undergone constant change. At the level of the state, Egypt has experienced a shift from the authoritarian populism of Nasser to the emerging neoliberal authoritarianism of the Mubarak period (with Sadat's tenure being a period of transition between the two). While theorists of authoritarianism tend to focus on the formal aspects of authoritarianism (e.g., the absence of free and fair multi-party elections, the absence or lack of enforcement of civil rights, the absence of the rule of law) to make their claims of authoritarian resilience, they neglect to give sufficient attention to the content of authoritarian politics. Authoritarian politics that restrains the unfettered play of market forces, redistributes land to peasants and profits to the workers, and provides de-commodified goods and services to the popular classes in general, is a qualitatively different type of authoritarianism than one that acts to dispossess the popular classes, eliminate social and economic rights through the commodification of goods and services and uses its coercive force to defend the private property rights of the owners of capital. In other words, the class content of authoritarian politics has dramatically changed in Egypt over the course of the post-war period.

This brings us to the development of "contentious politics" in Egypt and the broader Arab world. There has been a tendency amongst the scholarship on authoritarianism to view the Arab world as a region that is "frozen in time and space" (Gerges, 2015, p. 10). However, as this book has demonstrated, contemporary Egyptian politics has been unavoidably contentious, both in the sense of contention between elites as well as between the dominant class and the popular classes. The advent of liberalization in the 1970s and the implementation of more ambitious neoliberal reforms starting in the 1990s, coincided with the long-term erosion of the authoritarian bargain that formed the basis of the social contract between rulers and ruled in Egypt. As this social contract eroded, contentious politics – in terms of urban based protest movements like *Kefaya*, the disorganized "nonmovements" of the urban underclass, and especially the contentious politics of class struggle both amongst the working class and the peasantry – began to intensify and contest the neoliberal authoritarianism that had been institutionalized over the previous thirty years.

The composition of the Sisi regime has been shaped by the contentious politics of class just as it has been shaped by the fragmented nature of Egyptian capital discussed above. While the new military regime seeks to establish its hegemony by implementing policies that suggest a continuity of a global, neoliberal capitalism with stronger ties to Saudi Arabia, it has also sought to re-establish social and political order through the implementation of various populist measures that contradict the neoliberal orthodoxy of the current conjuncture. Significant wage increases for public sector workers, debt forgiveness for small farmers and the reintroduction of subsidies and price controls on commodities consumed by the popular classes sit precariously alongside the banning of strikes and the outlawing of independent trade unions. These are contradictions that will no doubt test the mettle of the Sisi regime over the years to come.

Bibliography

Abdel Khalek, G. (2001). *Stabilization and Adjustment in Egypt: Reform or De-Industrialization*. Northampton, MA: Edward Elgar.

Abdel Malek, A. (1968). *Egypt: Military Society; the Army Regime, the Left, and Social Change under Nasser*. New York: Random House.

Abdel Razek, S. (2005, August 25). The hardest nut to crack. *Al Ahram Weekly*.

   (2011, February 9). Living in poverty. *Al Ahram Online*. Retrieved from http://weekly.ahram.org.eg/Archive/2012/1084/ec1.htm

Abdelgouad, A. F. (2014). *Labor Law Reforms and Labor Market Performance in Egypt*. Lüneburg, Germany: University of Lüneburg Working Paper Series in Economics.

Abdelrahman, M. (2015). *Egypt's Long Revolution: Protest Movements and Uprisings*. London: Routledge.

   (2017). Policing neoliberalism in Egypt: The continuing rise of the "securocratic" state. *Third World Quarterly*, 38(1), 185–202. https://doi.org/10.1080/01436597.2015.1133246

Abraham, G., and Bakr, A. (2000). *Comprehensive Development Plan for the City of Luxor, Egypt*. Cambridge, MA: ABT Associates.

Abu Lughod, J. L. (1971). *Cairo: 1001 Years of the City Victorious*. Princeton, NJ: Princeton University Press. /z-wcorg/.

Abul-Magd, Z. (2012, February 13). The Brotherhood's businessmen. *Egypt Independent*. Retrieved from www.egyptindependent.com/brotherhoods-businessmen/

   (2016). Egypt's Adaptable Officers. In E. Grawert, and Z. Abul-Magd (eds.), *Businessmen in Arms: How the Military and Other Armed Groups Profit in the MENA Region*. Lanham, MD: Rowman & Littlefield, pp. 23–42.

   (2017). *Militarizing the Nation: The Army, Business, and Revolution in Egypt*. New York: Columbia University Press.

Adams, R. H. (2000). Evaluating the process of development in Egypt, 1980–97. *International Journal of Middle East Studies*, 32(2), 255–275.

Adly, A. (2014, July 7). Investigating the Muslim Brotherhood Economy. Retrieved April 16, 2018, from Tahrir Institute for Middle East Policy website: https://timep.org/commentary/investigating-muslim-brotherhood-economy/

Ahram Online. (2013, October 28). Egypt's millionaires make up 0.04% of total adult population: Report. *Ahram Online.* Retrieved from http://english.ahram.org.eg/NewsContent/3/0/84904/Business/0/Egypts-millionaires-make-up–of-total-adult-popula.aspx

Al Jazeera. (2008, March 12). Warning over world food shortages. Retrieved from www.aljazeera.com/news/middleeast/2008/03/2008525133438179651.html

al-Shater, K. (2011, April 21). The Nahda project. Retrieved July 11, 2018, from www.hudson.org/research/9820-khairat-al-shater-on-the-nahda-project-complete-translation-

Alavi, H., and Shanin, T. (1982). *Introduction to the Sociology of "Developing Societies."* London: MacMillan.

Al-Barawy, R. (1972). *Economic Development in the United Arab Republic.* Cairo: Anglo-Egyptian Bookshop.

Albrecht, H. (2013). *Raging against the Machine: Political Opposition under Authoritarianism in Egypt.* Syracuse, NY: Syracuse University Press.

Albrecht, H., and Bishara, D. (2011). Back on horseback: The military and political transformation in Egypt. *Middle East Law and Governance, 3* (1–2), 13–23.

Albrecht, H., and Schlumberger, O. (2004). "Waiting for Godot": Regime change without democratization in the Middle East. *International Political Science Review, 25*(4), 371–392.

Alexander, A. (2010). Leadership and collective action in the Egyptian trade unions. *Work, Employment and Society, 24*(2), 241–259. https://doi.org/10.1177/0950017010362144

(2012). The Egyptian workers' movement and the 25 January Revolution. *International Socialism, 133,* 101–126.

Alexander, A., and Bassiouny, M. (2014). *Bread, Freedom, Social Justice: Workers and the Egyptian Revolution.* London: Zed Books Ltd.

Alonso-Gamo, P., Fedelino, A., and Horvitz, S. P. (1997). Globalization and growth prospects in Arab countries. IMF working paper WP/79/127. Washington, DC: International Monetary Fund.

American Chamber of Commerce in Egypt. (2003). *The Construction Sector in Egypt: Development and Competitiveness.* Cairo: Business Studies and Analysis Centre.

Anderson, P. (1974). *Lineages of the Absolutist State.* London: Verso.

Ansari, H. (1986). *Egypt: The Stalled Society.* Albany: State University of New York Press.

AOI. (2018). Arab organization for industrialization. Retrieved August 20, 2018, from www.aoi.org.eg/index.php?lang=en

Apeldoorn, B. van. (2002). *Transnational Capitalism and the Struggle over European Integration*. London: Routledge.

Arab Republic of Egypt, The. (2005). *Egypt...Crossing Paths into Modernization*. Cairo: The Government of Egypt.

Assaad, R. (2011, February 14). Demographics of Arab protests. Retrieved March 15, 2018, from the Council on Foreign Relations website: www.cfr.org/interview/demographics-arab-protests

(2014). Making sense of Arab labor markets: The enduring legacy of dualism. *IZA Journal of Labor & Development*, 3, 6. https://doi.org/10.1186/2193-9020-3-6

Assaad, R., and Krafft, C. (2015). The structure and evolution of employment in Egypt: 1998–2012. In R. Assaad and C. Krafft (eds.), *The Egyptian Labor Market in an Era of Revolution*. Oxford, UK: Oxford University Press, pp. 27–51.

Asutay, M. (2013). Islamic moral economy as the foundation of Islamic finance. In V. Cattelan (ed.), *Islamic Finance in Europe: Towards a Plural Financial System*. Cheltenham, UK: Edward Elgar, pp. 55–68.

Ates, D. (2005). Economic liberalization and changes in fundamentalism: The case of Egypt. *Middle East Policy*, 12(4), 133–144. https://doi.org/10.1111/j.1475-4967.2005.00230.x

Aughey, A., Jones, G., and Riches, W. T. M. (1992). *The Conservative Political Tradition in Britain and the United States*. Madison, NJ: Fairleigh Dickinson Univ Press.

Aulas, M.-C. (1982). Sadat's Egypt: A balance sheet. *MERIP Reports*, (107), 6–31. https://doi.org/10.2307/3011724

Ayeb, H. (2012). The marginalization of the small peasantry: Egypt and Tunisia. In R. Bush and H. Ayeb (eds.), *Marginality and Exclusion in Egypt*. London: Zed Press, pp. 72–96.

Ayubi, N. (1991a). *Political Islam: Religion and Politics in the Arab world*. London: Routledge.

(1991b). *The State and Public Policies in Egypt since Sadat*. London: Ithaca Press.

(1992). Withered socialism or whether socialism? The radical Arab states as populist-corporatist regimes. *Third World Quarterly*, 13(1), 89–105.

(1995). *Over-Stating the Arab State: Politics and Society in the Middle East*. London: I.B. Tauris.

Azzam, H. T. (2002). *The Arab World: Facing the Challenge of the New Millennium*. London: I.B. Tauris.

Baffes, J. (2004). Cotton: *Market Setting, Trade Policies, and Issues*. In M. Ataman Aksoy and John C. Beghin (eds.), *Global Agricultural Trade and Developing Countries*, Washington, DC: The World Bank, pp. 259–274.

Bargawi, H., and McKinley, T. (2010). *The ADCR 2011: The Poverty Impact of Growth and Employment in Egypt (1990–2009)*. New York: UNDP.

Batatu, H. (1978). *The Old Social Classes and the Revolutionary Movements of Iraq: A Study of Iraq's Old Landed and Commercial Classes and of Its Communists, Ba'thists, and Free Officers*. Princeton, NJ: Princeton University Press.

(1999). *Syria's Peasantry, the Descendants of Its Lesser Rural Notables, and Their Politics*. Princeton, NJ: Princeton University Press.

Bayad, M. (1979). *Housing and Urban Development in Egypt*. Copenhagen, Denmark: The Royal Danish Academy of Art, School of Architecture.

Bayat, A. (2006). *The Political Economy of Social Policy in Egypt: Social Policy in the Middle East*. New York: Palgrave Macmillan.

(2013). *Life as Politics: How Ordinary People Change the Middle East*, 2nd edn. Stanford, CA: Stanford University Press.

(2017). *Revolution without Revolutionaries: Making Sense of the Arab Spring*. Stanford, CA: Stanford University Press.

Beach, W., and O'Driscoll, G. (2003). *The Role of Property Rights in Economic Growth: An Introduction to the 2003 Index*. Washington, DC: The Heritage Foundation.

Beinin, J. (1989). Labor, capital, and the state in Nasserist Egypt, 1952–1961. *International Journal of Middle East Studies*, 21(1), 71–90.

(2001). *Workers and Peasants in the Modern Middle East*. Cambridge, UK; New York: Cambridge University Press.

(2005). Political Islam and the new global economy: The political economy of an Egyptian social movement. *CR: The New Centennial Review*, 5(1), 111–139.

(2009a). Workers' protest in Egypt: Neo-liberalism and class struggle in 21st century. *Social Movement Studies*, 8(4), 449–454.

(2009b). Workers' struggles under "socialism" and neoliberalism. In R. El-Mahdi and P. Marfleet (eds.), *Egypt: The Moment of Change*. London: Zed Books, pp. 68–86.

(2016a). *Workers and Thieves: Labor Movements and Popular Uprisings in Tunisia and Egypt*. Stanford, CA: Stanford University Press.

(2016b). *Workers and Thieves: Labor Movements and Popular Uprisings in Tunisia and Egypt*. Stanford, CA: Stanford University Press.

Beinin, J., and Lockman, Z. (1987). *Workers on the Nile: Nationalism, Communism, Islam, and the Egyptian Working Class, 1882–1954*. Princeton, NJ: Princeton University Press.

Ben Nefissa, S. (1995). Les ligues régionales et les associations islamiques en Égypte: deux formes de regroupements à vocation sociale et caritative. *Revue Tiers Monde*, 36(141), 163–177. https://doi.org/10.3406/tiers .1995.4951

Berberoglu, B. (1987). *The Internationalization of Capital: Imperialism and Capitalist Development on a World Scale.* Westport, CT: Praeger.

(2003). *Globalization of Capital and the Nation-State: Imperialism, Class Struggle.* Lanham, MD: Rowman & Littlefield.

Bernstein, H. (2010). *Class Dynamics of Agrarian Change.* Sterling, VA: Kumarian Press.

Bianchi, R. (1985). Businessmen's Associations in Egypt and Turkey. *Annals of the American Academy of Political and Social Science, 482,* 147–159.

(1986). The corporatization of the Egyptian labor movement. *Middle East Journal, 40*(3), 429–444.

(1989). *Unruly Corporatism: Associational Life in Twentieth-Century Egypt.* Oxford, UK: Oxford University Press.

Blaydes, L. (2006). *Who Votes in Authoritarian Elections and Why? Determinants of Voter Turnout in Contemporary Egypt.* Presented at the American Political Science Association, Philadelphia.

Blumberg, A. (2011). Egypt's Military, Inc. *All Things Considered.* Retrieved from www.npr.org/sections/money/2011/02/10/133501837/why-egypts-military-cares-about-home-appliances

Boas, M., and McNeill, D. (2004). *Global Institutions and Development: Framing the World?* London: Routledge.

Breman, J., and Linden, M. (2014). Informalizing the economy: The return of the social question at a global level. *Development and Change, 45*(5), 920–940.

Bromley, S. (1994). *Rethinking Middle East Politics.* Austin: University of Texas Press.

Bromley, S., and Bush, R. (1994). Adjustment in Egypt? The political economy of reform. *Review of African Political Economy, 21*(60), 201–213.

Bruff, I. (2014). The rise of authoritarian neoliberalism. *Rethinking Marxism, 26*(1), 113–129. https://doi.org/10.1080/08935696.2013.843250

(2016). Neoliberalism and authoritarianism. In S. Springer, K. Birch, and J. MacLeavy (eds.), *Handbook of Neoliberalism.* New York: Routledge, pp. 107–117.

Bryceson, D. (2000). African peasants' centrality and marginality: Rural labour transformations. In D. Bryceson, C. Kay, and J. Mooij (eds.), *Disappearing Peasantries? Rural Labour in Africa, Asia and Latin America.* London: Intermediate Technology Publications, pp. 37–63.

Bush, R. (1999). *Economic Crisis and the Politics of Reform in Egypt.* Oxford: Westview Press.

(2000). An agricultural strategy without farmers: Egypt's countryside in the new millennium. *Review of African Political Economy, 27*(84), 235–249.

(ed.). (2002). *Counter-Revolution in Egypt's Countryside: Land and Farmers in the Era of Economic Reform.* London: Zed Press.

(2009). The land and the people. In R. El-Mahdi and P. Marfleet (eds.), *Egypt: The Moment of Change.* London: Zed Books, pp. 51–67.

(2011). Coalitions for dispossession and networks of resistance? Land, politics and agrarian reform in Egypt. *British Journal of Middle Eastern Studies, 38*(3), 391–405.

(2016). Uprisings without Agrarian Questions. In A. Kadri (ed.), *Development Challenges and Solutions after the Arab Spring.* New York: Springer, pp. 153–172.

Cahill, D. (2014). *The End of Laissez-Faire? On the Durability of Embedded Neoliberalism.* Cheltenham, UK: Edward Elgar Publishing.

Calvert, J. (2009). *Sayyid Qutb and the Origins of Radical Islamism.* Oxford, UK: Oxford University Press.

Cambanis, T. (2010, September 11). Succession Gives Army a Stiff Test in Egypt. *The New York Times.* Retrieved from www.nytimes.com/2010/09/12/world/middleeast/12egypt.html

Cammack, P. (1989). Bringing the state back in? *British Journal of Political Science, 19*(2), 261–290.

(1990). Statism, new institutionalism, and Marxism. *Socialist Register: The Retreat of the Intellectuals, 26*(26). Retrieved from http://socialist register.com/index.php/srv/article/download/5578

(2004). What the World Bank means by poverty reduction, and why it matters. *New Political Economy, 9*(2), 189–211.

CAPMAS. (2018a). Annual employment rate. Retrieved September 12, 2018, from www.capmas.gov.eg/Pages/IndicatorsPage.aspx?page_id=6149&ind_id=1116

(2018b). Average wages. Retrieved September 12, 2018, from www.capmas.gov.eg/Pages/IndicatorsPage.aspx?page_id=6149&ind_id=1116

Castel, R. (2003). *From Manual Workers to Wage Laborers: Transformation of the Social Question.* Piscataway, NJ: Transaction Publishers.

Central Bank of Egypt. (2018). Investments. Retrieved September 9, 2018, from www.cbe.org.eg/en/EconomicResearch/Statistics/Pages/TimeSeries.aspx

Cerny, P. G. (1997). Paradoxes of the competition state: The dynamics of political globalization. *Government and Opposition, 32*(2), 251–274. https://doi.org/10.1111/j.1477-7053.1997.tb00161.x

Chaudhry, K. A. (1994). Economic liberalization and the lineages of the rentier state. *Comparative Politics, 27*(1), 1–25.

Chesnais, F. (2016). *Finance Capital Today: Corporations and Banks in the Lasting Global Slump.* Leiden, the Netherland: Brill.

CIA. (1987). The Egyptian military: Its role and missions under Mubarak. Retrieved from Central Intelligence Agency website: www.cia.gov/library/readingroom/document/cia-rdp88t00096r000700820001-5

Clarke, S. (1978). Capital, fractions of capital and the state: "Neo-Marxist" analysis of the South African state. *Capital & Class*, 2(2), 32–77.

Cook, S. A. (2007). *Ruling but Not Governing: The Military and Political Development in Egypt, Algeria, and Turkey*. Baltimore, MD: Johns Hopkins University Press.

Cooper, M. N. (1982). *The Transformation of Egypt*. London: Croom Helm.

Credit Suisse. (2010). Global wealth databook 2010. Retrieved from Credit Suisse website: www.credit-suisse.com/corporate/en/research/research-institute/global-wealth-report.html

(2017). Global wealth databook 2017. Retrieved from Credit Suisse website: www.credit-suisse.com/corporate/en/research/research-institute/global-wealth-report.html

Crouch, C. (2004). *Post-Democracy*. New York: Wiley.

Dabbah, M. M. (2010). *International and Comparative Competition Law*. Cambridge: Cambridge University Press.

Dahl, R. A. (1961). *Who Governs? Democracy and Power in an American City*. New Haven, CT: Yale University Press.

(1973). *Polyarchy: Participation and Opposition*. New Haven, CT: Yale University Press.

Dalacoura, K. (2016). Islamism and neoliberalism in the aftermath of the 2011 Arab uprisings: The Freedom and Justice Party in Egypt and Nahda in Tunisia. In E. Akcali (ed.), *Neoliberal Governmentality and the Future of the State in the Middle East and North Africa*. New York: Springer, pp. 61–83.

De Smet, B. (2016). *Gramsci on Tahrir: Revolution and Counter-Revolution in Egypt*. London: Pluto Press.

De Soto, H. (2000). *The Mystery of Capital: Why Capitalism Triumphs in the West and Fails Everywhere Else*. New York: Basic Books.

(2001). Dead capital and the poor. *SAIS Review*, 21(1), 13–43. https://doi.org/10.1353/sais.2001.0011

Demmelhuber, T. (2011). Economic reform and authoritarianism in Egypt: Politics, power and patronage. In J. Harrigan and H. El Said (eds.), *Globalisation, Democratisation and Radicalisation in the Arab World*. New York: Springer, pp. 145–161.

Denis, E. (2006). Cairo as neo-liberal capital? From walled city to gated communities. In D. Singerman and P. Amar (eds.), *Cairo Cosmopolitan: Politics, Culture, and Urban Space in the New Globalized Middle East*. Cairo: American University in Cairo Press.

Diab, O. (2016a, May 23). Egypt's widening wealth gap. Retrieved May 25, 2018, from Mada Masr website: www.madamasr.com/en/2016/05/23/feature/economy/egypts-widening-wealth-gap/

(2016b, October 20). How every dollar became $12,000 in less than a decade for Gamal Mubarak. *Mada Masr.* Retrieved from www.madam asr.com/en/2016/10/20/feature/economy/how-every-dollar-became-12000-in-less-than-a-decade-for-gamal-mubarak/

Diamond, L. (1997). *Is the Third Wave of Democratization Over? An Empirical Assessment.* Notre Dame, IN: Helen Kellogg Institute for International Studies.

Droz-Vincent, P. (2009). The security sector in Egypt: Management, coercion and external alliance under the dynamics of change. In L. Guazzone, and D. Pioppi (eds.), *The Arab State and Neo-Liberal Globalization. The Restructuring of State Power in the Middle East.* Ithaca, NY: Ithaca Press, pp. 219–246.

Duboc, M. (2015). Challenging the trade union, reclaiming the nation: The politics of labor protest in Egypt, 2006–11. In M. Kamrava (ed.), *Beyond the Arab Spring: The Evolving Ruling Bargain in the Middle East.* Oxford, UK: Oxford University Press, pp. 223–248.

Economist. (2004). *Breathing Life into Dead Capital: Why Secure Property Rights Matter.*

Economist Intelligence Unit (EIU). (1988). *Egypt: Country Profile, 1989/90.* London: The Economist Group.

(1997). *Egypt: Country Profile, 1997–1998.* London: The Economist Group.

(2006). *Country Profile: Egypt.* London: The Economist Group.

Egypt. (2005). *Trade Policy Review.* Geneva: World Trade Organization.

Egyptian Stock Exchange. (2007). Stock market annual report 2007. Retrieved from www.egx.com.eg/English/Services_Reports.aspx

Ehab, M. (2012). *Labor Market Flexibility in Egypt: With Application to the Textiles and Apparel Industry (Working Paper 170).* Cairo: Egyptian Centre for Economic Studies.

El Madany, S. (2009, January). *No Monopoly in Egypt's Steel Sector, Says ECA.* Cairo: Egyptian Media Services Ltd.

El Nour, S. (2015). Small farmers and the revolution in Egypt: The forgotten actors. *Contemporary Arab Affairs, 8*(2), 198–211.

El-Shatir, K. (2005, November 23). Khairat el-Shatir: No need to be afraid of us. *The Guardian.* Retrieved from www.theguardian.com/world/2005/nov/23/comment.mainsection

El Shazly, A. (2001, January). *Incentive Based Regulation and Bank Restructuring in Egypt.* Presented at the Annual Conference of the Middle East Economic Association, Cairo.

El Tarouty, S. (2016). *Businessmen, Clientelism, and Authoritarianism in Egypt.* New York: Springer.

El-Erian, M. A., and Sheybani, S. (1997). Private capital flows in the development of the Arab countries. *Cairo Papers in Social Sciences*, 11–34.

El-Gawhary, K. (1997). Nothing more to lose. Landowners, tenants and economic liberalization in Egypt. *Middle East Report*, 7–9.

El-Ghobashy, M. (2005). The metamorphosis of the Egyptian Muslim brothers. *International Journal of Middle East Studies*, 37(3), 373–395.

El-Ghonemy, R. M. (2003). Development Strategies, 1950–2001. In R. M. El-Ghonemy (ed.), *Egypt in the Twenty First Century: Challenges for Development.* London: Routledge, pp. 73–110.

El-Hefnaway, A. I. K. (2004). *Protecting' Agricultural Land from Urbanization Or "Managing" the Conflict between Informal Urban Growth while Meeting the Demands of Communities.* Cairo, Egypt: Ministry of Housing Utilities and Urban Communities.

El-Karanshawi, S. (2011, March 23). Alaa Mubarak owns over LE 49 million worth of shares in Palm Hills. *Al Masry Al Youm.*

El-Laithy, H., Lokshin, M., and Banerji, A. (2003). Poverty and economic growth in Egypt, 1995–2000 (No. WPS3068; p. 1). Retrieved from the World Bank website: http://documents.worldbank.org/curated/en/846511468746774719/Poverty-and-economic-growth-in-Egypt-1995-2000

Elliot, L., and Stewart, H. (2017, October 11). IMF: Higher taxes for rich will cut inequality without hitting growth. *The Guardian.* Retrieved from www.theguardian.com/business/2017/oct/11/imf-higher-taxes-rich-inequality-jeremy-corbyn-labour-donald-trump

Enders, K. (2008, February 13). IMF Survey: Egypt: Reforms Trigger Economic Growth. Retrieved August 13, 2018, from the IMF website: www.imf.org/en/News/Articles/2015/09/28/04/53/socar021308a

England, A. (2007). TMG prices largest IPO in Egypt this year. *Financial Times, November 16.* Retrieved from www.ft.com/content/d347bea2-945c-11dc-9aaf-0000779fd2ac

Esping-Andersen, G. (1976). Modes of class struggle and the capitalist state. *Kapitalistate*, 4/5, 186–220.

(1990). *The Three Worlds of Welfare Capitalism.* Princeton, NJ: Princeton University Press.

Esposito, J. L. (1983). *Voices of Resurgent Islam.* Oxford, UK: Oxford University Press.

Esterman, I. (2015, June 10). A fight over land rights shaped by wars, an uprising and power politics. *Mada Masr.* Retrieved from www.madamasr.com/en/2015/06/10/feature/politics/a-fight-over-land-rights-shaped-by-wars-an-uprising-and-power-politics/

Euben, R. L. (1999). *Enemy in the Mirror: Islamic Fundamentalism and the Limits of Modern Rationalism: A Work of Comparative Political Theory*. Princeton, NJ: Princeton University Press.

Evans, B., Rueschemeyer, D., and Skocpol, T. (eds.). (1985). *Bringing the State Back in: Strategies of Analysis in Current Research*. Cambridge: Cambridge University Press.

Fahmi, M. (2001, January 4). Panacea or nostrum? *Al-Ahram Weekly*. Retrieved from http://weekly.ahram.org.eg/archive/2001/515/ec2.htm

Fahmy, N. (2002). *The Politics of Egypt: State-Society Relationship*. London: Routledge.

Fandy, M. (1994). Egypt's Islamic Group: Regional revenge? *Middle East Journal, 48*(4), 607–625.

FAOSTAT. (2018). Food and agriculture data. Retrieved from www.fao.org/faostat/en/#home

Farah, N. R. (2009). *Egypt's Political Economy: Power Relations in Development*. Cairo: American University in Cairo Press.

Farsoun, S. K. (1997). Class structure and social change in the Arab World. In N. S. Hopkins and S. E. Ibrahim (eds.), *Arab Society: Class, Gender, Power, and Development*. Cairo: American University in Cairo Press, pp. 11–28.

Farsoun, S. K., and Zacharia, C. (1995). Class, economic change, and political liberalization in the Arab World. In R. Brynen, B. Korany, and P. Noble (eds.), *Political Liberalization and Democratization in the Arab World* (Vol. 1). Boulder, CO: Lynne Rienner Publishers, pp. 261–282.

Fathi, Y. (2005, April). When the strangers came to town. *Al-Ahram Weekly*. Retrieved from http://weekly.ahram.org.eg/Archive/2005/739/eg7.htm

Fergany, N. (1998). *The Challenges of Human Development in the Arab World*. Cairo: Cairo Papers in Social Science.

Feteha, A. (2012, April 3). Muslims Inc: How rich is Khairat El-Shater? *Ahram Online*. Retrieved from http://english.ahram.org.eg/News/38278.aspx

Forte, D. F. (1978). Egyptian land law: An evaluation. *The American Journal of Comparative Law, 26*(2), 273–278. https://doi.org/10.2307/839674

Fukuyama, F. (1993). *The End of History and the Last Man*. New York: Harper Collins.

Gamble, A. (1988). *The Free Economy and the Strong State: The Politics of Thatcherism*. Durham, NC: Duke University Press.

(2009). *The Spectre at the Feast: Capitalist Crisis and the Politics of Recession*. New York: Macmillan International Higher Education.

Gerges, F. (2012). The new capitalists: Islamists' political economy. Retrieved March 6, 2018, from the Open Democracy website: www.opendemo cracy.net/fawaz-gerges/new-capitalists-islamists-political-economy

Gerges, F. (ed.). (2015). *Contentious Politics in the Middle East: Popular Resistance and Marginalized Activism beyond the Arab Uprisings*. New York: Palgrave Macmillan.

Gerschenkron, A. (1962). *Economic Backwardness in Historical Perspective: A Book of Essays*. Cambridge, MA: Belknap Press of Harvard University Press.

Gill, S. (1992). The emerging world order and European change. *Socialist Register*, 28(28). Retrieved from www.socialistregister.com/index.php/srv/article/download/5613

Giugale, M. (1993). The rationale for structural adjustment. *Cairo Papers in Social Science*, The Economic And Politics of Structural Adjustment in Egypt: Third Annual Symposium, *16*(3).

GOE. (2018). State Information Service. Retrieved August 20, 2018, from the Government of Egypt State Information Service website: www.sis .gov.eg/Story/99743?lang=en-us

Golia, M. (2011, April 5). Egypt's forgotten fellahin. *Egypt Independent*. Retrieved from www.egyptindependent.com/egypts-forgotten-fellahin/

Görmüs, E. (2016). The economic ideology of the Egyptian Muslim Brotherhood: The changing discourses and practices. *Journal of Emerging Economies & Islamic Research*, 4(3), pp. 60–74.

Gramsci, A. (1971). *Selections from the Prison Notebooks of Antonio Gramsci*. New York: International Publishers.

Grawert, E. (2016). Introduction: The political economy of the military and non-state armed groups in the Middle East and North Africa. In E. Grawert and Z. Abul-Magd (eds.), *Businessmen in Arms: How the Military and Other Armed Groups Profit in the MENA Region*. Lanham, MD: Rowman & Littlefield, pp. 1–22.

Gumuscu, S. (2010). Class, status, and party: The changing face of political Islam in Turkey and Egypt. *Comparative Political Studies*, 43(7), 835–861.

Halawa, O. (2012, September 5). Profile: The Arab Organization for Industrialization. *Egypt Independent*. Retrieved from www.egypt independent.com/profile-arab-organization-industrialization/

Halliday, F. (2013). *Arabia without Sultans*. London: Saqi.

Halperin, S. (1997). *In the Mirror of the Third World: Capitalist Development in Modern Europe*. Ithaca, NY: Cornell University Press.

(2004). *War and Social Change in Modern Europe: The Great Transformation Revisited*. Cambridge: Cambridge University Press.

Hamzawy, A. (2007). Egypt: Regression in the Muslim Brotherhood's Party platform? *Arab Reform Bulletin, 5.*

Hanieh, A. (2011). *Capitalism and Class in the Gulf Arab States.* New York: Palgrave Macmillan US.

(2013). *Lineages of Revolt: Issues of Contemporary Capitalism in the Middle East.* Chicago: Haymarket Books.

Hanna, M. (1985). Real estate rights in urban Egypt: The changing socio-political winds. In A. E. Mayer (ed.), *Property, Social Structure and Law in the Modern Middle East.* Albany: SUNY Press.

Harb, I. (2003). The Egyptian military in politics: Disengagement or accommodation? *Middle East Journal, 57*(2), pp. 269–290.

Harik, I. (1992). Privatization: The Issue, the Prospects, and the Fears. In I. Harik and D. J. Sullivan (eds.), *Privatization and Liberalization in the Middle East.* Bloomington: Indiana University Press, pp. 1–23.

(1998). *Economic Policy Reform in Egypt.* Cairo: American University in Cairo Press.

Harrington, J. (1992). *Harrington: "The Commonwealth of Oceana" and "A System of Politics."* Cambridge: Cambridge University Press.

Harvey, D. (1982). *The Limits to Capital.* New York: Blackwell.

(1992). *The Condition of Postmodernity: An Enquiry into the Origins of Cultural Change.* New York: Wiley.

(2003). *The New Imperialism.* Oxford, UK: Oxford University Press.

(2005). *A Brief History of Neoliberalism.* Oxford: New York University Press.

Hasan, S. S. (2003). *Christians versus Muslims in Modern Egypt: The Century-Long Struggle for Coptic Equality.* Oxford, UK: Oxford University Press.

Hassan, M., and Kandil, M. (2011). *The Relation between Public and Private Employment in Egypt: Evidence and Implications.* Cairo: Egyptian Center for Economic Studies.

Hayek, F. A. (2014). *The Constitution of Liberty.* London: Routledge.

Henry, C., and Springborg, R. (2001). *Globalization and the Politics of Development in the Middle East.* Cambridge: Cambridge University Press.

Heydemann, S. (2004). *Networks of Privilege in the Middle East: The Politics of Economic Reform Revisited.* New York: Springer.

Hill, E. (1999). The Supreme Constitutional Court of Egypt: Al-Mahkama Al-Dusturiyya Al-Ulya. In M. C. Kennedy (ed.), *Twenty Years of Development in Egypt (1977–1997): Part 2.* (Vol. 21). Cairo: American University in Cairo Press.

Hinnebusch, R. (2014). Towards a historical sociology of the Arab Uprising. *Routledge Handbook of the Arab Spring: Rethinking Democratization.* London: Routledge.

Hobsbawm, E. J. (1971). *Primitive Rebels: Studies in Archaic Forms of Social Movement in the 19th and 20th Centuries*. Manchester, UK: Manchester University Press.

Hobsbawm, E. J., and Rude, G. (1969). *Captain Swing*. Brooklyn, NY: Verso Books.

Holding Company for Maritime and Land Transport (HCMLT). (2018). Ownership structure. Retrieved August 10, 2018, from www.hcmlt .com/e_mysite/e_ownstr.htm

Hopwood, D. (1982). *Egypt: Politics and Society*. London: Allen and Unwin.

Howeidy, A. (2012, March 29). Meet the Brotherhood's enforcer: Khairat El-Shater. *Ahram Online*. Retrieved from http://english.ahram.org.eg/ NewsContent/1/64/37993/Egypt/Politics-/Meet-the-Brotherhood%E2% 80%99s-enforcer-Khairat-ElShater.aspx

Hubbard, B. (2018, October 19). Military reasserts its allegiance to its privileges. *The New York Times*. Retrieved from www.nytimes.com/ 2013/07/04/world/middleeast/Egyptian-military-reasserts-its-allegiance-to-its-privileges.html

Huntington, S. (1968). *Political Order in Changing Societies*. New Haven, CT: Yale University Press.

(1991). Democracy's third wave. *Journal of Democracy*, 2(2), 12–12. https://doi.org/10.1353/jod.1991.0016

Hyman, R., and Elger, T. (1981). Job controls, the employers' offensive and alternative strategies. *Capital and Class*, 15(4), 115–149.

Ibrahim, F., and Ibrahim, B. (2003). *Egypt: An Economic Geography*. London: I.B. Tauris.

Ibrahim, S. E. (1994). Egypt's Landed Bourgeoisie. In A. Oncu, C. Keyder and S. E. Ibrahim (eds.), *Developmentalism and Beyond: Society and Politics in Egypt and Turkey*. Cairo: American University in Cairo Press, pp. 19–43.

Ikhwan. (2007a, June 13). The Muslim Brotherhood's Program 2005 election. Retrieved July 9, 2018, from the Ikhwanweb website: www .ikhwanweb.com/article.php?id=811

(2007b, June 14). The Electoral Programme of the Muslim Brotherhood for Shura Council in 2007 – Ikhwanweb. Retrieved July 9, 2018, from the Ikhwanweb website: www.ikhwanweb.com/article.php?id=822

Ikram, K. (2006). *The Egyptian Economy, 1952–2000: Performance, Policies and Issues*. London: Routledge.

International Labor Organization (ILO). (2010). *Global Wage Report*. Geneva, Switzerland: ILO.

ILO. (2018a). Informal employment and informal sector as a percent of employment. Retrieved from the International Labor Organization website: www.ilostat.org

(2018b). Informal employment and informal sector as a percent of employment by sex – Harmonized series (%). Retrieved from the International Labor Organization website: www.ilo.org/ilostat

(2018c). Public employment by sectors and sub-sectors of national accounts. Retrieved from the International Labor Organization website: www.ilo.org/ilostat

(2018d). Trade union density rate. Retrieved from the ILO website: www.ilostat.org

ILOSTAT. (2018a). Days not worked due to strikes and lockouts by economic activity. Retrieved September 12, 2018, from www.ilo.org/ilostat

(2018b). Legal health coverage deficit by rural/urban areas (% of population without legal coverage). Retrieved September 12, 2018, from www.ilo.org/ilostat

(2018c). Number of strikes and lockouts by economic activity. Retrieved September 12, 2018, from www.ilo.org/ilostat

(2018d). Share of youth not in employment, education or training (NEET) by sex. Retrieved September 12, 2018, from www.ilo.org/ilostat

(2018e). Unemployment rate by sex and age (%). Retrieved from the ILO website: www.ilostat.org

(2018f). Workers involved in strikes and lockouts by economic activity (Thousands). Retrieved September 12, 2018, from www.ilo.org/ilostat

IMF. (1991a, October 2,). Concluding remarks by the acting chairman– Military Expenditure and the role of the fund, executive board meeting 91/138. Retrieved from the International Monetary Fund website: www.imf.org/external/SelectedDecisions/Description.aspx?decision= EBM/91/138

(1991b). International Monetary Fund Annual Report 1991 (p. 207). Retrieved from www.imf.org/external/pubs/ft/ar/archive/pdf/ar1991.pdf

(2007). Arab Republic of Egypt: 2007 Article IV Consultation: Staff report; staff statement; public information notice on the executive board discussion; and statement by the Executive Director for the Arab Republic of Egypt. Retrieved from the International Monetary Fund website: www.imf.org/en/Publications/CR/Issues/2016/12/31/Arab-Republic-of-Egypt-2007-Article-IV-Consultation-Staff-Report-Staff-Statement-Public-21507

International Business Publications. (2013). Egypt labor laws and regulations handbook: Volume 1 strategic information and basic laws. Retrieved from Lulu.com

Ismail, S. (2006). *Rethinking Islamist Politics: Culture, the State and Islamism*. London: I.B. Tauris.

Issawi, C. (1963). *Egypt in Revolution*. London: Oxford University Press.

Janowitz, M. (1977). *Military Institutions and Coercion in the Developing Nations: The Military in the Political Development of New Nations, expanded edition*. Chicago: University of Chicago Press.

(1988). *Military Institutions and Coercion in the Developing Nations: The Military in the Political Development of New Nations*. Chicago: University of Chicago Press.

Jaraba, M. (2014, May 14). The Egyptian military's economic channels of influence. Retrieved July 2, 2018, from the Middle East Institute website: www.mei.edu/content/map/egyptian-military%E2%80%99s-infor mal-channels-influence

Jehl, D. (1997, November 18). 70 die in attack at Egypt Temple. *The New York Times*. Retrieved from www.nytimes.com/1997/11/18/world/70-die-in-attack-at-egypt-temple.html

Johnson, P. (1973). Retreat of the revolution in Egypt. *MERIP Reports*, (17), 3–6. https://doi.org/10.2307/3011502

Johnston, C. (2008, April 6). In Egypt, long queues for bread that's almost free. *Reuters*. Retrieved from www.reuters.com/article/us-agflation-sub sidies/in-egypt-long-queues-for-bread-thats-almost-free-idUSL0404033 220080406

Jones, T. C. (2011). *Desert Kingdom*. Cambridge, MA: Harvard University Press.

Joya, A. (2008). Egyptian protests: Falling wages, high prices and the failure of an export-oriented economy. *Bullet, 2*.

(2013). *Accumulation by Dispossession and the Transformation of Property Relations in Egypt: Housing Policy Under Neoliberalism*. Toronto, Ontario, Canada: York University.

(2017). Neoliberalism, the state and economic policy outcomes in the post-Arab uprisings: The case of Egypt. *Mediterranean Politics, 22*(3), 339–361.

(2018). The military and the state in Egypt: class formation in the post-Arab uprisings. *British Journal of Middle Eastern Studies*, DOI: 10.1080/13530194.2018.1509692.

Kamil, J. (2008, November 6). The development plan for Luxor. *Al Ahram Weekly*.

Kandil, H. (2012). *Soldiers, Spies, and Statesmen: Egypt's Road to Revolt*. Brooklyn, NY: Verso Books.

Karshenas, M. (1994). Structural adjustment and employment in the Middle East and North Africa. *Working Paper Series/Economic Research Forum; 9420*. Cairo: Economic Research Forum.

Kay, C. (2000). Latin America's agrarian transformation: Peasantization and proletarianization. *Disappearing Peasantries*, 123–138.

Kechichian, J., and Nazimek, J. (1997). Challenges to the military in Egypt. Retrieved July 2, 2018, from the Middle East Policy Council website: www.mepc.org/challenges-military-egypt

Kennedy, G. (2008). *Diggers, Levellers, and Agrarian Capitalism: Radical Political Thought in Seventeenth Century England*. Lanham, MD: Lexington Books.

Kepel, G. (1985). *Muslim Extremism in Egypt: The Prophet and Pharaoh*. Berkeley: University of California Press.

Kepel, G., and Richard, Y. (1990). *Intellectuels et militants de l'Islam contemporain*. Paris: Seuil.

Kesselman, M. (ed.). (1992). *European Politics in Transition*, 2nd edn. Lexington, MA: DCHeath.

Kheir-El-Din, H., and El-Laithy, H. (2006). An assessment of growth, distribution, and poverty in Egypt: 1990/91-2004/05. Retrieved from www.eces.org.eg/Publication.aspx?Id=45

Kienle, E. (1998). More than a response to Islamism: The political deliberalization of Egypt in the 1990s. *Middle East Journal*, 219–235.

King, S. J. (2003). *Liberalization against Democracy: The Local Politics of Economic Reform in Tunisia*. Bloomington: Indiana University Press.

(2009). *The New Authoritarianism in the Middle East and North Africa*. Bloomington: Indiana University Press.

Kohut, A., Wike, R., and Horowitz, J. M. (2011). *Egyptians Embrace Revolt Leaders, Religious Parties and Military, As Well*. Washington, DC: Pew Research Center, p. 38.

Kourgiotis, P. (2018). Understanding Egyptian capitalism through the Muslim Brotherhood's eyes: The quest for an "Islamic economy" in the 1940s and its ideological and social impact. *British Journal of Middle Eastern Studies*, 45(3), 464–479. https://doi.org/10.1080/13530194.2017.1320973

La Monica, P. (2013, October 1). You're fired. Stock rises. Wall Street loves layoffs - The Buzz - Investment and Stock Market News. Retrieved April 15, 2018, from the CNNMoney website: http://buzz.money.cnn.com/2013/10/01/layoffs-stocks/

Langot, F., and Yassin, S. (2015). Reforming employment protection in Egypt: An evaluation based on transition models with measurement errors. *Economic Research Forum Working Paper Series No, 918*.

Law 12/2003., Pub. L. No. 12/2003 (2003).

LCHR. (2003). *Development and Agricultural Credit Bank: Between Corruption and Policies of Abusing of Poor Farmers* (No. 19). Cairo: Land Center for Human Rights.

(2004a). Land Center for Human Rights asks the general prosecutor to stop violations committed by some officials against farmers in Damytta province. Retrieved from the Land Center for Human Rights website: www.lchr-eg.org/archive/112/04-43.htm

(2004b). Nazlet El Ashtar farmers demand the minister of agriculture to protect their right in safe agrarian possession. Retrieved from the Land Center for Human Rights website: www.lchr-eg.org/archive/112/04-27.htm

(2004c). The conditions of human rights in Egypt during the last ten years (No. 33). Retrieved from www.lchr-eg.org/archive/indexe.htm

(2004d). The Land Center requests the officials to stop the eviction of Basune farmers from their homes. Retrieved from the Land Center for Human Rights website: www.lchr-eg.org/archive/112/04-30.htm

(2005a). Farmers and the election in Qena: Qena is afflicted . . . beautification and hunger. Retrieved from the Land Center for Human Rights website: www.lchr-eg.org/archive/112/05-63.htm

(2005b). Farmers of Sarando village: Help us from the tyranny of Damanhour police station. Retrieved from the Land Center for Human Rights website: www.lchr-eg.org/archive/112/05-1.htm

(2005c). Freedom and safety for all farmers in Sarando. Retrieved from the Land Center for Human Rights website: www.lchr-eg.org/archive/112/05-20.htm

(2005d). LCHR demands the Officials, To stop evicting Borg El Arab farmers from their lands and threatening them with eviction and imprisonment. Retrieved from the Land Center for Human Rights website: www.lchr-eg.org/archive/112/05-26.htm

(2005e). "Sarando" a flower in the heart of the Egyptian countryside Could the general prosecutor and the minister of agriculture help its' lands and farmers. Retrieved from the Land Center for Human Rights website: www.lchr-eg.org/archive/112/05-2.htm

(2005f). Who will protect farmers rights in Egypt? After the decrease of the prices of cotton "white gold," the collapse of farmers incomes and the deterioration of the textile industry. Retrieved from the Land Center for Human Rights website: www.lchr-eg.org/archive/112/05-47.htm

(2005g). Your Excellencies Mr. Minister of the Interior and Mr. Prosecutor General "Stop the violence against peasants." Retrieved from the Land Center for Human Rights website: www.lchr-eg.org/archive/112/05-10.htm

(2006a). Do employees of the Ministry of Endowments Own the lands managed by this ministry so they can evict farmers for the benefit of ownership claimers? Retrieved from the Land Center for Human Rights website: www.lchr-eg.org/archive/112/06-26.htm

(2006b). LCHR demands the officials to protect agrarian lands and farmers' rights in Egypt. Retrieved from the Land Center for Human Rights website: www.lchr-eg.org/archive/112/06-3.htm

(2006c). Security forces violate farmers' rights by transferring them to the State Security Prospector under the Emergency Law. Retrieved from the Land Center for Human Rights website: www.lchr-eg.org/archive/112/06-32.htm

(2007a). A letter from the farmers to the Prime Minister: Who will stop our displacement in the governorate of Sohag? Retrieved from the Land Center for Human Rights website: www.lchr-eg.org/archive/112/07-43e.htm

(2007b). A L=letter to the President of the Republic: The story of farmers who have no more way to Go!! What are they going to do in front of imprisonment, poverty, and lack of security?!! Retrieved from the Land Center for Human Rights website: www.lchr-eg.org/archive/112/07-19.htm

(2007c). Farmers of Ezbet Ahmed Rashed demand their right to safe housing. Retrieved from the Land Center for Human Rights website: www.lchr-eg.org/archive/112/07-7.htm

(2007d). LCHR asks for an independent and free union that defends farmers' rights. Retrieved from the Land Center for Human Rights website: www.lchr-eg.org/archive/112/07-8.htm

(2007e). Mr. Prime Minister Sohag Airport could be established on desert and fallow land... So why establish it on the lands of the farmers? Retrieved from the Land Center for Human Rights website: www.lchr-eg.org/archive/112/07-25.htm

(2007f). Mr. Prime Minister, the safety of the people an the protection of their land in Egypt is more important than constructing tourist establishments and trading in their properties on the grounds of public utility!!! Retrieved from the Land Center for Human Rights website: www.lchr-eg.org/archive/112/07-28.htm

(2007g). The Governor of El Wadi El Gedid to The farmers after they reclaimed the land: You have no place in the Governorate...so who will protect their rights!! Retrieved from www.lchr-eg.org/archive/112/07-42e.htm

(2007h). The white gold is the symbol of grief in the Egyptian countryside, cotton harvest seasons, seasons of ruined homes, the cotton that is in the homes and fields, who will buy it? Retrieved from www.lchr-eg.org/archive/112/07-39e.htm

(2008a). In West Tahta no life for farmers.....intentional neglect from the authorities cause further impoverishment of farmers!! Retrieved from the Land Center for Human Rights website: www.lchr-eg.org/archive/112/08-30.htm

(2008b). Mr. Minister of Irrigation, did you know that the trespassing on the lands of citizens surrounding the villages of Almnashi and Wardan is

Giza Governorate is for the benefit of "Hathor Land." Retrieved from www.lchr-eg.org/archive/112/08-6.htm

(2008c). Mr. President of the Egyptian government farmers on the Dom island eat tree leafs. Retrieved from the Land Center for Human Rights website: www.lchr-eg.org/archive/112/08-19.htm

(2008d). Who protects the residents of Ezbet Khairi from the tyranny of property claimers? Retrieved from the Land Center for Human Rights website: www.lchr-eg.org/archive/112/08-23.htm

(2009a). Does this Corruption and prejudice have an end? The story of selling the remains of the Egyptian land and wealth. Retrieved from the Land Center for Human Rights website: www.lchr-eg.org/archive/112/09-47.htm

(2009b). Governmental authorities violate the rights of farmers: A new, old, and continuous story. Retrieved from the Land Center for Human Rights website: www.lchr-eg.org/archive/112/09-9.htm

(2009c). Is this the way of developing the countryside? Villagers were intimidated to abandon their agriculture lands power. Retrieved from the Land Center for Human Rights website: www.lchr-eg.org/archive/112/09-49.htm

(2009d). On the Occasion of Holding International Conferences to Treat the Effects of the Economic Crisis: The Impossible Development in the Egyptian Countryside. Retrieved from Land Center for Human Rights website: www.lchr-eg.org/archive/112/09-32.htm

(2009e). Sabera El Masreya between the anvil of bullying and the hammer of neglect. Retrieved from www.lchr-eg.org/archive/112/09-21.htm

(2009f). The use of fraud, imprisonment and detention to force farmers to leave their land, so as to be seized by authorities and people in power. Retrieved from the Land Center for Human Rights website: www.lchr-eg.org/archive/112/09-48.htm

(2009g). The World Bank and the Egyptian Government in before the Egyptian Judiciary because of violating the rights of farmers in the delta. Retrieved from the Land Center for Human Rights website: www.lchr-eg.org/archive/112/09-33.htm

(2010a). Corruption has been rampant in the country: Destruction and burning of crops and lands without any legal reason. Retrieved from the Land Center for Human Rights website: www.lchr-eg.org/archive/112/10-26.htm

(2010b). Stealing the lands of farmers fraudulently, without compensation. Retrieved from the Land Center for Human Rights website: www.lchr-eg.org/archive/112/10-32.htm

(2010c). The series of acquisition of the farmers' agricultural lands continues. Retrieved from the Land Center for Human Rights website: www.lchr-eg.org/archive/112/10-4.htm

(2010d). Underground metro steals the lands of farmers. Retrieved from the Land Center for Human Rights website: www.lchr-eg.org/archive/112/10-10.htm

Lee, E., and Weinthal, B. (2011, February 10). Trade unions: The revolutionary social network at play in Egypt and Tunisia. *The Guardian.* Retrieved from www.theguardian.com/commentisfree/2011/feb/10/trade-unions-egypt-tunisia

Leiken, R. S., and Brooke, S. (2007). The moderate Muslim brotherhood. *Foreign Affairs*, 107–121.

Levinson, C., and Bradley, M. (2013, July 19). In Egypt, the "deep state" rises again. *Wall Street Journal.* Retrieved from www.wsj.com/articles/SB10001424127887324425204578601700051224658

Lipietz, A. (1987). *Mirages and Miracles: The Crisis in Global Fordism.* Brooklyn, NY: Verso Books.

Loza, P. (2004, March 4). The not-so real estate market. *Al Ahram Weekly.*
    (2005, December). Laden claims. Retrieved from http://weekly.ahram.org .eg/Archive/2005/773/feature.htm

Luciani, G. (1994). The oil rent, the fiscal crisis of the state and democratization. In Ghassan Salamé (ed.), *Democracy without Democrats? The Renewal of Politics in the Muslim World.* New York: I. B. Tauris & Co., pp. 130–155.

Lust, E. (2009). Competitive clientelism in the Middle East. *Journal of Democracy*, 20(3), 122–135. https://doi.org/10.1353/jod.0.0099

Lynch, M. (2014). *The Arab Uprisings Explained: New Contentious Politics in the Middle East.* New York: Columbia University Press.

Macpherson, C. B. C. B. (1964). *The Political Theory of Possessive Individualism: Hobbes to Locke.* Oxford: Clarendon Press.

Malik, A. (2011, October 13). The economics of the Arab Spring. Retrieved from www.aljazeera.com/indepth/opinion/2011/10/201110101424254 19849.html

Mandour, M. (2016, February 27). The revolution and rural Egypt: A lost opportunity? Retrieved July 9, 2018, from the openDemocracy website: www.opendemocracy.net/north-africa-west-asia/maged-mandour/the-revolution-and-rural-egypt-lost-opportunity

Marx, K. (1964). *Pre-capitalist Economic Formations.* New York: International Publishers.
    (1973). *Surveys from Exile: Political Writings.* London: Penguin Books, Limited.
    (1976). *Capital: A Critique of Political Economy.* London: Penguin Books, Limited.

Marx, K., and Engels, F. (1967). *The Communist Manifesto.* London: Penguin Books, Limited.

Maskus, K. E., and Konan, D. E. (1997). Trade liberalization in Egypt. *Review of Development Economics*, 1(3), 275–293. https://doi.org/10.1111/1467-9361.00019

Mason, P. (2012). *Why It's Kicking Off Everywhere: The New Global Revolutions*. Brooklyn, NY: Verso Books.

Mayer, A. J. (2010). *The Persistence of the Old Regime: Europe to the Great War*. Brooklyn, NY: Verso Books.

McCall, B. (1988). The Effects of Rent Control in Egypt: Part I. *Arab Law Quarterly*, 3(2).

McGreal, C. (2008, May 26). Egypt: Bread shortages, hunger and unrest. *The Guardian*. Retrieved from www.theguardian.com/environment/2008/may/27/food.egypt

McMichael, P. (2012). *Development and Social Change: A Global Perspective*. Newbury Park, CA: Pine Forge Press.

Meital, Y. (2006). The struggle over political order in Egypt: The 2005 elections. *Middle East Journal*, 60(2), 257–279.

Migdal, J. (1988). *Strong Societies and Weak States: State-Society Relations and State Capabilities in the Third World*. Princeton, NJ: Princeton University Press.

Miliband, R. (1969). *The State in Capitalist Society*. London, UK: Weidenfeld & Nicolson.

(1970). The capitalist state-reply to Nicos Poulantzas. *New Left Review*, (59), 53.

(1973). Poulantzas and the capitalist state. *New Left Review*, (82), 83.

Miller, J. (1984, May 27). Mubarak's venture in democracy. *The New York Times*. Retrieved from www.nytimes.com/1984/05/27/magazine/mubaraks-venture-in-democracy.html

Ministry of Defense. (2018). The Official Home Page of the Egyptian Armed Forces. Retrieved August 9, 2018, from www.mod.gov.eg/ModWebSite/Default.aspx

Mitchell, R. (1969). *The Society of the Muslim Brothers*. Oxford, UK: Oxford University Press.

Mitchell, T. (1991a). America's Egypt: Discourse of the development industry. *Middle East Report*, 18–36.

(1991b). *Colonizing Egypt*. Berkeley: University of California Press.

(2002). *Ruler of Experts: Egypt, Techno-Politics, Modernity*. Berkeley: University of California Press.

Mohamed, F. A.-S. (2004). *Role of Agricultural Cooperatives in Agricultural Development: The Case of Menoufiya Governorate*. Bonn, Germany: University of Bonn.

Mohsen, A. A. (2010, February 17). Villagers protest upper Egypt land seizures. *Al Masry Al Youm*. Retrieved from www.egyptindependent.com/villagers-protest-upper-egypt-land-seizures/

Momani, B. (2003). Promoting economic liberalization in Egypt: From US foreign aid to trade and investment. *Middle East*, 7(3), 89.

(2005). IMF-Egyptian debt negotiations. *Cairo Papers in Social Science*, 26(3).

(2013). *In Egypt, "Deep State" vs. "Brotherhoodization."* Washington, DC: Brookings Institution.

Mooers, C. (1991). *The Making of Bourgeois Europe: Absolutism, Revolution, and the Rise of Capitalism in England, France, and Germany.* Brooklyn, NY: Verso Books.

Moore, C. H. (1990). Islamic banks and competitive politics in the Arab world and Turkey. *Middle East Journal*, 44(2), 234–255.

Moustafa, T. (2003). *Law versus the State: The Radicalization of Politics in Egypt.* Chicago: American Bar Foundation.

Munck, R. (2002). *Globalization and Labour: The New "Great Transformation."* London: Zed Books.

Munson, H. (1988). *Islam and Revolution in the Middle East.* New Haven, CT: Yale University Press.

Murphy, D. (2005, May 6). Discontent flaring in rural Egypt. *Christian Science Monitor.* Retrieved from www.csmonitor.com/2005/0506/p01s02-wome.html

Naguib, S. (2009). Islamism (s) old and new. In P. Marfleet, and R. El-Mahdi (eds.), *Egypt: The Moment of Change.* London: Zed Books.

Nasr, S. V. R. (2005). The Rise of "Muslim Democracy." *Journal of Democracy*, 16(2), 13–27.

Nassar, S., and Mansour, M. (2003). Agriculture: An assessment of past performance and the task ahead. In R. M. El-Ghonemy (ed.), *Egypt in the Twenty-First Century: Challenges for Development.* London: Routledge, pp. 141–159.

Nassif, H. B. (2013). Wedded to Mubarak: The second careers and financial rewards of Egypt's military elite, 1981–2011. *Middle East Journal*, 67 (4), 509–530.

National Bank of Egypt (NBE). (1990). *Economic Bulletin.* Cairo: National Bank of Egypt.

(1992). *Economic Bulletin.* Cairo: National Bank of Egypt.

(2001). *Economic Bulletin* (No. 54 (4)). Cairo: National Bank of Egypt.

Neumann, J. (2009, January 9). Unfounded optimism. Cairo: *Businesstodayegypt.*

Niblock, T., and Murphy, E. (1993). *Economic and Political Liberalization in the Middle East.* London: British Academic Press; Distributed by St. Martin's Press.

Nitzan, J., and Bichler, S. (2002). *The Global Political Economy of Israel: From War Profits to Peace Dividends.* London: Pluto Press.

Nordlinger, E. A. (1982). *On the Autonomy of the Democratic State.* Cambridge, MA: Harvard University Press.

NSPO. (2018). National Service Projects Organization. Retrieved August 9, 2018, from www.nspo.com.eg/nspo/about.html

OECD. (2007a). *African Economic Outlook 2006/07*. Abidjan, Côte d'Ivoire: African Development Bank.

(2007b). *OECD Investment Policy Reviews: Egypt 2007*. Retrieved from https://doi.org/10.1787/9789264034624-en

(2007c). *OECD Investment Policy Reviews: Egypt 2007*. Retrieved from https://doi.org/10.1787/9789264034624-en

(2008). *African Economic Outlook 2008*. Paris: Organisation for Economic Co-operation and Development.

(2009). *African Economic Outlook 2009*. Retrieved from https://doi.org/10.1787/aeo-2009-en

Ostry, J., Loungani, P., and Furceri, D. (2016). Neoliberalism: Oversold? – finance & development, June 2016. *Finance and Development*, 53(2), 38–41.

Overbeek, H. (2000). Transnational historical materialism. In R. Palan (ed.), *Global Political Economy: Contemporary Theories*. New York: Routledge. pp. 168–183.

Owen, R. (2002). *State Power and Politics in the Making of the Modern Middle East*. London: Routledge.

(2004). *State, Power and Politics in the Making of the Modern Middle East*, 3rd edn. London: Routledge.

Paczynska, A. (2006). Globalization, structural adjustment, and pressure to conform: Contesting labor law reform in Egypt. *New Political Science*, 28(1), 45–64.

Panitch, L. (1998). "The state in a changing world": Social-democratizing global capitalism? *Monthly Review*, 50(5), 11.

Partridge, M. (2011, June 7). How the economic policies of a corrupt elite caused the Arab Spring. Retrieved from www.newstatesman.com/blogs/the-staggers/2011/06/economic-arab-egypt-region

Paul, J. (1983). The Egyptian Arms Industry. *Merip Reports*, (112), 26–28.

Perelman, M. (2000). *The Invention of Capitalism: Classical Political Economy and the Secret History of Primitive Accumulation*. Durham, NC: Duke University Press.

Peters, P. E. (2004). Inequality and social conflict over land in Africa. *Journal of Agrarian Change*, 4(3), 269–314.

Pfeifer, K. (1997). Is there an Islamic economics. *Political Islam. Essays from Middle East Report*, 144, 153.

Picard, E. (1988). Arab military in politics: From revolutionary plot to authoritarian state. In A. Dawisha and W. Zartmann (eds.), *Beyond Coercion: The Durability of the Arab State*. London: Croom Helm, pp. 116–146.

Pilon, D. (2013). *Wrestling with Democracy: Voting Systems as Politics in the Twentieth-century West.* Toronto, Ontario, Canada: University of Toronto Press.

Polanyi, K. (1944). *The Great Transformation: The Political and Economic Origins of Our Time.* Boston: Beacon Press.

Pontusson, J., and Swenson, P. (1996). Labor markets, production strategies, and wage bargaining institutions: The Swedish employer offensive in comparative perspective. *Comparative Political Studies, 29*(2), 223–250.

Portes, A., and Böröcz, J. (1988). The informal sector under capitalism and state socialism: A preliminary comparison. *Social Justice, 15*(3/4 (33–34)), 17–28.

Post, E. (1987). Egypt's elections. *Middle East Report,* (147). Retrieved from www.merip.org/mer/mer147/egypts-elections

Posusney, M. P. (1997). Labor and the state in Egypt: Workers, unions, and economic restructuring. Retrieved from https://books.google.com/books?id=FeNj5PGd76YC&printsec=frontcover&dq=Posusney+1997&hl=en&sa=X&ved=0ahUKEwjt18qzhPnZAhWIrlQKHQsLCnkQ6AEIKTAA#v=onepage&q=Posusney%201997&f=false

Poulantzas, N. (1969). The problem of the capitalist state. *New Left Review,* (58), 67.

(1973). *Political Power and Social Classes* (T. O'Hagan, Trans.). Ljubljana, Slovenia: NLB London.

(1976). The capitalist state: A reply to Miliband and Laclau. *New Left Review,* (95), 63.

Prashad, V. (2008). *The Darker Nations: A People's History of the Third World.* New York: The New Press.

Putz, U. (2008, April 18). Crisis in Egypt: The daily struggle for food. *Spiegel Online.* Retrieved from www.spiegel.de/international/world/crisis-in-egypt-the-daily-struggle-for-food-a-548300.html

Qutb, S. (2006). *Milestones.* Birmingham, UK: Maktabah Publishers.

Radchenko, N. (2014). Heterogeneity in informal salaried employment: Evidence from the Egyptian labor market survey. *World Development, 62,* 169–188.

Radwan, S. (1997). Towards full employment: Egypt into the 21st century. *Eces.Org.Eg.* Retrieved from www.eces.org.eg/Publication.aspx?Id=81

(2002). *Employment and Unemployment in Egypt: Conventional Problems, Unconventional Remedies.* Cairo: The Egyptian Center for Economic Studies.

Reuters. (2018, May 16). Special Report: From war room to boardroom. Military firms flourish. *Reuters.* Retrieved from www.reuters.com/article/us-egypt-military-economy-specialreport/special-report-from-war-room-to-boardroom-military-firms-flourish-in-sisis-egypt-idUSKCN1 IH185

Ricciardone, F. (2008). Scene-setter for Mindef Tantawi's visit to the U.S. March 24–28 (Wikileaks Public Library of US Diplomacy No. 08CAIRO524_a). Retrieved from the Egypt Cairo website: https:// wikileaks.org/plusd/cables/08CAIRO524_a.html

Richards, A. (2004). Economic reform in the Middle East: The challenge to governance. In N. Bensahel and D. Byman (eds.), *The Future Security Environment of the Middle East: Conflict, Stability and Political Change*. Santa Monica, CA: Rand Corporation, pp. 57–128.

Richards, A., and Waterbury, J. (1996). *A Political Economy of the Middle East*, 2nd edn. Boulder, CO: Westview Press.

(2008). *A Political Economy of the Middle East*, 3rd edn. Boulder, CO: Westview Press.

Roccu, R. (2013). *The Political Economy of the Egyptian Revolution: Mubarak, Economic Reforms and Failed Hegemony*. New York: Springer.

Rodrik, D. (1997). *Has Globalization Gone Too Far?* New York: Columbia University Press.

Roll, S. (2010). Finance matters! The influence of financial sector reforms on the development of the entrepreneurial elite in Egypt. *Mediterranean Politics*, 15(2), pp. 349–370.

Roushdy, R., and Selwaness, I. (2014). *The Coverage Gap in the Egyptian Social Insurance System during a Period of Reforms and Revolts*. Giza, Egypt: Economic Research Forum.

Roussillon, A. (1998). Republican Egypt Interpreted: revolution and beyond. In M. W. Daly (ed.), *The Cambridge History of Egypt: Vol. 2, Modern Egypt from 1517 to the End of the Twentieth Century*. Cambridge: Cambridge Studies , pp. 334–393.

Roy, D. A. (1991a). Egyptian emigrant labor: Domestic consequences. *Middle Eastern Studies*, 27(4).

(1991b). Islamic banking. *Middle Eastern Studies*, 27(3), 427–456.

Roy, O. (1994). *The Failure of Political Islam*. Cambridge, MA: Harvard University Press, pp. 551–582.

Rudé, G. F. E. (1995). *Ideology and Popular Protest*. Chapel Hill: University of North Carolina Press Books.

Rutherford, B. K. (2008). *Egypt after Mubarak: Liberalism, Islam, and Democracy in the Arab World*. Princeton Studies in Muslim Politics, Princeton, NJ: Princeton University Press.

Saad, R. (1999). State, landlord, parliament and peasant: The story of the 1992 Tenancy Law in Egypt. *Proceedings of the British Academy*, 96, 387–404.

(2000). Agriculture and politics in contemporary Egypt: The 1997 tenancy crisis. Hill, E. (ed.). *Discourses in Contemporary Egypt: Politics and Social Issues. Cairo Papers in Social Science,* 22(4), 22–35.

(2002). Egyptian Politics and the Tenancy Law. In R. Bush (ed.), *Counter-Revolution in Egypt's Countryside: Land and Farmers in the Era of Economic Reform.* London: Zed Books, pp. 103–125.

Saad-Filho, A., and Johnston, D. (2005). *Neoliberalism: A Critical Reader.* London: Pluto Press.

Sachs, J. (1996, June). Achieving rapid growth: The road ahead of Egypt. Distinguished Lecture Series. Cairo: Egyptian Centre for Economic Studies.

Sadowski, Y. (1991). *Political Vegetables? Businessmen and Bureaucrats in the Development of Egyptian Agriculture.* Washington, DC: The Brookings Institute.

Salama, A. M. S., and Ahmed, M. S. (1972). *Arab Socialism.* London: Blandford Press.

Schmid, K. (2015). Accumulation by dispossession in tourism. *Anthropologica,* 57(1), 115–125.

Schumpeter, J. A. (1950). *Capitalism, Socialism, and Democracy,* 3rd edn. New York: Harper.

Scobey, M. (2008). Academics see the military in decline, but retaining strong influence (Wikileaks Public Library of US Diplomacy No. 08CAIRO2091_a). Retrieved from the Egypt Cairo website: https://wikileaks.org/plusd/cables/08CAIRO2091_a.html

Scott, J. C. (1977). *The Moral Economy of the Peasant: Rebellion and Subsistence in Southeast Asia.* New Haven, CT: Yale University Press.

(1985). *Weapons of the Weak: Everyday Forms of Peasant Resistance.* New Haven, CT: Yale University Press.

Seddon, D. (1990). The politics of adjustment: Egypt and the IMF, 1987–1990. *Review of African Political Economy,* 17(47), 95–104. https://doi.org/10.1080/03056249008703850

Sedgwick, M. (2010). Measuring Egyptian regime legitimacy. *Middle East Critique,* 19(3), 251–267. https://doi.org/10.1080/19436149.2010.514474

Sfakianakis, J. (2004). The whales of the Nile: Networks, businessmen, and bureaucrats during the era of privatization in Egypt. In *Networks of Privilege in the Middle East: The Politics of Economic Reform Revisited.* New York: Springer, pp. 77–100.

Shanin, T. (1972). *The Awkward Class: Political Sociology of Peasantry in a Developing Society: Russia 1910–1925.* Oxford: Clarendon Press.

Sharp, J. M. (2006). *Egypt: 2005 Presidential and Parliamentary Elections.* Washington, DC: Congressional Research Service, Library of Congress.

Shawkat, Y. (2015). Egypt's Deregulated Property Market: A Crisis of Affordability. Retrieved March 4, 2018, from the Middle East Institute website: www.mei.edu/content/at/egypts-deregulated-property-market-crisis-affordability

Shehata, D. (2009). *Islamists and Secularists in Egypt: Opposition, Conflict & Cooperation.* London: Routledge.

Shehata, S., and Stacher, J. (2006). The Brotherhood goes to parliament. *Middle East Report,* (240). Retrieved from www.merip.org/mer/mer240/brotherhood-goes-parliament

Sieverding, M., and Selwaness, I. (2012). Social protection in Egypt: A policy overview. *Gender and Work in the MENA Region Working Paper Series,* (23).

Smith, A. (1937). *An Inquiry into the Nature and Causes of the Wealth of Nations.* New York: The Modern Library

Soliman, A. M. (2004). *A Possible Way Out: Formalizing Housing Informality in Egyptian Cities.* Lanham, MD: University Press of America.

Soliman, S. (1998). *State and Industrial Capitalism in Egypt* (Vol. 2). Cairo: The American University of Cairo Press.

Springborg, R. (1987). The president and the field marshal: Civil-military relations in Egypt today. *MERIP Middle East Report,* (147), 5–42.

(1989). *Mubarak's Egypt: Fragmentation of the Political Order.* Boulder, CO: Westview Press.

(1991). State-society relations in Egypt: The debate over owner-tenant relations. *Middle East Journal, 45*(2), 232–249.

(2014, October 10). The role of militaries in the Arab Thermidor. Retrieved July 2, 2018, from the Project on Middle East Political Science website: https://pomeps.org/2014/12/12/the-role-of-militaries-in-the-arab-thermidor/

Stacher, J. A. (2002). Post-Islamist rumblings in Egypt: The emergence of the Wasat party. *Middle East Journal,* 415–432.

(2004). Parties over: The demise of Egypt's opposition parties. *British Journal of Middle Eastern Studies, 31*(2), 215–233. https://doi.org/10.1080/1353019040042000268222

(2012). *Adaptable Autocrats: Regime Power in Egypt and Syria.* Stanford, CA: Stanford University Press.

Standing, G. (2011). *The Precariat: The New Dangerous Class.* London: Bloomsbury Publishing.

Stiglitz, J. (2002). *Globalization and Its Discontents.* New York: W. W. Norton.

Streeck, W., and Yamamura, K. (2001). *The Origins of Nonliberal Capitalism: Germany and Japan in Comparison.* Ithaca, NY: Cornell University Press.

Sullivan, D. J. (1990). The Political Economy of Reform in Egypt. *International Journal of Middle East Studies*, 22(3, August), pp. 317–334.

Sullivan, D. J., and Abed-Kotob, S. (1999). *Islam in Contemporary Egypt: Civil Society vs. the State*. Boulder, CO: Lynne Rienner Publishers.

Tadros, S. (2012, February 15). Egypt military's economic empire. *Al Jazeera*. Retrieved from www.aljazeera.com/indepth/features/2012/02/2012215195912519142.html

Tarrow, S. G. (2011). *Power in Movement: Social Movements and Contentious Politics*. Cambridge: Cambridge University Press.

Taylor, F. W. (1913). *The Principles of Scientific Management*. New York: Harper.

Therborn, G. (1977). The rule of capital and the rise of capitalism. *New Left Review*, *103*, 3–41.

   (1978). *What Does the Ruling Class Do When It Rules? State Apparatuses and State Power under Feudalism, Capitalism and Socialism*. London: NLB; Schocken Books.

Thompson, E. P. (1963). *The Making of the English Working Class*. New York: Penguin Books.

   (1971). The moral economy of the English crowd in the eighteenth century. *Past & Present*, (50), 76–136.

Tignor, R. L. (1990). Capitalism in colonial Africa: A historical overview. *Political Economy of Public Sector Reform and Privatization*, 187.

Toynbee, P. (2016, January 28). Selling off the family silver? Cameron and Osborne have gone way beyond that | Polly Toynbee. *The Guardian*. Retrieved from www.theguardian.com/commentisfree/2016/jan/28/selling-family-silver-cameron-osborne-thatcher

Trimberger, E. K. (1978). *Revolution from above: Military Bureaucrats and Development in Japan, Turkey, Egypt, and Peru*. Piscataway, NJ: Transaction Publishers.

Tripp, C. (2006). *Islam and the Moral Economy: The Challenge of Capitalism*. Cambridge: Cambridge University Press.

Tuğal, C. (2012). Fight or acquiesce? Religion and political process in Turkey's and Egypt's neoliberalizations. *Development and Change*, *43* (1), 23–51.

UNCTAD. (2005). *Report on the Implementation of the Investment Policy Review: Egypt*. Geneva, Switzerland: United Nations Conference on Trade and Development.

UNDP. (2009). Arab human development report 2009. Retrieved from the United Nations Development Program website: www.undp.org/content/undp/en/home/librarypage/hdr/arab_human_developmentreport2009.html

UNU-WIDER. (2017, January 18). World income inequality database - WIID3.4. Retrieved March 4, 2018, from the UNU-WIDER website: www.wider.unu.edu/database/world-income-inequality-database-wiid34

Van der Pijl, K. (1989). Ruling classes, hegemony, and the state system: Theoretical and historical considerations. *International Journal of Political Economy*, 19(3), 7–35.

Van der Weide, R. (2016, September 27). Is inequality underestimated in Egypt? Evidence from housing prices [Text]. Retrieved May 25, 2018, from the Let's Talk Development website: https://blogs.worldbank.org/developmenttalk/inequality-underestimated-egypt-evidence-housing-prices

Vannetzel, M. (2017). The Muslim Brotherhood's "Virtuous society" and State Developmentalism in Egypt: The Politics of 'Goodness.' *International Development Policy | Revue Internationale de Politique de Développement*, 8(8), 220–245. https://doi.org/10.4000/poldev.2327

Vannetzel, M., and Yankaya, D. (2017). Crafting a business Umma? Transnational networks of "Islamic businessmen" after the Arab Spring. *Mediterranean Politics*, 23(3), 1–21. https://doi.org/10.1080/13629395.2017.1403229

Väyrynen, R. (1979). The Arab organization of industrialization: A case study in the multinational production of arms. *Current Research on Peace and Violence*, 2(2), 66–79.

Vergara-Camus, L. (2014). *Land and Freedom: The MST, the Zapatistas and Peasant Alternatives to Neoliberalism*. London: Zed Books.

Vignal, L., & Denis, E. (2006). *Cairo as Regional/Global Economic Capital? In Cairo, Cosmopolitan: Politics, Culture, and Urban Space in the New Globalized Middle East*. Cairo: American University in Cairo Press.

Vitalis, R. (1995). *When Capitalists Collide: Business Conflict and the End of Empire in Egypt*. Berkeley: University of California Press.

Wahba, J. (2009). Impact of labor market reforms on informality in Egypt [Working Paper]. Retrieved from the Population Council, Cairo, EG website: https://idl-bnc-idrc.dspacedirect.org/handle/10625/41993

Wahba, J., and Assaad, R. (2015). Flexible labor regulations and informality in Egypt. *Economic Research Forum (ERF)*. Retrieved from http://erf.org.eg/publications/flexible-labor-regulations-and-informality-in-egypt/

(2016). Flexible labor regulations and informality in Egypt. *Review of Development Economics*, 21(4), 962–984. https://doi.org/10.1111/rode.12288

Wahba, M. (1994). *The Role of State in the Egyptian Economy, 1945–81*. Reading, UK: Ithaca Press.

Waterbury, J. (1983). *The Egypt of Nasser and Sadat: The Political Economy of Two Regimes*. Princeton, NJ: Princeton University Press.

Weiss, D., and Wurzel, U. (1998). *The Economics and Politics of Transition to an Open Market Economy*. Retrieved from https://doi.org/10.1787/9789264163607-en

Whyte, D., and Wiegratz, J. (2016, June 20). How neoliberalism's moral order feeds fraud and corruption. Retrieved May 3, 2018, from The Conversation website: http://theconversation.com/how-neoliberalisms-moral-order-feeds-fraud-and-corruption-60946

Wickham, C. R. (2002). *Mobilizing Islam: Religion, Activism, Pnd Colitical change in Egypt*. New York: Columbia University Press.

(2015). *The Muslim Brotherhood: Evolution of an Islamist Movement*. Princeton, NJ: Princeton University Press.

Wittfogel, K. A. (1959). *Oriental Despotism: A Comparative Study of Total Power*. New Haven, CT: Yale University Press.

Wood, E. M. (1990). The Uses and Abuses of "Civil Society." *Socialist Register*, 26(26). Retrieved from www.socialistregister.com/index.php/srv/article/download/5574

(1991). *The Pristine Culture of Capitalism: A Historical Essay on Old Regimes and Modern States*. Brooklyn, NY: Verso Books.

(1995). *Democracy against Capitalism: Renewing Historical Materialism*. Cambridge: Cambridge University Press.

(2002). *The Origin of Capitalism: A Longer View*. Brooklyn, NY: Verso Books.

World Bank. (1990). Summary Proceedings: 1989 Annual Meetings of the Board of Governors (No. 53426). Retrieved from the World Bank website: http://documents.worldbank.org/curated/en/969681468170972480/pdf/534260BR0board101Official0Use0Only1.pdf

(ed.). (1997). *The State in a Changing World* (1. print). Oxford: Oxford University Press.

(2006). Egypt Public Land Management Strategy: Volume 2. Background Notes on Access to Public Land by Investment Sector–Industry, Tourism, Agriculture, and Real Estate Development. Retrieved from The World Bank website: https://openknowledge.worldbank.org/handle/10986/19443

(2018a). Agriculture, value added (% GDP). Retrieved September 9, 2018, from http://databank.worldbank.org/data/source/world-development-indicators

(2018b). Exports of goods and services (% of GDP). Retrieved September 9, 2018, from http://databank.worldbank.org/data/source/world-development-indicators

(2018c). External balance on goods and services. Retrieved from http://databank.worldbank.org/data/reports.aspx?source=world-development-indicators#

(2018d). External debt stocks (% of GNI). Retrieved from http://databank
.worldbank.org/data/reports.aspx?source=world-development-indicators#

(2018e). Foreign direct investment net inflows (% of GDP). Retrieved
March 3, 2018, from http://databank.worldbank.org/data/reports.aspx?
source=world-development-indicators#

(2018f). GDP growth rate. Retrieved from the World Bank website: http://
databank.worldbank.org/data/reports.aspx?source=world-development-
indicators

(2018g). GINI index. Retrieved from http://databank.worldbank.org/data/
reports.aspx?source=world-development-indicators

(2018h). Gross fixed capital formation. Retrieved from the World Bank
website: http://databank.worldbank.org/data/reports.aspx?source=world-
development-indicators

(2018i). Gross Fixed Capital Formation - Private Sector. Retrieved March
3, 2018, from http://databank.worldbank.org/data/reports.aspx?source=
world-development-indicators

(2018j). Income shares. Retrieved from http://databank.worldbank.org/
data/reports.aspx?source=world-development-indicators

(2018k). Inflation. Retrieved from the World Bank website: http://
databank.worldbank.org/data/reports.aspx?source=world-development-
indicators#

(2018l). Manufacturing, value added (% growth). Retrieved September 9,
2018, from http://databank.worldbank.org/data/source/world-develop
ment-indicators

(2018m). Manufacturing, value added (% of GDP). Retrieved September
9, 2018, from http://databank.worldbank.org/data/source/world-devel
opment-indicators

(2018n). Market capitalization of listed domestic companies (% of GDP).
Retrieved September 9, 2018, from http://databank.worldbank.org/
data/source/world-development-indicators

(2018o). Military expenditure [Database]. Retrieved August 13, 2018,
from the World Bank Development Indicators website: http://databank
.worldbank.org/data/source/world-development-indicators#

(2018p). Military expenditures - Percentage of central government spending and percentage of GDP. Retrieved August 15, 2018, from the World
Development Indicators website: http://databank.worldbank.org/data/
source/world-development-indicators

(2018q). Poverty Headcount Ratio at National Poverty Lines (% of population). Retrieved from http://databank.worldbank.org/data/reports
.aspx?source=world-development-indicators#

(2018r). Rural poverty headcount ratio at national poverty lines (% of
rural population). Retrieved from http://databank.worldbank.org/data/
reports.aspx?source=world-development-indicators#

(2018s). Stocks traded, total value (% of GDP). Retrieved September 9, 2018, from http://databank.worldbank.org/data/source/world-develop ment-indicators

(2018t). Unemployment rate. Retrieved from the World Bank website: http://databank.worldbank.org/data/reports.aspx?source=world-develop ment-indicators

(2018u). Unemployment, youth total (% of total labour force ages 15–24). Retrieved from http://databank.worldbank.org/data/reports.aspx?source= world-development-indicators#

(2018v). Urban poverty headcount ratio at national poverty lines (% of urban population). Retrieved from http://databank.worldbank.org/ data/reports.aspx?source=world-development-indicators#

Wright, J. (2005, September 11). Egyptians vote for leader, opposition complains. *Reuters*. Retrieved from https://web.archive.org/web/20050 911043259/http://in.today.reuters.com/news/newsArticle.aspx?type= worldNews&storyID=2005-09-07T233301Z_01_NOOTR_RTRJO NC_0_India-215318-4.xml

Wurzel, U. G. (2004). Patterns of resistance: Economic actors and fiscal policy reform in Egypt in the 1990s. In *Networks of Privilege in the Middle East: The Politics of Economic Reform Revisited*. New York: Springer, pp. 101–131.

(2009). The political economy of authoritarianism in Egypt: Insufficient structural reforms, limited outcomes and a lack of new actors. In *The Arab State and Neo-liberal Globalization: The Restructuring of State Power in the Middle East*. Ithaca, NY: Ithaca Press, pp. 97–123.

Zaalouk, M. (1989). *Power, Class and Foreign Capital in Egypt: The Rise of the New Bourgeoisie*. London: Zed Press.

Ziadeh, F. (1978). Law of property in Egypt: Real rights. *The American Journal of Comparative Law*, 26(2, Spring).

Zovighian, D. (2013). The politics of "Good Governance" in Mubarak's Egypt: Western donors and SME politics under authoritarian rule. In S. Hertog, G. Luciani, and M. Valeri (eds.), *Business Politics in the Middle East*. London: Hurst & Company, pp. 183–209.

Zubaida, S. (1990). The politics of the Islamic investment companies in Egypt. *British Society for Middle Easter Studies, Bulletin*, 17(2), pp. 152–161.

(2011). *Beyond Islam: A New Understanding of the Middle East*. London: I.B. Tauris.

Index